The publisher gratefully acknowledges the generous support of the Sue Tsao Endowment Fund in Chinese Studies of the University of California Press Foundation.

Bitter and Sweet

CALIFORNIA STUDIES IN FOOD AND CULTURE

Darra Goldstein, Editor

Bitter and Sweet

FOOD, MEANING, AND MODERNITY
IN RURAL CHINA

Ellen Oxfeld

UNIVERSITY OF CALIFORNIA PRESS

University of California Press, one of the most distinguished university presses in the United States, enriches lives around the world by advancing scholarship in the humanities, social sciences, and natural sciences. Its activities are supported by the UC Press Foundation and by philanthropic contributions from individuals and institutions. For more information, visit www.ucpress.edu.

University of California Press
Oakland, California

Chapter 5 was revised from an earlier version which appeared in *Ethical Eating in the Postsocialist and Socialist World,* edited by Yuson Jung, Jakob Klein, and Melissa Caldwell (University of California Press, 2014). I gratefully acknowledge University of California Press for permission to reprint this material.

All photographs by Ellen Oxfeld.

Library of Congress Cataloging-in-Publication Data

Names: Oxfeld, Ellen, 1953– author.
Title: Bitter and sweet : food, meaning, and modernity in rural China / Ellen Oxfeld.
Other titles: California studies in food and culture ; 63.
Description: Oakland, California : University of California Press, [2017] | Series: California studies in food and culture ; 63 | Includes bibliographical references and index.
Identifiers: LCCN 2016048660 (print) | LCCN 2016050441 (ebook) | ISBN 9780520293519 (cloth : alk. paper) | ISBN 9780520293526 (pbk. : alk. paper) | ISBN 9780520966741 (ebook)
Subjects: LCSH: Food supply—China. | Food consumption—China. | Rural families—China. | Urbanization—China. | Agriculture—Economic aspects—China—History—21st century.
Classification: LCC HD9016.C62 O94 2017 (print) | LCC HD9016.C62 (ebook) | DDC 338.1/951091734—dc23
LC record available at https://lccn.loc.gov/2016048660

Manufactured in the United States of America

26 25 24 23 22 21 20 19 18 17
10 9 8 7 6 5 4 3 2 1

For my Meixian family and friends

Navarro Vineyards
Box 47, Philo, California 95466

Tasting Room: 5c c1 Hwy. 128
(707) 895-3685 (3 0) 537-9463
w w w . N a v a r r o i n e . c o m

B
I
L Andrew Scull
L 918 Muirlands Drive
T La Jolla, CA 92037
O

S
H
I Andrew Scull
P 918 Muirlands Drive
T La Jolla, CA 92037 (858)459-1307
O

INVOICE
Invoice #: 506917

Order Date	Invoice Date	Sales Person	Customer Number	Ordered By		Terms		S H I P V I A
07/12/17	N/A	DRW	024143 - 001	Andrew		45 days		FEDXG

Item Description		Quantity	Unit Price	Gross Ext Price	Disc Rate	Net Ext Price
2016 Rosé Anderson Valley Pinot Noir	750 ml ROAV-16-₂	6	22.00	132.00	10.000 %	118.80
2016 Rosé Mendocino	750 ml ROME-16-₂	6	17.50	105.00	10.000 %	94.50
	SubTotals:	12		237.00	-23.70	213.30

This invoice has $.01 shipping for all wine cases.

Payments					Sales Tax	15.73
07/ /17 Crd Card			229.04		Shipping	0.01
					Grand Total $	**229.04**
					Amount Paid	229.04
					Amount Due	**0.00**

CONTENTS

ILLUSTRATIONS

MAPS

FIGURES

TABLES

The need for food is a biological reality that all people have in common regardless of age or identity. But while the necessity of consuming food is part of our dependence on nature, our ability to access good food, the meanings we impart to food, and the ways in which food consumption is socially structured and culturally framed differ widely both within and between societies. The production and consumption of food are imbued with different meanings, reflect variable social roles, and are shaped by historical processes.

This book strives to convey the cultural and social centrality of food in Moonshadow Pond, which is the pseudonymous name of a village in southeastern China. Focusing on food in one rural Chinese community provides us with a unique lens through which to understand many aspects of contemporary culture and society in China. These include the play of cultural continuity versus rupture and transformation, ties to the land and peasant identities versus the pull of the city and urban identities, family duties versus the growth of individualism, and an economy based on money and profit versus older forms of exchange that privilege social obligation. Of course, aside from all of these important issues, the role of food in any society is intrinsically important.

In trying to learn about the food culture of Moonshadow Pond, I have been assisted by many people. First and foremost are the residents of Moonshadow Pond. Over the many years I made visits to the village to conduct research for this book, I was warmly welcomed by them. They were always patient with me as they explained the complexities and nuances of their food culture, and as I participated in celebrations, harvests, and ordinary living. My host family in Moonshadow Pond, which I refer to in this text as the family of Songling and Baoli, truly created a home away from home for me. They have never stopped sharing knowledge with me about both the past and the present life of the village.

As I have sorted through my notes from fieldwork, I have tried to analyze and describe what I have learned through scholarly papers, lectures, classes, and discussions with colleagues, especially Paula Schwartz, with whom I have frequently taught a food and culture seminar. Throughout this process I have received excellent feedback. Parts of this book benefited from the comments and input of the following people: Melissa Caldwell, Jakob Klein, Yuson Jong, David Stoll, Eriberto Lozada, Charles Stafford, John Lagerway, David Stoll, Anna Lora-Wainwright, and Adam Chau. I am immensely grateful to all of these individuals.

I also thank Middlebury College for its constant support, both in terms of leave time for sabbaticals and financial support during specific research trips. Without the local hospitality of the Hakka Research Institute of Jiaying University in Meizhou, and in particular the help of Professor Fang Xuejia, I would not have been able to undertake this research, and for that, I am forever indebted to him. Once again, I thank Lee Jyu-Fong for introducing me to Moonshadow Pond and sometimes visiting with me. Thanks also go to my family for going on this journey with me in different ways. My husband, Frank Nicosia, accompanied me on a number of trips, and enjoyed the warmth and hospitality of all our Moonshadow Pond and Meixian friends, and my mother, Edith Oxfeld, has always been happy to read my written work and to provide editorial comments. Ann Donahue copyedited my manuscript and the writing is greatly improved and more streamlined because of her efforts.

Finally, I owe a huge thanks to Yashu Zhang, my student research assistant at Middlebury College. Yashu helped me with so many tasks—from looking up the Latin names of Chinese food plants, to constructing readable tables on the basis of local agricultural statistics, to compiling a glossary of Chinese terms used in the text. All of those items came about with Yashu's help, and I cannot thank her enough.

According to an old Chinese proverb, which aptly applies a food metaphor, "A full person cannot truly understand a starving person's hunger."[1] In so doing, it succinctly sums up the difficulty of ever comprehending or empathizing with those whose life experiences differ from our own. But if we can't overcome this obstacle, then all understanding and empathy are impossible. Anthropological knowledge, after all, is grounded not only in the quest to understand diverse cultural worlds through personal experience but also in the idea that this knowledge can be communicated to others who were not there.

Without the help I received from everyone cited above, and from many who are not mentioned, I would not have been able to experience and gain knowledge about the food culture of Moonshadow Pond, nor been able to write about it here. But, of course, I take sole responsibility for my success or failure in analyzing and communicating what I have learned in the text that follows.

NOTE ON THE TEXT

Chinese words and phrases are romanized in Mandarin in the text. There is an extensive glossary at the back of the book that contains the Chinese characters for these words and phrases, as well as short notes about their significance.

ONE

The Value of Food in Rural China

AFTER A THREE-YEAR ABSENCE, I was returning to Moonshadow Pond, a village in southeastern China, where I have periodically undertaken field research for almost twenty years.

As soon as I entered the house of my hosts, Songling and Baoli, they cut open a local pomelo, a citrus fruit resembling a grapefruit. It was late May, and Songling had zealously saved it for my arrival; the date for storing pomelos had long since passed, and the fruit would have spoiled had I appeared any later. Soon afterward, several neighbors stopped by with tasty treats in hand. Miaoli came to the house with a dish of fermented rice flour pasta that she had stir fried with scallions (*weijiao ban*). Songling's sister-in-law Yinglei brought over some Qingming buns (*ban*), sweet, steamed buns made from chopped and boiled wild grasses mixed into a batter of glutinous rice flour and sugar.[1] The following day, Songling slaughtered one of her chickens and cooked another local specialty made up of chicken and ginger braised in homemade glutinous rice wine (*jijiu*).

Such food exchanges were not unusual in Moonshadow Pond. First, food was given to me to celebrate my return visit and to reconstitute warm social ties. In addition, many of these dishes contained seasonal, ethnic, and other symbolic references, and also embodied very specific medicinal qualities. For instance, the chicken and wine dish that Songling made for me was more commonly prepared on two occasions—either for new mothers to consume after childbirth or for everyone to enjoy during the celebrations of the Lunar New Year. The use of this dish in a postchildbirth diet stems from the ingredients, wine and ginger, as well as the braised preparation, all of which are viewed as conducive to the production of ample breast milk because of their "heating" qualities (more on this below). Moreover, the particular chicken used in this dish must ideally be raised at home and be large for it to impart its nourishing qualities to the mother.

Yinglei's Qingming buns were also not simply sweet treats. These are usually made during the Qingming Festival (Clear Bright Festival)—a time of year near the spring equinox when people clean their ancestors' gravesites. The green color of the buns is based on a homonym—although the character *qing* in the word *qingming* means "clear" or "pure," it is the same sound as a different character that means "green."[2]

These dishes were additionally associated with a particular ethnic identity, the Hakka, the Han Chinese linguistic and ethnic group that lives in Meizhou, an area in northeastern Guangdong Province, where Moonshadow Pond is located. And they can be used to distinguish the Hakka from other Guangdong ethnic groups, such as the Cantonese. As one friend said to me regarding the custom of making special food for women after childbirth, "We Hakka make *jijiu* [ginger chicken and wine], but the Cantonese prefer making pig's feet in ginger!"[3]

Certainly, the use of homegrown or even foraged ingredients, and the gifting of food that occurred that day, was not atypical. In Moonshadow Pond, food circulates constantly because it reaffirms old and creates new social ties. Indeed food is an important medium of social communication in the village. It is a constant focus of effort—from agricultural labor, to cooking, daily provisioning, gift exchange, worship, banqueting, and celebration of yearly holidays. It has great value and creates value in numerous domains of activity.

This book attempts to understand the value of food in rural China, or at least one small place in rural China—the village of Moonshadow Pond. That food is valuable in any society is certainly obvious. After all, food is vital to human biological existence. Further, a cursory look at food in almost any culture will show that it is implicated in many dimensions of social life beyond mere survival—from relationships among people within and outside the family to health, from economic and ecological systems to notions of morality and expressions of ethnic, religious, class, and national identities.

Given the universal salience of food in all cultures, therefore, why write a book about food in one small corner of rural China? One answer is simply that most people who have lived or even traveled in China will quickly agree that, while food is important in all societies, it is a highly charged focus of interest there. As the archaeologist K. C. Chang rather famously said about food in China, "That Chinese cuisine is the greatest in the world is highly debatable and is essentially irrelevant. But few can take exception to the statement that few other cultures are as food oriented as the Chinese. And this orientation appears to be as ancient as Chinese culture itself."[4]

From China's extremely varied and elaborate cuisine to memories of starvation and want, food assumes a central place in Chinese life. There is certainly no dearth of writing that focuses on food in China: cookbooks and even novels; academic studies encompassing everything from the history of food and agriculture in China[5] to analyses of social and cultural rituals, such as banqueting;[6] and investigations of the rapid development of fast food and the explosion of concern over food safety issues.[7] In what follows, however, I hope to provide something different. Instead of looking at a particular issue with regard to food—banqueting, fast food, health, or food scandals, to name a few—I aim to understand the role of food in one community as it shapes people's everyday lives.

The very fact that, in the late 1950s, less than a half century ago, China experienced a cataclysmic famine means that the experiences of older people in rural areas relative to food have incorporated everything from misery and extreme want to relative abundance. On the other hand, because China is rapidly industrializing, and so many young rural people are migrating to cities for work, the connection between food and agriculture is attenuated for many members of the younger generation, who have left behind the backbreaking exertions of peasant agriculture. Such divergent generational experiences are developments that make highlighting the role of food in rural China particularly interesting now.

As we shall see, despite these rapid transformations, food in Moonshadow Pond is an essential building block of social relations and a source of value within, but also well beyond, the market economy. The reform and opening (*gaige kaifang*) of China's political economy began in 1978 with the Third Plenary Session of the 11th Central Committee of the Communist Party of China. It had momentous consequences as China opened up its labor markets to the global capitalist economy and de-collectivized agriculture. Food has certainly been drastically affected by this change. Diets have improved and China is now a donor, and not a recipient, of international food aid. Noting rising living standards, changing sexual and family practices, and the migration of tens of millions of rural migrants to the city, scholars have also pointed to moral and ideological shifts, such as the rise of a new individualism in China.[8]

A focus on food, however, can give us a different framework for thinking about these transformations. Certainly the role of food in society has partially reflected the stunning rapidity of social and cultural change in China; trends such as the expansion of the commodity economy and rising individualism can be indexed through changing foodways (for instance, the growth of fast food outlets in cities). But in other respects, food's role as a measure and source of value in China, certainly in rural China, has defied oversimplfication. Indeed, the production and consumption of food in rural culture also creates spaces for community, connection, and meanings beyond commoditized values.

In recent years in North America, there has been a renewed interest in our own food practices. Much discussion in academic circles and in the larger public has focused on the ecological toll of a highly industrialized food system, one that depends on petrochemical inputs and entails long distances between farm and table, factors that contribute to both pollution and greenhouse gas emissions. The ever-expanding supply of highly processed and fast foods has been associated with adverse impacts on human health, such as obesity. Meanwhile, the use of pesticides and other chemical inputs on crops has raised fears about their links with cancer and other illnesses. Along with the development of fast foods, China is itself also undergoing a rise in industrialized food production.[9] Many of the same ills associated with these practices in the West are now emerging in China. Rather than fear of famine, the Chinese must contend now with fear of food itself; food dangers currently range from the deliberate adulteration of food for profit to the longer-term health and environmental impacts on the food supply of pesticides; herbicides; nitrogen-based fertilizers; and, finally, soil and water pollution from industry and mining.[10]

To grasp some of the changes that have occurred in China's food situation over the last century, particularly in rural China, let us compare peasant livelihoods before the Communists came to power in 1949 (referred to as Liberation), during the following collectivized period, and after the implementation of reforms in 1980. A few examples can give us a sense of the changes in China's food and agricultural system.

For instance, between 1929 and 1933, the economist John Lossing Buck and his colleagues at the University of Nanjing undertook a vast survey of Chinese villages and families (over 38,000 families in 168 localities in 22 provinces of China). Their picture of the Chinese peasant's diet and agricultural system at that time is fascinating and also grim. In densely populated rural China, Buck noted, relying on a predominantly vegetable diet enabled peasants to use less land to support more people; very little energy, no more than 2–3 percent of total calories, came from animal products.[11] Most animals were used not for meat but for draft purposes,[12] and most crops went directly to human food rather than to feed.[13] Because of the uncertainties of life, such as high infant mortality rates and crop failures caused by weather disasters, over half the rural population died before reaching the age of 28.[14] Indeed, peasant informants in Buck's study remembered an average of three famines in their lifetimes.[15] When these famines occurred, portions of the population were reduced to eating tree bark and grass, relocated, or even starved to death.[16] Land tended to be divided into numerous small parcels. Tenancy rates were higher in the south, where tenancy was as high as 32 percent of families.[17]

These data were gathered in the 1920s. But after Liberation in 1949, Chinese agriculture entered a period of whirlwind change. The rapid collectivization efforts of the Great Leap Forward (1958–61) led to what was probably the greatest famine in world history, with estimates of deaths directly attributable to famine varying from thirty to as high as forty-five million.[18] After that, a gradual increase in consumption occurred, but per capita food availability did not surpass 1958 levels until 1974.[19]

Changes after 1980 were dramatic. Vaclav Smith estimates that by 1984 the per capita food supply in China rose to within 5 percent of Japan's mean.[20] Between 1980 and 2000, a "dietary transition" occurred, in which the consumption of eggs and fruits increased sixfold, the purchase of pork tripled, and the consumption of pulses, once a dietary staple, declined by two-thirds.[21] All of this occurred while China's population was increasing by leaps and bounds, from 660 million in 1961, to 870 million in 1972, and to over 1.2 billion today. In the context of the growing population and the use of formerly agricultural land for industrialization and urbanization, this dietary transition is even more stunning, since it has occurred in a rapidly growing population using less land for agriculture.

Still, despite a marked dietary transition in China as a whole, dietary patterns in China today do vary depending on place of residence. Compared with rural residents, urban dwellers consume fewer grains but more meat, poultry, fish, fruits, eggs, dairy, and even vegetables than their rural counterparts.[22] Dietary consumption also varies by region. For instance, rural residents of the southeast, where Moonshadow Pond is located, have a much more varied diet than those in the north and west, where growing seasons are short and economic development and expansion have not occurred as rapidly.

Furthermore, it is important to keep in mind that the Chinese dietary regime today is not a replica of North American or European ones. For instance, entering the twenty-first century, Americans ate over a hundred grams of meat or chicken each day, while the Chinese consumed less than twenty-five.[23] The share of animal products, sugars, and sweets in the Chinese diet is certainly growing and is estimated at between one-fifth to one-third of the diet. But this is still not as much as in the United States, where fat, sugars, and sweets make up over 40 percent of American diets.[24] China, with fewer than ninety-nine tractors per thousand persons in the agricultural population (as compared to over a thousand tractors per thousand people in the agricultural population of the United States), also remains behind in the mechanization of agriculture.[25] And while under 10 percent of the American population is engaged in agriculture, the percentage is about 50 percent for China.[26]

In approaching my project, I wondered how all of these developments might affect the role and significance of food in a specific community. In addition to the important issues of food safety and health, very basic questions of meaning also arise. Scholars such as Sidney Mintz have long pointed out that "modernity" in food systems—that is, the rationalization of food production and consumption, and its increasing uniformity over vast reaches of time and space—has led to the demise of food as a signifier of meaning in particular times and spaces. In other words, food is no longer a language in a local symbolic system[27] because it is becoming increasingly commoditized and is exchanged over ever-larger geographical areas. Might not my earlier examples of food being used as a specific and locally significant symbolic language become increasingly rare, even in rural China, as food turns into a mere commodity that is uniform over great distances?

Writing about food as a local symbolic system in a somewhat isolated rural community of rural North China, Xin Liu called it both a "social institution and a system of values"[28] and remarked, "Day by day, occasion by occasion, individuals must learn rules and conventions of preparing and presenting food in order to communicate with others and become full members of the community. As a social institution, food—like language—is a kind of collective contract that one must accept in its entirety if one wishes to survive in the community it dominates."[29]

Indeed, the importance of food as a means of symbolic communication has a history of several thousand years in China. Speaking about ancient

China, historian Roel Sterckx states, "Culinary activity governed not only human relationships but also fermented the communication between humans and the spirit world. Cooking, the offering and exchanging of food, and commensality were among the most pervasive means of social and religious communication in traditional China."[30]

Food has been central to ritual occasions, as offerings to ancestors and gods as well as in banqueting, from ancient China until the present. But as rural China is now experiencing an ever-more freewheeling and unregulated market economy, following directly on the heels of several decades of collectivized agriculture, asking if these historical developments have influenced the role and meanings of food at the local level makes sense.

In examining foodways in contemporary China, however, extending our focus beyond the issues of globalization and modernity is important. A singular focus on modernity can unwittingly produce new forms of Orientalism, by which we evaluate China as moving in a straightforward trajectory toward "modern," albeit Chinese-inflected, orientations. (Ironically, such a focus can cause us to overlook the continuing importance of "nonmodern" practices in North America or Europe.)[31] Thus, before we assume that China is moving in a straight line toward a food modernity of industrialized, generic foods and food practices, dis-embedded from local meaning systems, we must also consider that modernity itself has always generated strong countercurrents. Further, modernity in its present incarnation of globalized capitalism is absorbed in different degrees and ways, even as it continues its spread throughout global space.

THE FOOD UNIVERSE OF MOONSHADOW POND

To understand how food practices and meanings really work in people's daily lives, we have to move from examining the big picture to a more localized focus.

The southeastern Chinese village of Moonshadow Pond, which I have been visiting periodically since 1993, is a good place to look more deeply at the significance of food in one place. Moonshadow Pond is actually my pseudonym for the village. The village and its neighboring village make up an administrative district that was a production brigade during the collective era. Together with twenty-one other administrative districts, they constitute a township of about forty-thousand people. And this township is located within Meixian, a county in northeastern Guangdong Province.

Meixian in turn is part of a much larger area comprising six counties that are now called Meizhou.[32] The residents of the Meizhou area of Guangdong are Hakka, a distinct ethnic and linguistic group in southeastern China that is nevertheless considered to be ethnic Chinese or Han. They believe they originated in north central China many hundreds of years ago. In addition to the Hakka, two other distinct linguistic and cultural groups of Han reside in Guangdong Province—the majority Cantonese, who inhabit the Pearl River Delta, and the Chaoshan people, who live on the coast in the northeast of the province. The residents of Moonshadow Pond in particular trace the establishment of their village to one ancestor, who migrated there at the end of the seventeenth century. Ancestral records go further back to an even more distant ancestor, who lived in Jiangxi Province (northwest of Guangdong) in the eleventh century.[33]

Since first arriving in Moonshadow Pond in the summer of 1993, I have returned several times. I lived there from 1995–96, during the summers of 1997 and 2006, for five months in the spring of 2007, and during visits in the spring of 2010 and in the fall and winter of 2012.[34] Because I had established relationships with residents over many years, it was a good venue for studying food in rural China. My visits from 2007 onward were explicitly focused on local food culture, and I was also able to comb through earlier field notes to find relevant information.

Moonshadow Pond was the ancestral village of a friend, who had introduced me, and each time I returned I lived with the same family—her closest relations in the village. My hosts, Songling and her husband Baoli, were a middle-aged couple when I began my fieldwork in the mid-1990s. Living in Songling and Baoli's house, I shared meals; witnessed relationships between and among families; and participated in festive occasions, attended banquets, and took part in important yearly and life-cycle rituals. I also gained an overview of key parts of the agricultural calendar, including rice planting and harvesting, as well as seasonal changes in produce. Additionally, I conducted surveys and did much informal visiting, keeping notes on over fifty families.

Songling and Baoli had come of age during the collective era, had spent their entire lives in the village, and had participated in the agricultural life of the collective during the Mao era. After the Communists came to power in 1949, China transitioned rapidly to a system of collective agriculture. In 1958, the Great Leap Forward began. Communes, often with as many as twenty thousand people, were organized as the basic units of production and

MAP 1. Meizhou's location in Guangdong Province and within the People's Republic of China.

distribution throughout the country. Eating was also collectivized; family kitchens were abolished. Grain harvests were often left to rot in the fields because peasants were urged to spend their time trying to smelt iron from their personal cooking pots and pans in "backyard furnaces." All of these activities were supposed to fuel the country's industrial revolution and to enable them to catch up with the West in fifteen years. However, no iron was successfully produced from this effort, and after peasants ate their fill in collective canteens for a few months, food started to run out. Further, local officials often overstated their production in order to appear successful to higher-ups, resulting in even less food being available for peasants to eat after state procurements. Procurements were determined on the basis of a percentage of total production, and if production was exaggerated, even more would be taken away. Thus, of the grain actually produced, little remained in the countryside. The result was massive starvation.

In Moonshadow Pond, Songling and Baoli lived through these terrible times and, like many others, remember resorting to "famine foods" in order to survive. They made buns by grinding the indigestible husks of rice, mixing these with water and steaming them, a practice to which Songling attributed her continuing digestive problems. Other villagers tried to make a similar steamed bun using the ingredients from the top of banana tree roots. They also tried to create a feeling of fullness by mixing starch from rootstock plants, such as cassava and edible canna, with boiling water. The resulting brew was a bit thick, like drinking cornstarch and water, but it had little caloric or nutritional value.

The disastrous results of the Great Leap led China to reorganize communes into smaller, more manageable units in 1962. As the Great Leap canteens fell apart, cooking returned to family kitchens. Though labor was still organized on a collective basis, it was through production teams of twenty-to-thirty families each, and payment systems were roughly geared to the amount of effort or type of work one did. For instance, Moonshadow Pond was organized into six production teams and, together with its neighboring village, formed a single production brigade. Significantly, private garden plots were created for each family during that time so that families could grow their own vegetables, and these have continued to the present.

From the end of the Great Leap to the late 1970s, diets slowly improved, and famine was no longer part of the picture. Statistics from the Meixian Gazetteer paint a picture of steady increases in the consumption of basic grains and production of meat from the end of the Great Leap to the early years of the reform era.[35] Still, until the reform period, daily fare continued to be simple, and meat was a rarity. "Through the 1950s, 1960s, even into the 1970s," Baoli told me, "we had sweet potatoes for one or two meals per day, and then congee [*zhou* or rice porridge] was for the other meals. We never had *fan* [dry cooked rice]."

But during the reform and opening initiated in 1978, dramatic changes were implemented. The reforms opened China to the world market and to capitalist modes of production, which also meant the end of collective agriculture. In Moonshadow Pond, as elsewhere in rural China, villagers were given use rights in collective land, including rice paddy land and dry land, which could be used for other crops. They also retained their garden plots. Productivity and crop diversity increased because peasants had much more latitude than in the collective era about what to grow and how (see appendix A, figs. A.1–A.8, for more details on changes in agricultural productivity from 1949 through the reform era in Meixian.)

Initially, however, peasants still had to pay a tax in grain on the land they used, and this meant that, in Moonshadow Pond, they still had to produce a certain amount of rice. Later, peasants had a choice between paying the tax in grain or in money. A cash assessment on rice production did not fall heavily on villages like Moonshadow Pond. With the loosening of regulations about rural-to-urban migration in the reform era, many younger villagers began migrating to cities to work for wages, supplementing family incomes. With wages rising, and the younger generation leaving the countryside for work, families could always come up with the cash to pay the tax, even if they did not produce grain from their land. However, in the hinterlands of China, where families were less likely to have wages from outside work, the taxes, both in kind and in cash, were much more burdensome. Ultimately, these factors may have been one of the reasons the national government eliminated taxes on family rice production in 2005.[36] Villagers could now make decisions about what to cultivate according to their own needs.

By 2012, Songling, now in her late sixties, still maintained a large vegetable garden and raised her own chickens. Until recently, she had grown her own rice. By contrast, Songling and Baoli's three married children (two daughters and a son) and their four grandchildren spent most of their time in the county capital, a bustling center of 380,000 that was not far from Moonshadow Pond. In the capital, their son, Yanhong, and his sister Meiying owned a small store that sold bedding materials. Their younger sister, Fengying, operated the same type of business, which she jointly managed with her husband. Fengying was quite successful as a businesswoman, both running the bedding material business and also collecting rent on some other properties.

Daughters in rural southeastern China are traditionally expected to "marry out" of their natal homes, and into their husband's homes. Sons are customarily expected to bring their wife "in" to their household. But, work schedules and job situations may mean that all family members do not always live and eat together. Thus, as Yanhong had a store in the county capital, he and his wife and son spent most nights in quarters above the store instead of in the village at his parents' home. From their abode in town, Yanhong's wife spent less time commuting to her factory job, and their son could cycle to middle school more quickly.

But despite all of Songling and Baoli's adult children moving to the county capital, coming and going between village and city were constant; on weekends and holidays, one or more grandchildren would stay over in Moonshadow Pond. Songling and Baoli could also visit the county capital fairly easily now by hopping on a public bus; and by 2012, two of their three married children had cars.[37] So family members traveled back and forth, and food always accompanied their travels. If Songling were going to town to visit her children, she would bring fresh pork from the village or vegetables from her garden. If Fengying were coming to Moonshadow Pond, she might bring her parents a special snack, associated with another region of Meizhou, that was unavailable in the village. No one ever came or went empty handed.

Songling and Baoli's family situation was hardly an unusual one in Moonshadow Pond, where most of the younger population worked and lived outside the village, or at least worked outside the village. Not only is the local county seat a location of employment but the metropolises of Shenzhen and Guangzhou are also sites of much labor migration from the village. These cities are several hours away by bus—too far to commute on a daily basis. Thus, by 2007, 24 percent of all households in Moonshadow Pond had at least one family member who had migrated beyond Meixian for employment.[38]

In Moonshadow Pond, therefore, a labor transition took place that is not unlike the ones experienced in many other rural localities in China, as growing numbers of young and even middle-aged people work for wages and are inevitably less involved in the world of agriculture. Hence, although the population of Moonshadow Pond has hovered around eight hundred persons since I started my fieldwork in the mid-1990s,[39] at first glance the number of people engaged in agriculture and their commitment to it seem to have diminished.[40] In 1997, the majority of Moonshadow Pond families relied on a mixture of agriculture and wage labor. While only 10 percent of households earned their livings *entirely* from farming, just 14 percent of families did *no* farming. Ten years later, the majority of families still combined agriculture with wage labor. However, the number of families who did not farm at all had grown to 33 percent, while the number who earned their living only from agriculture had dropped to 6 percent.

However, a caveat needs to be added to this picture of a decline in farming. In Moonshadow Pond, "farming" is identified by the word *gengtian,*

FIGURE 1. In the garden plot.

which literally means to "plow the fields." Local residents understand *geng-tian* as referring to those who still grow their own rice. (The particular significance of growing rice for Moonshadow Pond residents will be explored more deeply in later chapters.) Growing vegetables, however, is an activity that is engaged in much more extensively—even by those who are no longer considered to be farming, and even by those who have outside employment (see fig. 1). Essentially, we might think of this activity as gardening, and there are few families in Moonshadow Pond that do not maintain a minimal garden for vegetables, even if they have abandoned rice cultivation.

Indeed, the variety of cultivated plants in Moonshadow Pond is huge. Leafy greens and cabbages of many types; tubers and root vegetables, such as taro, sweet potatoes, carrots, and daikon radish; rhizomes, such as ginger; a large variety of gourds; garlic green onion varieties; corn; fava beans and other legumes; eggplants; and peanuts are just some of the varieties of plants that are cultivated by villagers in their gardens. Villagers also own individual banana trees (again, there are several types) and papaya trees (see fig. 2). Many items, furthermore, have multiple uses. Daikan radish (*luobo*) is boiled in soup, stir fried with meat, dried to use in congee, and dried even longer as a cure for the digestive system. Papaya can be eaten raw, but it can also be stir fried.

FIGURE 2. Fresh bananas.

Most families in Moonshadow Pond, therefore, fall between the two extremes of having abandoned agricultural activity altogether and self-provisioning all their own food. The majority still use the land allocated to them to cultivate their own rice and vegetables, but they also rely on wage labor or the small business activities of some family members to augment their livelihoods, using the cash income to purchase food they do not self-provision. Additionally, about 17 percent of households in 2007 engaged in market-based agricultural production, such as raising chickens or pigs for sale; fish farming; raising goats to produce milk; and tending fruit orchards of pomelos, mandarin oranges, and oranges. Some individuals butcher and sell fresh pork, or produce value-added agricultural products such as fresh bean curd.

Food provisioning is crucial to the subsistence of Moonshadow Pond residents, but it is viewed as more than simple provisioning. Villagers often speak about the "sweetness" of local vegetables as opposed to the "bitterness" of vegetables that have been exposed to pesticides and herbicides, which they might buy in city markets. As one village resident said to me disparagingly about vegetables from these markets, "Those are sold by people who want to earn money, and schoolchildren have been sickened by the poison in these, but we grow our vegetables to eat for ourselves, so we prefer these whenever possible." Another villager told me she had visited a relative abroad in Indonesia, where she ate what she described as very "bitter" vegetables that had clearly been adulterated with farming chemicals. Young migrants who returned to the village for holidays from the metropolises of Shenzhen and Guangzhou often comment both on the "sweetness" of the village vegetables and on how much they miss these when they are away. Once when relatives from Guangzhou came to visit Songling and Baoli, they spoke excitedly not only about how fresh the vegetables tasted but even about how good the rice was. In fact, one relative said, "The rice is so good you don't even have to add anything to it!"

It is not procurement from the market *per se* that brands some foods as more dangerous or less tasty than others. Food originating from the village, even if it is sold by local vendors, is usually viewed as better in almost all ways—tastier, healthier, and less fraudulent! Small-scale local producers in Moonshadow Pond play up their differences from larger factory farmers outside the village. For instance, in describing his business raising chickens, one villager explained how much care must be taken in feeding chickens, and also in ensuring that the chickens have room to run around. He emphasized that the chicken droppings from his operation were sold to local people for cultivating fruit trees so that nothing was wasted. The "circle of good things" (*liangxing xunhuan*) was his description of this self-contained system. He also boasted that the chickens he raised for sale, while not quite as good as those he raised at home, were certainly much better than "factory chickens" (*gongchang ji*) Similarly, villagers who raise and sell pigs on the local market also often point to this circle of good things. A Hui, who is the eldest son of my neighbor in the village, raises pigs, manages a small pomelo orchard, and tends two fishponds. He told me that his pomelo trees were fertilized with pig manure, and that the pig manure could be used to fuel his stove. Like many people, he spoke of the dangers to one's health from "farm chemicals" (*nongyao*).[41]

Negative attitudes about *nongyao* does not mean that villagers always practiced organic agriculture in every domain. While no villagers used farm chemicals on their gardens, many used nitrogen-based fertilizers on rice. What might explain this seeming contradiction between villagers' love of their unadulterated vegetables and some villagers' choice to use chemical fertilizers on rice? Such chemical fertilizers were viewed by villagers as increasing productivity; rice production is now primarily the work of middle-aged women, who view these fertilizers as a labor saver, since it enables them to produce more per acre.[42] Nonetheless, villagers were cognizant of the dangers of overusing such chemicals. In a survey I conducted in 2007, over half the respondents reported using no chemical fertilizers on their rice fields, or at least reported attempting to keep their use to a minimum.[43]

As *gengtian* essentially refers to growing rice, it should not be surprising to learn that rice remains a staple for all. The distinction between rice and trimmings (*fan/cai*) is a basic element of the Chinese dietary regime, especially in southeastern China. Nowadays, Moonshadow Pond families typically consume dry rice as their staple for two meals each day, while consuming rice porridge or congee as their staple for one meal, usually breakfast. Of course, a bowl of rice that was not watered down as congee was a real luxury in the past. But at a bare minimum, a bowl of congee with salted vegetables can define a meal, as even this is made up of the crucial *fan/cai* combination. What is more, rice is not only a staple but is seen as a part of "Hakka" identity. For instance, Songling often stated that part of being a "real Hakka" was to desire and eat rice.[44] (With the rise in the standard of living, noodles can occasionally substitute for rice, especially in breakfast dishes such as rice or wheat noodles in soup, or fried noodles served as an accompaniment to soup.)

It should be kept in mind, however, that the *fan/cai* distinction pertains to ordinary meals and not banquets. Unlike the structure of ordinary meals, the foundation of banquets is not based on rice. The Hakka use the same verb, "to eat," for both ordinary meals and banquets. However, ordinary meals are referred to as "eating rice" (*shifan*), while banquets are literally referred to as "eating spirits," or "eating liquor" (*shijiu*). Thus, while the ordinary meal is glossed as a combination of rice and trimmings, the banquet is characterized as a combination of these trimmings or dishes with wine or liquor. If rice appears at a banquet, it is usually as fried rice served toward the end of a whole series of dishes. Occasionally, the option of getting up and serving oneself white rice is also afforded at a banquet, but, if so, it occurs only toward the tail end.

Referring to banquets as liquor consuming events does not mean that everyone at a banquet drinks alcoholic substances. Indeed, while work-related banqueting in China can entail profuse alcohol drinking,[45] not all banqueting in Moonshadow Pond, particularly around family- and lineage-related events, does. For instance, at a wedding or at other banquets in Moonshadow Pond, men drink and toast ostentatiously, while women and children tend to confine themselves to nonalcoholic beverages, such as sodas or peanut milk. Women may also toast with homemade glutinous rice wine; once it is cooked, its alcoholic effect is neutralized. Subsequent chapters will explore banqueting in more detail, but the distinction between ordinary meals that are categorized by the act of eating rice versus banquets that are categorized by the act of drinking liquor is important to keep in mind.

As for ordinary meals, in addition to rice, there are a few other non-negotiable elements in the Hakka cuisine of Moonshadow Pond. Clear soups are customarily served with lunch and dinner—they are usually made with pork bones and may contain dried medicinal grasses or preserved vegetables, beans of various types, or root vegetables. These soups are typically consumed after the rice/trimming (*fan/cai*) combination. If you are a guest at a family meal and have already eaten one bowl of rice, the host may ask you, "Would you like soup or more rice?" So while rice and trimmings go together, soup usually finishes off the meal, though it can also substitute for a second bowl of rice.

Greens and other vegetables, either fresh or dried, are also part of every meal; as stated above, despite changes in the economy, gardening is still the main source for these.[46] While preserving vegetables through drying or pickling is still practiced in the village, dried and pickled vegetables are no longer as central to the diet as they were in the less prosperous past. Nowadays, dried vegetables are more likely to show up as an optional condiment with congee for the morning meal, or as an ingredient in one particularly famous Hakka dish consisting of braised pork and dried salted greens (*meicai kourou*). Meanwhile, the variety of vegetables that is cultivated has expanded greatly as the standard of living has improved and as people have started cooking vegetables that need more oil to prepare, or those (such as cilantro) that are delicious but not necessarily filling.

One common staple of the past that has almost disappeared is the humble fava bean. I rarely saw it consumed in the 1990s or 2000s. Fava beans are quite filling and were often cooked along with dried salted vegetables in order to enhance their flavor. Most likely, one reason for the decline of this pulse has to do with the great rise in meat consumption (as pulse production in all of China has declined dramatically with the rise of meat). Moonshadow

FIGURE 3. Purchasing local pork in early morning.

Pond villagers in their thirties and forties can remember the fava bean from their childhoods—which dates its commonplace consumption through to the end of the collective era. Indeed, the county gazetteer confirms this impression—the hundreds of thousands of acres of land in all of Meixian that were once devoted to fava cultivation had declined by the late 1980s to under 6,000 acres (see appendix A, fig. A.9).[47]

As the standard of living has increased in the village, meat (which usually means pork in this context), poultry, or fish can now be found in most people's daily fares. Villagers rely much more on the market for these items than for rice and vegetables,[48] but they also go to great lengths to procure their meat from local sources (which, as stated above, are presumed to be more trustworthy). Pork is purchased primarily from local butchers (there are several in Moonshadow Pond), and village residents often emphasize that meat from locally slaughtered pigs is preferable to the meat sold in city markets, for reasons of both taste and safety (see fig. 3).

Other meats are also eaten but much less commonly. Some people raise dogs for meat, but this is not daily fare—though dog may find its way onto a banquet menu, or be used for addressing particular health conditions, such as back pain. Beef is only available from the county capital and is not raised locally (although it is slaughtered locally because people in Meixian are reluctant to purchase meat that is shipped from far). Goats are raised in the village for milk, but goat meat and lamb are usually eaten only during a small space of time during the winter solstice.

Pork, which is what really counts as meat most of the time, is used in numerous ways. It is stir fried, its bones are used for soup stock, and it is also used to make a popular morning soup called the "three-levels" soup (*san ji di tang*) that always accompanies a simple fried-noodle dish with scallions and garlic. The soup is made from small pieces of fresh meat, liver, and intestines, and because of its freshness, it actually tastes sweet. The soup also contains dried red yeast rice (*hong qu mi*), a byproduct of making one's own wine at home from glutinous rice. The "three levels" refers to the three highest levels of examination that a candidate for the imperial court had to pass if he wanted to become a high-level bureaucrat at the emperor's court—the highest mark of meritocratic success during the imperial era. The implication is that this soup is nourishing enough to fuel the highest levels of scholarly success.

"This is just our Hakka dish," Songling used to tell me. Baoli was so fond of it that, whenever my husband and I spoke about how we would miss the fresh food from the village when we returned home, Baoli would excitedly exclaim, "Over there, you won't be able to get the three levels!"

Almost every day, during my morning walk at the crack of dawn, I would see a gathering of villagers around one or more local pork vendors. These men usually placed their fresh pork meat on a flat of wood draped across the back of their motorcycles. In 2012, the local regulations changed, and pork vendors were directed to purchase their meat from a city slaughterhouse, a regulation put in place to control fraud; but most vendors preferred to make their own arrangements with local pig farmers so they could sell meat that was only a few hours old. Villagers considered the route from village pig farmer to city slaughterhouse and back to the village for sale too time-consuming to yield fresh meat. (If a government inspector were suddenly to enter the village, someone would usually call up the vendor on a cell phone and tip him or her off; the vendor would disappear before the inspector could find him and return after the inspector had left.)

As for poultry, most families raise their own chickens and ducks. Yet while these animals are almost always slaughtered for specific festivities, such as the Lunar New Year, or for special purposes, such as making chicken in glutinous rice wine for a new mother, at other times poultry may be purchased from a vendor.[49]

In addition to meat and vegetables, fruit and eggs are now commonly eaten, and milk is beginning to be a more frequent part of the diet in a minority of families.[50] Citrus fruits, particularly pomelos, are not only grown for sale, but have become a very important part of the daily diet and social ritual. If you visit a family during the many months pomelos are available, your hosts will probably break open a pomelo to share, as Songling did when I returned to the village in the incident discussed at the beginning of this chapter. In fact, the pomelo has become such an exemplary part of social ritual that, when visiting dignitaries come to Meixian, they are almost always presented with a pomelo!

Milk in the diet does not necessarily mean powdered milk (which has been made famous by recent scandals) but rather fluid milk. Indeed, local goat milk has recently become popular. Two families in Moonshadow Pond raise goats and deliver milk twice a day, primarily either to families with elderly people who think it buttresses their health or to families with very small children (more on this in chapter 2).

During my early morning walks in Moonshadow Pond, I would usually bump into a group of four or five elderly women (all over 80), who were also taking a morning walk. On these occasions, it was not unusual for one of these women to pick out something that looked to me like a blade of grass or even a twig to bring home and use for medicinal purposes. The wild environment indeed remains a source of sustenance, but village elders undoubtedly have the richest knowledge of this environment. Often the wild grasses and twigs they gather are boiled and then used topically, or ingested to treat everything from scratchy throats to cuts and abrasions.[51] Wild plants have also found their way into soups[52] and even into seasonal treats, such as the Qingming buns referred to at the beginning of this chapter.

Among foraged items, water is one item that is particularly worthy of note. Older villagers remember a time when the river that flowed through the village was considered a source of pure drinking water. But that time passed with the rise of nitrogen-based fertilizers and other contaminants; now the river water is considered unsafe for drinking. All village houses now have wells, and, if this well water is boiled, it is considered safe for drinking (as long as it is not too close to rice paddy land). However, the taste of water is very important for many people. This is true for water used for cooking in general, but it is especially the case for water used to make tea. The market for high-status tea has grown with greater wealth, and more attention than ever is paid to the quality of the water used for brewing tea.[53]

Indeed, tea is ever present in the life of Moonshadow Pond. Serving tea is the minimal gesture of hospitality when guests, or even neighbors, walk into the house. But it was not always so. As our neighbor Aihua reminded me, many people were so poor in the past that they could offer only boiled water to guests. Now, however, tea and tea-making implements are essential features of all Moonshadow Pond homes. In each house, a public room is generally arranged with a tea table surrounded by seating; a teapot, small tea cups, and either a thermos to store hot water or an electric water heater to boil water are always present.

Serving tea in Meixian, and in many parts of China, is a much more social experience than merely pouring tea into a large cup or mug as it might be in the United States. The host must continuously pour boiling water onto the leaves in the teapot and then refill tiny tea cups for each guest. This tea ritual can be highly informal, as when someone enters a shop and the shopkeeper makes a cup of tea for her in a tiny plastic disposable cup, or very formal, as when one visits friends and relatives during the Lunar New Year, when the tea will be accompanied by many special treats.[54]

For the sake of cooking and tea drinking, therefore, many village residents will go to great lengths to procure water from natural aquifers (see fig. 4). One such place is a rock at a cliff's bottom near the village. Villagers may travel weekly to this aquifer by motorcycle, or even by car (now that car ownership has begun to spread), in order to collect water and bring it home in large containers. Water from this source is so popular that people may have to queue for hours if they go to collect it during daylight. So people have started to travel late at night to avoid the rush. In this case, we see not so much the continuation of an old custom with regard to foraging but a new development born out of modern concerns about the taste and purity of water.

The concern with purity is part of a larger focus on food's influence on one's health, and on the particular qualities of food as it affects specific parts of the body. Such concerns are not merely those of specialists in Moonshadow Pond but are also a part of daily food practices. People will effortlessly talk about the appropriate foodstuffs to counteract particular health conditions and to favorably affect one's *qi,* understood as a vital energy, vapor, or breath that circulates through one's body. All foodstuffs are seen as having a quality (*xing*). They can be cold, cool, hot, warm, dry, or neutral. For instance,

FIGURE 4. Collecting pure water from a natural aquifer.

pineapple and mango are viewed as heating, whereas pomelo is cooling. Some greens, such as sweet potato leaves, mustard greens, celery, cucumber, pumpkin, and Chinese cabbage, are neutral. Other greens, like Chinese chives, scallions, and garlic stems, are heating, and still others, such as bitter gourd and green cabbage, are cooling. Of the many different medicinal soups made from grasses and twigs (*yaocai*), each is seen as having different properties. Medicinal soups are also used for their positive effects on specific organs (e.g., lungs, kidneys, liver) or for treatment of various conditions (e.g., inflammation, coughs, thirst).[55]

As Vivienne Lo states, "While the term *wu wei* (the five flavors) may refer in a general sense to the pleasures of eating, medical historians have preferred to translate *wei* as 'sapors' to emphasize the medical rather than culinary virtues of the term." And she continues to tell us that by the eighteenth century, "Every foodstuff, like every drug, had a sapor associated with the pentic system, a *qi,* a relative potency, and was associated with healing different parts of the body. This *qi* in a medical context indicated thermostatic qualities: hot, warm, neutral, cool, and cold. The five flavors were each associated with an organ: the lungs, spleen, kidneys, liver and heart."[56]

Such ideas clearly permeated society over time, and in Moonshadow Pond they are part of everyday approaches to food. When my husband suffered from an upset stomach after a trip to a tea plantation in 2007, our neighbors said his illness was the result of getting a cold wind on the mountains during the day, then consuming excessively "hot" dishes when we ate dinner at a restaurant in the county capital that evening. This, they said, created an imbalance in his system. One of the reasons Moonshadow Pond residents disdain fast foods such as Kentucky Fried Chicken (that can be found in the county capita) is that they believe these foods to be excessively "heating" and to negatively impact digestion.

As we can see from this brief overview, the "food universe" of Moonshadow Pond is a complex mix of cultivated and foraged, self-provisioned and purchased, the locally available and the more distantly procured (see fig. 5). It is fair to say that villagers share a common food culture. Sidney Mintz describes a "common cuisine" as one that is shared by a community of people who eat it "with sufficient frequency to consider themselves experts on it. They all believe and care to believe, that they know what it consists of, how it is made, and how it should taste."[57]

Within this food universe, daily meals are routinely cooked at home. There are a few items, such as bean curd and fish and meat balls served in soup, that cannot be made at home. These are made daily by local businesses and sold in the village. Also, two roadside restaurants in the village have recently been upgraded and are now three-story banquet halls. The clientele for these restaurants is primarily white-collar workers from the nearby county capital. But rural dwellers also use their services for special occasions, such as weddings and other banquets. Recently, a few villagers have opened roadside noodle shops on the highway that passes through the village. These serve popular breakfast noodle dishes, mainly for travelers and commuters heading to work on the heavily trafficked highway to the capital.

For most Moonshadow Pond residents, eating out is reserved for celebratory events. As one Moonshadow Pond resident said of the banquet halls, "We villagers don't eat at that kind of place unless there is a wedding or something like that. We eat at home. These kinds of places are for *ganbu* [cadres], people with a *danwei* [office work unit], and other people who are not spending their own money."

The preceding provides a cursory description of the foods that are produced and consumed in Moonshadow Pond, as well as some of the social and cultural contexts of consumption. The chapters that follow will look more deeply at "food in action," or, rather, the ways in which people use food to organize their work; communicate meanings about the present and

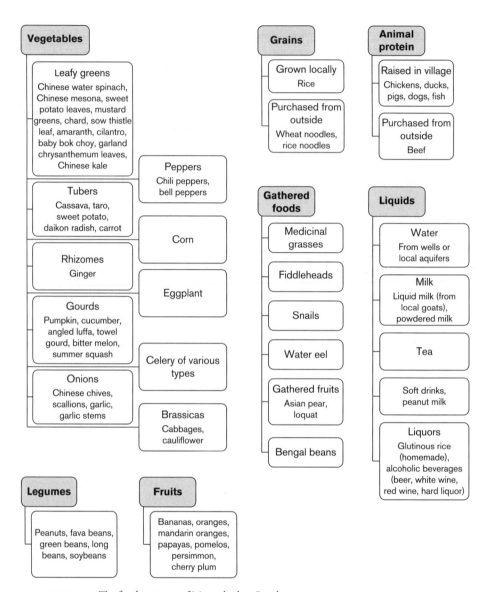

FIGURE 5. The food universe of Moonshadow Pond.

the past; create, shape, and sustain relationships; and communicate moral values.

FOOD AS A CULTURAL SYSTEM

Food has always had a dual nature. It is a necessity for biological existence, but in all cultures it has also been invested with a range of meanings. But in discussing the specific relationship of food to culture, analysts have often fallen into two camps. Those who emphasize deep structure, or long-lasting meanings of food that transcend particular shifting contexts, are applying a semiotic or meaning-based approach to understanding the role of food in culture. Others, while also looking at the meanings attributed to food, choose to emphasize historical and contextual elements of the relationships of food, culture, and society.

Two anthropologists who have written widely on food, and whose work illustrates these frameworks, are Mary Douglas and Sidney Mintz. It was Mary Douglas who so famously articulated the idea that food is a "system of communication"[58] that encodes messages about social relationships, including degrees of hierarchy, inclusion, and exclusion.[59] A model for this kind of meaning-based approach is Douglas's analysis of dietary rules in the Old Testament's book of Leviticus.[60] As she pointed out, the notion of *holiness* in Leviticus was equated with wholeness, perfection, and completeness. Hence, animals that were considered "whole," or pure, were allowed, while those defined as incomplete (such as the cud-chewing, cloven-footed pig) were considered anomalous and were prohibited. These rules about food define a particular community within which the rules apply, hence creating boundaries between insiders and outsiders. For Douglas, therefore, no part of a food system can be understood in isolation from other parts, or from an overall cultural-meaning system. In this particular case, perfect whole animals are considered analogous to the perfection of the temple altar, and these examples of wholeness and perfection are ultimately analogized with the need or desire to preserve the territorial integrity of the promised land itself.[61]

Douglas perceived food as being not merely symbolic but as having a language, with both a syntax and a grammar, that expresses core cultural meanings.[62] Approaching food as a language entails carefully observing such things as the order of elements within a meal, and the relationship between meals (in a day, over a week, or in a year), as these relationships themselves constitute meanings. One example of how these "syntagmatic relations" constitute meanings is simply illustrated in her example: "'It can't be lunchtime, I haven't had breakfast yet!'"[63]

Additionally, within this linguistic system, the individual elements of each meal can function as signs or paradigms for one another. So, for instance, in the British working-class food system of the 1970s, a biscuit with icing and a jam center might function in a small meal as a desiccated, condensed substitute for plum cake with sweet custard in a more elaborate meal.[64] As Douglas famously put it, "On the two axes of syntagm and paradigm, chain and choice, sequence and set, call it what you will, . . . food elements can be ranged until they are all accounted for either in grammatical terms, or down to the last lexical item."[65]

Interestingly, this "grammar," or language, of food is one reason, according to Douglas, that innovaton is often difficult to accomplish within food systems. There simply is no way to easily insert elements for which there is no conceptual space. For instance, there was no place for whole raw fruits within the meals of the working-class British families she studied—fruit could only be inserted into a meal as a sliced decorative topping for cake, cooked into a pudding, or spread as jam on a biscuit or toast.[66] And, seemingly more limiting, each of these elements can occur only within specific courses in particular meals. For these reasons, one can examine cultural categories and distinctions to answer the question, for specific contexts, "What is it that makes a meal a meal?"[67]

Douglas, and others who used her approach,[68] was able, through the analysis of food as a meaning system, to expose cultural categories that are not always readily apparent on the surface. But if one looks at food systems *only* as enclosed meaning systems, one can encounter difficulties explaining significant global transformations in diet. For instance, Douglas cited neither external factors, such as economy or ecology, nor specific historical circumstances when discussing cultural meanings of food and their impact on social relations.

Here the approach of Sidney Mintz, who emphasized the role of global political economy in changing dietary patterns, is illustrative of a different framework for thinking about the relationship of food to culture, society, and history. Mintz's work on sugar was pathbreaking in bringing changing political and economic relations into the analysis of the relationship between food and culture. He examined the role of sugar in Europe and the Americas as it shifted over several centuries, from an elite spice and condiment in medieval Europe, to an ingredient in the artfully constructed deserts of the nobility, to the cheap dietary energy of tea and jam consumed by the industrial proletariat in England. Indeed, Mintz's depiction of the diffusion of sugar makes the case that it fueled the industrial revolution in England every bit as much as coal. And its role has now expanded to become a ubiquitous substance throughout the modern food system.

Certainly the omnipresence of processed foods in the modern diet would have been impossible without an exponential rise in the consumption of both fats and sugars, and according to Mintz, these transformations have ultimately broken down some of the very conceptual regularities that Douglas spoke about in her work. Citing Douglas in the conclusion of his study of sugar, Mintz concluded that "The whole momentum of modern life has been away from any such 'lexicon' or 'grammar,' and the analogy is not a good one. Describing the foods in a meal in linguistic terminology hardly 'accounts for' them, because the structural constraints on ingestion are not comparable to those on language; we can eat without meals, but we cannot speak without grammar."[69] Mintz went on to explain that, in the world of mass-produced fast food, "The 'paradigm' of the meal, the 'syntagm' of the meal schedule, and time restraints on eating may all be considered as obstructions to the exercise of individual preference."[70] "Ingestion," he wrote, has become "individualized and noninteractive."[71]

Mintz's historical approach and Douglas's symbolic approach need not be viewed as incompatible. A number of theorists have combined materialist and symbolic or semiotic approaches.[72] I have found both perspectives useful in approaching the relationship between food and culture in Moonshadow Pond. For instance, it would be impossible to ignore the Douglas-inspired framework of food as a meaningful symbolic system. As subsequent chapters will show, the exchange of food in Moonshadow Pond is certainly a "language" that can be used to manipulate social relationships, create distance or closeness, and advance hierarchy or greater equality. Further, many core cultural concepts inform food consumption and production in Moonshadow Pond, not only medicinal notions, such as hot versus cold foods, but also ideas about the proper components of a meal. Food is also a moral instrument that expresses and acts out core cultural values such as filiality. What Douglas would call the "syntagmatic relations" of food is also clearly relevant here—because food structures both short and long cycles of time, from the rhythm of the day to yearly ritual cycles. Thus, despite the fact that the villagers possess greater wealth, and a diet far richer than most ordinary villagers consumed in the past, many customary meanings have retained their relevance.

Yet an approach informed with an eye toward historical transformation is also necessary for examining the relationship between food and culture in rural China, as it has experienced profound transformations over the last fifty years. As noted earlier, older residents of Moonshadow Pond have lived through civil war and revolution in the 1930s and 1940s, the establishment of the Communist government in 1949, large-scale collectivization followed by famine from 1958–61, a modified version of collectivization in the 1960s and 1970s, and finally the era of "reform and opening" that began in 1979. As subsequent chapters document, many of these historical developments were experienced and are remembered through food—as periods of relative food security or dearth and even famine, and also as changes in the organization of food production itself. At the same time, nowadays many young people have never experienced food through a participatory relationship with agriculture. To wonder if and how these historical transformations have influenced the role and meaning of food in their lives is not farfetched.

In looking at both long-lasting and deep-rooted cultural categories as well as at historical contexts, I have found a focus on the concept of value to be particularly useful. I turn to this issue below.

THE VALUE OF FOOD IN MOONSHADOW POND

In Moonshadow Pond, the value of food is expressed and appreciated daily, not only in words, but in the actions and interactions of people within the family, in the village and in their connections with the outside world. Indeed, it might not even be a stretch to say that in Moonshadow Pond daily life is experienced as a series of events and transactions around food.

On entering the village, visitors might be brought to the boundaries of the old village to make food offerings to the local gods who protect it; they might also be brought to the local ancestral temple to offer the "three sacrificial meats" (*san sheng*)—pork, chicken, and fish—to the lineage ancestors as well. As guests, they might be at the receiving end of generous hospitality centered on food, not only during banquets, but in attempts to ply them with as many delicious local specialties as possible during each meal. They might also learn how these different foods affect health—and which ones they should eat to strengthen weak areas of their constitutions. If the outsiders stay longer, they would start to notice that all kinds of exchanges take place daily between family members, kin, and neighbors, from sharing vegetables grown in their own gardens to elaborate gifting practices accompanying more formal events. They would also observe that despite these exchanges, which take place outside the domain of the market, food is also an important commodity, and the relative prices of different food items are a frequent topic of conversation. For instance, it would not be unusual for our guests to hear a visitor from a different part of Meixian and a local from Moonshadow Pond engaged in a heated discussion about the prices and quality of pig intestines in their respective areas.

Surveying the village landscape at different times of year, these guests would discern that much food production now falls to middle-aged and older women, who are responsible for the bulk of rice cultivation and tend to their family vegetable plots. In speaking with elderly villagers, our visitors would learn that their perspectives on the past are heavily influenced by the villagers' experiences of food scarcity or abundance. They might also catch villagers complaining about the younger generation's lack of commitment to gardening or cooking for their elders! They would likely observe that class and wealth distinctions are frequently remarked on through the lens of food—as criticism of local cadres who dine at the government's expense is accompanied by vivid descriptions of their consumption of exotic and highly priced culinary fare, from wild animals to elaborate soups with rare ingredients.

If our guests stay longer, they might start marking the passage of time through food. There is a collective dimension to all of this. Most families mark off the parts of the day in similar ways through mealtimes, and the yearly calendar is also distinguished by different holidays associated with special foods.

Finally, while the outsiders might see that much of the activity around food entails intensive labor—from growing to harvesting to cooking—they would not miss the emphasis on food's pleasures, the gusto with which villagers talk about their local produce or critique different dishes, the joy of sociality in large and small banquets, and the ways in which food creates conviviality and mutual good feelings. It would be a rare day, for instance, that someone in Moonshadow Pond would not be heard praising or disparaging the pork ball soup of another locality or the city food he or she ate on a trip. Food is pleasurable, as is talking endlessly about food!

In short, food in Moonshadow Pond is a medium of immense value. It is certainly a commodity, but it cannot be reduced to a mere commodity because it reflects and communicates social identities and creates and maintains social relationships through a variety of exchanges. It organizes time, from daily activities to the yearly calendar. As a symbol, it embodies the contradictions and tensions of contemporary rural life. As a language, it can be purposely manipulated to convey a range of meanings. It serves not only as a source of sustenance but as a vehicle for action. It is clearly a necessity, but it is also a focus of enjoyment, elaboration, and artistry.

Of course, as noted above, it is not food per se that is acting on its own here but, rather, humans who invest in food a vast array of meanings. Jean Baudrillard, in discussing what he called an "ideological genesis of needs," differentiated four logics of "value" that can be very useful to our project here.[73] In Baudrillard's words, an object can assume "a logic of utility, a logic of the market, a logic of the gift, and a logic of status. Organized in accordance with one of the above groupings, the object assumes respectively the status of an instrument, a commodity, a symbol, or a sign."[74]

For Baudrillard, any one object can function according to several of these logics at once. For instance, Baudrillard gives the example of the exchange of wedding rings as a symbol of the relationship between the two partners, but the rings are also obtained through market exchange and in that sense are commodities. We might also add, though Baudrillard does not point this out, that according to his own definition a wedding ring can also function as a sign. As he states, a sign "no longer gathers its meaning in the concrete relationship between two people. It assumes its meaning in its differential relation to other people. It assumes its meaning in its differential relation to other signs."[75] Here we might think of a wedding ring that is made of a large, expensive, precious stone, which the wearer rather ostentatiously flaunts. In this sense, it is less a symbol of the relationship between the couple than a sign of status.

As with the example of the wedding ring, the value of food in rural China has multiple logics at work simultaneously. We might think here of a banquet. Because it involves relations among people, it is clearly an instance of gift or symbolic exchange. Yet the items may be purchased in the market (part of commodity exchange) or self-provisioned. This self-provisioning, when not related to a banquet, is also motivated by what Baudrillard would call the "logic of utility." At the same time, however, the particular dishes presented at a banquet, such as a soup with rare ingredients, might also function as signs because they are used to create distinctions from others and to enhance status.[76]

As an embodiment of value, however, food is certainly unusual. Unlike wedding rings or cash, food is perishable. David Graeber has pointed out that, in most cultural systems, perishable things are usually ranked lower on orders of value, for the very reason that by definition they do not last. Indeed, even something as permanent as money may not be permanent enough, and this is why those who have great monetary wealth often invest some of it in art or in other unique and transcendent items.[77]

How, then, can we reconcile the impermanence of food with its nature as a source of great value in rural China? One possibility is by reformulating our notion of value, and seeing it as inhering not only in discrete objects but in actions, for objects are themselves usually the products of action. Graeber gives an example of value as action: "If one gives another person food, and receives a shell in return, it is not the value of the food that returns to one in the form of the shell, but rather the value of the act of giving it. The food is simply the medium."[78] As Graeber points out, Marx also had a theory of value in action. For Marx, the effort that goes into producing a commodity is invisible at the time of its consumption—no one sees the worker and the efforts he she undertook in producing it. Nonetheless, despite this invisibility, every object "embodies human intentions."[79] For Marx, these intentions and the actions that resulted from them were the actual sources of an object's value.[80] And Graeber also argues that we can use this insight in thinking about value.

How does all this help us to understand the value of food in rural China, and the seeming conundrum of its having great value despite its perishability? As we shall see, much of food's value in the rural Chinese context inheres precisely in its uncanny ability to embody human intentions. While food is perishable, the actions surrounding it can create connectedness and sharing, debts and obligations, even resentments and recriminations. Whether hosting a banquet, or cooking for one's mother-in-law, one is engaged in a value-laden activity. Food in this sense becomes a critical medium through which, in large and small ways, people communicate throughout their lives about what and who really matter.

Additionally, food is particularly useful in what anthropologists call "value transformations" from one realm to the other. Within the ethnographic literature are many examples of such value transformations. For example, Jonathan Parry and Maurice Bloch explain how money earned through commerce or wage labor, which thus belongs to the realm of "short-term exchanges," can in turn be plowed into a different "transactional order" associated with a "long-term or cosmic order."[81] Examples of this include investing money in sacred ceremonies, making charitable donations, or sharing within one's own family to sustain long-term bonds.

The idioms of cooking and eating are frequently used to speak about such transformations in value. As Parry and Bloch point out, "It is no accident that such tranformations should so often be expressed in an alimentary idiom, for everywhere this is one of the most powerful of all possible metaphors for transformation."[82] Janet Carstens, for example, has examined rural Malay households, where men work as fishermen and women are responsible for most of the rice cultivation. The men provide women with the fish they catch and with their cash earnings, both of which are said to be "cooked" by the women, along with the rice they produce, and shared within the family.[83] In this particular context, the women actually do cook the rice and fish. But the idiom of cooking is also used to refer to their management of the household budget as a whole because they transform the men's cash earnings to use-values that can be shared by the family. Similarly, as stated above, food procured through market exchange or self-provisioning can be used in a banquet that functions as a medium of symbolic gift exchange.

We see, then, that food can partake of a variety of different and coexisting logics of value and reveals its value as a focal point of action and intention. It can also function as a medium through which transformations between different transactional orders are effected, The chapters that follow will look more closely at the value of food in Moonshadow Pond specifically. Our analysis begins in chapter 2 by examining food through the lens of labor. The work of farming, food processing, and cooking certainly has great "use-value" and is essential for survival. However, the labor of farming, which is integral to peasant identity and was valorized symbolically in the Mao era, has never been highly compensated on the market. It is now more than ever coded in terms of both gender and generation. Further, the labor of cooking is at the intersection of family dynamics and tensions. Therefore, we need to take a careful look at the complex and conflicting terrain of values in the production and preparation of food.

Food is also a vehicle for evaluating and remembering the past, and memory is an active and ongoing process. Chapter 3 turns to the way in which food—through its production, preparation, and consumption—serves as a powerful means of embodying memory. As a repository of individual and collective memories, food works as a vehicle through which villagers understand and judge the historical transformations of the last half century. But it does more than that: the replication of food practices in daily life and in calendrical celebrations connects people to time. As David Sutton suggests, food is often a medium for "tying past, present and future together."[84]

Foodstuffs move (or rather, people move foodstuffs) through a complex set of exchanges outside and within the market. Chapter 4 examines circulation, both symbolic, or gift exchange, and market exchange, to understand the value of food. The domination of the global and Chinese economies by capitalism has not meant that the logic of market exchange dominates all transactions within the village. Gift exchange is still an important arena for the circulation of food; and an economy of obligations, or "moral economy," coexists with the market. At the same time, as we shall see, food itself sometimes takes on the qualities of currency. The circulation and exchange of food, furthermore, involve many different kinds of relationships, from hierarchical to egalitarian, competitive to cooperative, and informal sharing to obligatory provisioning.

The issue of obligation is key. For if value emerges in actions, those actions will also be judged. This entails considering food as a moral signifier, a topic taken up in chapter 5, which focuses on the ways in which food expresses and enacts moral obligations and is also a focus of moral judgments. Finally, we will try to understand food as sociality and pleasure in chapter 6. The value of food as pleasure in Moonshadow Pond is inherently social and cannot be attained through solitary acts of consumption.[85]

These categories—labor, memory, exchange, morality, and sociality—are, of course, a way of organizing our study conceptually, but in actual lived experience they are not always easy to separate. In what category, for instance, would we put a discussion of the daughter-in-law who refuses to cook for her elderly mother-in-law after a family dispute? Clearly, this involves the labor of food preparation through cooking, but it also involves exchange and issues of moral obligation. Likewise, banqueting is very much about sociality, but it also involves exchange (both market and gift exchange), requires the labor of food production and preparation, and, through periodic reenactment, is a way of preserving memories. Lately, ostentatious banqueting has also been held up for moral critique.

In disentangling these categories, it makes sense to begin with labor—more specifically the production and preparation of food. Until recently, not only was agriculture the basis of subsistence for almost all the residents of Moonshadow Pond, but it was also the source of their collective identity as peasants. Further, sharing a common stove was a key component in defining family boundaries and thus was a source of family identity. The next chapter elaborates on these issues by examining the production and preparation of food, the labors of tilling the fields and tending the stove.

TWO

Labor

FOR EVERY GRAIN OF RICE, there are three grains of sweat.[1]

This proverb, recited to me by Songling, is not only an accurate reflection of the backbreaking toil necessary to cultivate rice but also of how this work is now viewed by most residents of Moonshadow Pond. As Moonshadow Pond's youth venture out of the village to work for wages, and as some even step up the educational ladder to college and beyond,[2] the idea of spending their lives as subsistence farmers is increasingly foreign to them. The labor of "tilling the fields" (*gengtian*) is now left to their parents and even grandparents, primarily middle-aged and older women, who are not employed for wages.

This chapter examines the work of producing food and preparing meals in Moonshadow Pond. There has hardly been an age-old way of organizing this. The gendered and generational configurations of agricultural labor changed profoundly from what is colloquially referred to as the "old society," the time before Liberation, through the collective era, to the present. Additionally, with the exodus of youth to nonagricultural employment, the future of agriculture in Moonshadow Pond is unclear.

In addition to the production of food—growing, harvesting, and processing—meal preparation is integral to the labor surrounding food in Moonshadow Pond. Both subsistence agriculture (rice and vegetable gardening) and cooking are at the center of domestic food production and preparation. Both of these need to be differentiated from production for the market—the work of raising pigs, tending fishponds, or growing citrus and other fruit trees, all of which are oriented toward earning cash income. Further, just as *cultivating* rice (*gengtian*) is central to peasant identity, so, too, *cooking* rice is at the center of family identity. When rice is cooked, those who eat from a common rice pot make up the boundaries of the undivided family.

Throughout most of Moonshadow Pond's history, producing one's own food was a non-negotiable necessity for survival. Even now, and despite the profound transformations that have altered village life, the needs of subsistence food production and preparation shape both small and large cycles of time in the village. The cycle of planting and harvesting rice demarcates time over the course of the year, and the work of cooking and gardening still helps create a daily rhythm.

As a creator of values, the production of food contains contradictory elements. A great deal of importance is placed on eating one's own rice and vegetables. On the other hand, the work of producing this food has never been highly valued in the market, and the identity of peasants (*nongmin*), society's main food producers, is a low status one, sometimes even in the eyes of the peasants themselves (as we will see later in the chapter).

Like rice cultivation and vegetable gardening, preparing food for the family on a daily basis takes place mainly outside the market. Cooking is also at the heart of family relationships and power dynamics. Yet like agriculture, it has not been immune to influences stemming from the political and economic transfigurations of the last half century, including collectivization and subsequent market reforms. Below, we probe the meanings of these varied aspects of the labor of producing and preparing food in Moonshadow Pond.

GENGTIAN

To say that the basic tasks involved in growing rice have not changed for centuries would not be inaccurate. The soil must be ploughed, seeds planted, and seedlings transplanted, with the plants then carefully cultivated until they turn from green to golden yellow. Then the grain must be reaped, threshed (separated from the stalks), and dried in the sun; the husks must be removed; and, finally, the rice must be polished.

Meixian, and indeed all of Guangdong Province, is part of an area of China not only associated with rice cultivation but with the double cropping of rice. This means that, because of the subtropical climate, villagers plant two crops of rice per year. For the majority of families in Moonshadow Pond, which rely on family members to plant and harvest their own rice, this means that the yearly calendar is structured around the several periods of intense activity involving rice agriculture. In Meixian, the end of the Lunar New Year, the most important yearly holiday, heralds the onset of the agricultural season. After the festivities of the holiday, with its feasting, fireworks, and interfamilial visiting, the weather usually turns cold and rainy. There is no heat in Meixian because the temperature never reaches freezing, but the concrete houses hold in a penetrating damp chill. Nonetheless, this raw weather indicates that it will soon be time to wade into the cold, muddy paddy fields to plant the first crop of rice.

At this time, usually late February or early March, or as common wisdom would have it, just when "the lotus flower blooms," the rice fields are plowed and made ready for planting. These fields are called "wet fields" (*shuitian*) because water must be let in to flood the field while rice is growing. During the same period after the New Year, as the wet fields are prepared for the first rice crop, the "dry fields" (*handi*) are tilled in preparation for planting peanuts and fava beans. These will all be harvested in July, when a second crop of rice, as well as a crop of sweet potatoes, is planted. These dry field crops—peanuts, sweet potatoes, and fava beans, corn, and taro—are relatively minor parts of the diet now, but they were once important supplements. As mentioned in the last chapter, beans were key sources of protein when meat was scarce, and sweet potatoes were an alternative to rice. During the collective era, brigade members pressed their own peanuts into oil, which was allocated in small amounts to each family on a monthly basis.[3] However, villagers now purchase their peanut oil, which is not made locally. Additionally, during the collective period, the first rice crop was preceded by a crop of winter wheat. This was not a traditional crop in Meixian, and the practice of growing winter wheat was abandoned during the reform era.[4]

Before collectivization, peasants in Moonshadow Pond tilled the fields with hoes or used water buffalo to pull ploughs. Later, the brigade purchased tractors, which tilled all the land in the cooperating production teams. During the reform era, as individuals each received use rights in specific plots of land, many formerly collective assets were dispersed among team members. For instance, the tractors were taken over by a few families. This process was contested and controversial, but the result has been that those who want their land tilled by tractor must now rent the service. Ironically, many people have returned to the old-fashioned practice of readying their fields with a hoe or water buffalo. Because rice is produced for family needs, largely by middle-aged and elderly women who don't work for a wage, they reason that it does not pay to spend more on inputs, such as renting a tractor. One woman said to me in the spring of 2007, "If I wasn't doing this, I would be [passing the time] playing mahjong or cards, so I'll just till the soil and not pay for a tractor!"

FIGURE 6. Transplanting rice seedlings from a tray.

Once the rice has been planted, it is only a matter of three weeks before the seedlings are mature enough to be transplanted (see fig. 6). This work is also very labor intensive, although not as backbreaking as in the past. Rather than bending over and transplanting each and every seedling, villagers now plant their seedlings in plastic pans, which they bury in the mud. When the time comes for transplanting, they take the pans out of the soil and, standing upright, aim and throw the seedlings into the wet paddy fields so that they can spread out and have room to grow. This new process of tossing the seedling (*paoyang*) is opposed to the centuries old process of transplanting each seedling by hand, literally "inserting the seedling" (*chayang*). *Paoyang* is more expensive because the seeds must be purchased from the government, since the process does not work with one's own seeds. However, it makes the process of planting and transplanting less onerous, and has therefore become popular since de-collectivization, especially as the work of rice cultivation has fallen to fewer people.

Within three months after the first rice crop is transplanted, by early July, the rice is ready for harvest. It is a nerve-racking time because, just as the first crop is harvested, the land must be immediately retilled and readied for

FIGURE 7. Milling rice.

planting the second crop. Villagers in Moonshadow Pond still use sickles to chop down the rice stalks, although other villages have turned to mechanical scythes. Once the stalks are chopped down, they are run through a thresher that separates stalks from the grain. Next, the grain must be dried under the sun and milled (the outer husk must be removed and polished).

Since 1973, the milling in Moonshadow Pond has been done by machines; thus it now takes only a few minutes to de-husk and simultaneously polish a large load of grain (see fig.7). The introduction of milling machines, in fact, occasioned the first use of electricity in Moonshadow Pond. At that time, the six production teams invested in milling machines, and they were able to access electricity for two hours per day in order to operate them. However, before that time, milling was accomplished by hand. A large grinding stone called a *long* was rotated and the husk removed. Then, the rice was put through a winnower *(fengche)*, a covered wooden wheel that removed any outer layer or dust that the *long* had missed. Finally, the rice was polished with a *dui,* a large stone pestle (also used to make glutinous rice flour). To produce 100 jin of rice, people would work an entire day to separate the inner kernel of rice from the outer kernel—something that now can be done in a few minutes with machinery.[5]

Bad weather can disrupt this process at any point. For instance, one year there was too much rain, and Songling's seedlings did not grow fast enough to be transplanted until mid-April. Waiting so long meant that her second crop was in danger of being planted too late to be successful. As she therefore needed to transplant her seedlings very rapidly, she decided to pay some workers to help her finish everything within one day. Timing is therefore critical. Because of the short time frame between harvesting the first crop and planting the second, people now use a variety of mutual-help strategies. While the work is mainly organized by older and middle-aged women who are not wage earners, they occasionally receive help from their husbands or adult children, who can chip in on the weekend or during nonworking hours. Neighbors may also help each other on different days, or if time really gets tight, as in Songling's example, people will pay for help—a better option than losing the chance to plant a second crop.

An example of using family help for the rice harvest can be seen in the case of Yinzhao, a woman in her early eighties. Yinzhao's two married sons live in the county capital, and she has two married daughters who live outside the village as well. When the time comes for the rice harvest, villagers joke that she employs the help of an entire "production team." In a big family such as Yinzhao's, many individual members have use rights to land. This is because all official residents of the village received shares of land during de-collectivization in the early 1980s. They received shares, even if they were actually living outside the village, as long as they had not changed their official registration to an urban one. So Yinzhao still plants and harvests rice on the land allocated for each of her sons, as well as on her own share of land and on a share of land belonging to her youngest daughter. During one harvest, I observed many family members who lived in the county capital come back to the village to help Yinzhao on the six mu of land they held in common. These included one of Yinzhao's married daughters; a granddaughter, who usually worked as a nurse in the county capital; and Yinzhao's second son and daughter-in-law, who both took four days off from work to help out. Additionally, Yinzhao's second daughter cooked for the entire crew. When it was all over, Yinzhao's son felt very sore, as he had carted heavy loads of rice to the thresher all day long—not something he was used to doing in his normal work as a machinist.

In addition to threatening the timing of harvesting and transplanting, bad weather can also interfere with drying the grain, thus endangering the entire crop. Once while I was visiting during the month of July, the weather was extremely wet, and nothing could proceed until the grains were dry. After a few days of wet weather, the harvested grain was in danger of germinating again, and, if the rains had continued, the grain would have been fit only to feed to chickens and ducks. Fortunately, the sun came back just in time to dry and then to mill the grain. Commenting on the ultimate precariousness of this situation, one villager simply observed to me, "Now you can see why we worship heaven (*tian*)!"

Viewing all of this in terms of historical continuity might seem easy—peasants tilling the fields to meet their subsistence needs, and dealing with the precariousness of the weather, as they have done for centuries. But as we explain below, there is much about the contemporary context of food production that is also unprecedented. As mentioned in the last chapter, taxes are no longer assessed on family rice production. This is a different situation than Chinese farmers have ever faced. In the past, whether it was the "old society" before Liberation, the collective era, or even the first twenty years of the reform era, peasants always had to pay either cash or an in-kind payment on the grain they produced. The payment might have gone to a landlord or the state prior to Liberation, or to the state during the collective and early reform eras. But there was always some kind of required payment.

Elderly villagers remember a variety of tenancy arrangements before Liberation. Comparing the relative prosperity of the present to the era before Liberation, one old timer remarked to me with irony, "If you didn't have any land [of your own], you had to give more than half of your produce to the landlord. At that time, having no land meant you had a hard time eating, but now people let land lie fallow and don't even want to work on it!"

During the collective era, of course, there were no longer any landlords to extract rent, but the government collected taxes in kind from all peasants. Indeed, the Great Leap Forward is noted especially because, in the midst of horrible crop failure, the government extracted what little was left—one of the many causes of the famine. After the demise of the draconian Great Leap Forward regime, however, more workable collective structures were created. Still, peasants produced not solely for themselves and their individual families but also for the collective and the government. In Moonshadow Pond, there were six production teams, each numbering about twenty-five families. Our neighbor Aihua was the team head of production team 2, and Baoli was the team accountant. Aihua told me, "During the rice transplanting, people would rise at 2:00 a.m. and work until evening after it was dark.... Our number 2 team had the most production as well as the number 15 team. Payment was in grain and cash; the cash came from selling grain to the government. If your team gave away more grain than you owed in tax, you would get [extra cash].... more for what you sold. So, our number 2 team produced a lot!"

Team 2 prided itself on its productivity and, with higher overall payments of grain to the government, they received more cash back for their team. Payments to individual team members were then divided according to how much each person worked—measured by hours worked and the job's degree of difficulty. (The exception to this was during the height of the Cultural Revolution, from 1966–68, when revolutionary fervor supplanted productivity as the chief measure of work points!) Team leaders themselves assessed the relative value of different tasks. But team members who worked very little because of ill health or infirmity still received a basic grain ration, even if the amount they worked was not equivalent to the food they received. If these team members produced more the following year, they would have to pay the team back. Examples of this type of situation included families with many small children and few adult family members who could actually work. These families might find themselves borrowing from the team for several years in a row. Thus, the system guaranteed a basic grain ration for everyone on the basis of a redistributive logic.

The government also attempted to direct, to a greater or lesser degree, the process of agricultural production. During the 1960s, Aihua's husband, whom everyone called "Uncle Wei," was the general secretary of the production brigade (made up of the six production teams of Moonshadow Pond and the nine teams from the neighboring village). In an effort to bolster production, the authorities told him to turn dry land into wet land, or rice paddy fields. He insisted it could not be done, and ultimately prevented this foolish scheme from being implemented. Indeed, the literature on the collective era is filled with many such incidents. Examples include trying to induce production brigades to grow cotton plants or wheat in unsuitable land and climate,[6] or making peasants dredge lucrative fishponds in order to grow more grain.[7]

Such futile or counterproductive attempts to direct agricultural production, however, do not mean that all government directed agricultural projects were useless. In Moonshadow Pond several collective era projects did pay off and succeeded in increasing agricultural production. For instance, before Liberation, mud gullies conducted water to the rice paddy fields. In some cases, paddy fields were placed at the bottoms of hills and mountains, where there was natural runoff. Waterwheels also helped guide water from streams onto fields. However, in the 1950s, work began on permanent ditches. They were first constructed with wood, and in the 1960s, villagers built stone ditches, which are still in use today. Collective labor also built two reservoirs—one in the production brigade (in 1958), which included Moonshadow Pond, and another in the neighboring production brigade (in 1969–70). These assured a more permanent supply of water that could be controlled for irrigation.

Throughout the collective era, rice production was central to the local agricultural economy. Keeping maximum land available for rice production was a key objective for all state planners. However, over the last few decades, this has changed throughout China. In Moonshadow Pond, producing fruit (especially pomelos), raising poultry and pigs, and tending fishponds are areas of food production that have expanded rapidly. The area set aside for grain production has gradually declined even as productivity has increased (see appendix A, figs. A.3–4). For instance, between Liberation and 1987, the total area used for fish cultivation quadrupled in Meixian as a whole.[8] Fruit production between the same years increased fifteenfold,[9] and the number of pigs that was raised in the county increased sixfold during those years.[10] These trends have continued through to the present (see appendix A, figs. A.5–8). In the administrative district composed of Moonshadow Pond and its neighboring village in particular, fruit production increased by a third between 1997 and 2011, and the area devoted to fish cultivation has more than quadrupled.[11] (Fruit cultivation and fish farming are often undertaken by individuals and families who rent or lease land that is still held collectively by production teams. For while production teams no longer work together or organize labor, they still retain title to all land, both paddy fields and dry land, in which individuals now have use rights).[12]

Large recorded increases in meat, poultry, fish, and fruit production correlate with villagers' subjective perceptions of change. For instance, Baoli told me that, during the collective era, he spent ten years in charge of raising pigs for his production team. At any given time, he raised at most twenty pigs for the entire team, yet some of the local pig farmers now raise several dozen each. The reform era therefore marked some important changes in the relationship of Moonshadow Pond residents to the work of growing and producing food, although these changes were not all implemented at once.

As mentioned above, land technically remains the property of the collective even in the reform era. But individual peasants sign use contracts lasting as long as thirty years at a stretch. Furthermore, with the elimination of all assessments on rice production, the activity of *gengtian* is now solely for the purpose of family provisioning, part of a family's domestic economy. It no longer entails payments or obligations to power holders, either to a landlord or to a collective. We therefore need to explore the value of *gengtian* in its current context more deeply, and begin by thinking through the ways it is structured by generation, gender, and class.

GENDER, GENERATION, AND THE PRODUCTION OF FOOD

While gender and generational roles with respect the production of food seem quite distinct in Moonshadow Pond now, with older and middle-aged women playing the key roles in rice cultivation and gardening, these roles have actually changed significantly from the pre-Liberation era, through Maoist collectivization, to the present reform era. Speaking about themselves, Hakka men *and* women both describe Hakka women as the most industrious (*qinlao*) of all the Han.[13] They point to the fact that Hakka women have never bound their feet and have always performed hard work, not only involving fieldwork, but also the carrying of heavy loads. Vegetable gardens also have always been tended by women. Indeed, even during the collective era, as soon as private plots (*zi liu di*) were allocated to families at the end of the Great Leap Forward, these became the domain of women.

The work of food production related to gardening means not only that vegetables are provided to families but also that they are preserved by drying, pickling, and salting. These dried vegetables are still eaten as accompaniments to morning congee. However, as mentioned previously, while drying and preserving vegetables still takes place, it is not nearly as pervasive as it once was. Further, as indicated in the last chapter, even women who may no longer cultivate rice may still energetically garden. For instance, Ailing works as a teacher's aide in a school. While she no longer cultivates rice, she uses her time during weekends, as well as after hours on workdays, to cultivate an extensive garden outside her house. She also tends a fishpond and raises ducks and chickens, activities testifying to the continuing importance of gardening and even animal husbandry in provisioning her family.

Men are not completely absent from the agricultural economy. However, much of their agricultural work, such as raising pigs and chickens for the market or tending fishponds or fruit orchards, is associated with the cash economy. Nonetheless and importantly, men's somewhat minimal participation in rice cultivation and vegetable gardening (both related to domestic provisioning) does not mean that women are absent from the agricultural cash economy. In Moonshadow Pond, market-based agricultural activities are not off limits to women. Indeed, some of the most successful operations that raise chickens and pigs for their meat, and cultivate citrus fruits, are run jointly by married couples, or even by women on their own. For instance, Qiufang is a woman in her forties who has leased 60 mu of land from a production brigade north of Moonshadow Pond. It is hilly land with a good water supply that is conducive to growing these kinds of citrus fruit. Interestingly, Qiufang, who had no previous experience raising fruit trees, learned how to do so primarily from her brother and sister-in-law and from reading books.

Similarly, Lishan and her husband, Wende, used to drive vans for hire. However, the business foundered after taxis, auto rickshaws, and public buses came onto the scene (and even as some of the wealthier villagers began to purchase cars of their own). Their daughter-in-law works in the county capital, but their son has been unsuccessful at finding and keeping jobs. So they have decided to raise goats and sell the milk. Goat milk is not a "traditional" choice, and, in fact, it is a new food in the context of southeastern China. While it is more expensive than powdered milk, however, it is also viewed as a safer and more nutritious alternative, especially in the wake of the national scandals of adulterated milk powder that sickened many babies and even led to some deaths.

The work of raising goats for their milk is certainly not easy (see fig. 8). Lishan and Wende have ten goats. They rise at three every morning, milk the goats at five, and then bag and bottle the milk to distribute to about fifty local customers. In the afternoon, they undertake a second round of milking and delivery, and then go out to cut grass and bring it back for the goats. Like Qiufang, they learned the business from reading, as it was not traditionally practiced in Meixian.

Lishan and her husband add to their income by producing a Chinese medicine that comes from a fungus they grow themselves. The medicine

FIGURE 8. Raising goats for their milk.

(*lingzi baozi fen*) is very expensive, selling at over 700 yuan per jin. (Those who consume it usually mix the powder from its spores in hot water and add honey.)

Such value-added food businesses may also contribute to a family's income when another family member is earning a wage or salary. I spent one day watching Liqiao make bean curd (tofu). Liqiao's husband works in town government, while Liqiao has been making and selling fresh bean curd daily for ten years. It is a complex process to master, one that Liqiao learned from her father. Several hours of prep time soaking the soy beans are followed by an entire afternoon of work. The beans are turned into a paste, added to boiled water, and fermented, and the curds are separated. The curds are then boiled, thickened, and set. Each day, after this process is complete, Liqiao sets out in the neighborhood and sells the fresh bean curd immediately (see fig. 9). Repeating this daily, she earns a decent monthly income.[14]

The collective era, however, involved a very different division of labor than the current one detailed above. The emphasis then was on grain production, and men as well as women were supposed to work in the fields, a departure from customary Hakka norms, in which women were expected to be the

FIGURE 9. Selling homemade bean curd.

primary agricultural fieldworkers while men ideally took on more remunerative activities. Indeed, during the collective era, grain production usually meant all hands on deck. Even children would help at the crucial times of planting, transplanting, and harvesting in spring, summer, and autumn. Both Aihua's eldest son and her nephew, who were schoolchildren during the late 1960s, spoke about their memories of working long hours in order to earn extra work points for their families. Contrastingly, the idea of children helping out with rice planting or harvest would be unfathomable now. Children face intense pressure to do well in school and score highly on entrance exams for high school, and even college; agricultural activities for children are now viewed as a waste of precious study time.

Speaking about men's participation in *gengtian* during the collective era, one village woman said to me that, although men worked in the field at that time, she thought they were just lazier than women: "They would *liao* [spend time talking aimlessly] when they were supposed to be working, or perhaps they would work, but work too slowly." Aihua recollected her difficulties motivating men when she was a team leader: "I would say, 'hey, you are not really working, just pretending to work and getting work points for it!'"

One of the obstacles to integrating men into agricultural work during the collective era in Moonshadow Pond was precisely its departure from previous practices. As in the reform era, the work of planting, transplanting, and harvesting rice before Liberation was heavily dominated by women. This was especially the case because Moonshadow Pond was a high emigration area, and many men migrated abroad, particularly to Indonesia, with some going to India. This meant that there was often a shortage of male labor. Men who remained in Moonshadow Pond would plow fields with water buffalo, or they worked in construction or in the local tannery, but daily agricultural work was viewed as women's domain. An old Hakka rhyme sums up what was understood as the accepted cultural norm for the time: "Father earns the cash flow, while Mother plants and hoes" *(nanba zhuanqian, mama gengtian).*[15]

For instance, Chunyu, who was already in her late eighties in 2012, had vivid memories of both the food and agricultural situation before Liberation. She told me, "In the old society we grew peanuts, sweet potatoes, greens, and ate very little meat. We gathered wood for cooking and saved it for the rainy season when we could not gather it. . . . We worked in the fields until just a few days before our babies were born." Many other older women also recounted working until a few days before giving birth. Of course, to be "industrious" is a cultural ideal for Hakka women, and older women were unlikely to recount stories to me in which their behavior departed from this archetype.

At first glance, therefore, the present day and the old society seem to have more in common with each other, in terms of the gender division of agricultural labor, than either does with the intervening collective era. In both the pre-Liberation and reform eras, women have been responsible for direct provisioning of food for the family, while men have been associated with wage work or market-oriented agricultural work. But there are important differences between these two eras that cannot be overlooked. First, as mentioned above, women now are not altogether absent from market-oriented agricultural production. More importantly, however, the present day is characterized by a large divide between generations. The generations born after the start of the reform era (post-1980) in Moonshadow Pond do not participate in either subsistence agriculture or market-based agricultural production. Since neither young men nor women work in agriculture now, what does this mean for their own relationships to the land and to food? How do they construct their identities, and what is their connection, if any, to *gengtian?* We take up these questions next.

PEASANT IDENTITY AND *GENGTIAN*

Scholars have long argued about how to define *peasant,* but they have generally agreed on a few common characteristics. To be a peasant means to be someone who produced food for his or her own subsistence needs while also fulfilling any number of obligations to those who had more power—whether as rent or shares of crops to landlords or as taxes to political authorities. This definition still raises questions. What about people, such as the local tannery workers in pre-Liberation Moonshadow Pond, who receive money or food for their work and live in rural areas but do not engage directly in subsistence food production?

Indeed, many who were classified as "peasants" in pre-Liberation China actually engaged in activities other than growing food because their agricultural activities did not provide a subsistence living. For instance, in their study of peasants in rural Yunnan Province in the 1930s, Fei Hsiao-tung and Chang Chih-I pointed out that rural industry was critical for peasant survival. In the villages they studied, basket weaving and papermaking were important crafts, but the particular mix of industries might vary from area to area.[16] Furthermore, questions also arise over how land ownership might have affected the definition of who was a peasant. What was the cutoff that turned someone from a peasant to a member of the rural elite?[17]

In the case of China, this definitional matter was settled by the state after Liberation, with immediate and often life-transforming consequences. In 1951 and 1952, soon after the Liberation, the party sent work teams to every village. Working in tandem with the poorest families, they began to secretly categorize their fellow villagers into classes according to whether they were landlords, rich, middle-income or poor peasants, or tenants.[18] This work was secret because the party did not want the landlords to know in advance and to hide or divide up their wealth and property. Relationships to land, food production, and consumption became integral to defining the rural classes that emerged after Liberation. In Moonshadow Pond, three families were categorized as landlords, on the basis of how much rice they produced. To be a landlord in Moonshadow Pond meant producing fifty *dan* or more of rice per year from one's land (a *dan* being the equivalent of fifty kilograms).[19]

Once identified as such, landlords were struggled against and criticized by their fellow villagers and lineage members. Aihua, speaking about this time, recollected, "We would say to them, you eat well, you use nice things, we would just go on in this way." Landlord houses and possessions were then confiscated. Initially, the land was divided among all the villagers—for the first few years after the revolution it was not collectivized. Like everyone else, landlord families received some land on which to cultivate their rice and to grow vegetables. But they were given the worst land, high up in the hills rather than in the center of the village where it was level. Landlord families also had to vacate their houses and live in the most dilapidated ones, while the very poorest families were given nicer homes. Throughout China, many landlords were executed or imprisoned. In Moonshadow Pond, of the three landlord family heads (the eldest males of the senior generation), one fled to Burma, another fled to Hong Kong, and a third committed suicide.[20]

Within a few years of land redistribution, the process of collectivization in Moonshadow Pond began, as it did throughout China. But despite the equalization of everyone's relationship to the land during the collective era, the class labels of these early years remained. They were officially inherited through the patrilineal line until 1985, when the class label system was abolished. Through the years of collectivization, therefore, the descendants of the landlords in Moonshadow Pond remained "landlords," even though they owned no land. Throughout rural China, these class labels became a stigma. Those such as landlords, who were from "bad" classes, were shunned for marriage, and faced limited opportunities for higher education and jobs. But since most villagers were not landlords but poor peasants, and since there were few opportunities for higher education or jobs outside rural villages anyway, this class-label system did not really affect the vast majority of peasants during the collective era.[21]

Unlike specific class labels, the more general identity of peasant is still shared by almost all residents of Moonshadow Pond. China still has a household registration system, in which everyone has either a rural or urban residence (*hukou*). Even now, changing one's official residence from a rural to an urban one, even if one works as a migrant in the city, is very difficult. So, to some extent, rural people take their identities with them. Like the "landlord" families during the collective era, who were no longer actually landlords, so, too, many rural migrants who move to the cities to work are technically still considered peasants, even though they no longer till the fields.

Though rural migrants in the cities are really workers, their rural identities create an association with the countryside, and therefore with tilling the soil. For instance, the anthropologist Pun Ngai reports on an interesting incident in an electronics factory in Shenzhen, the bustling new city of three million on the border of Hong Kong, which is a magnet for young rural migrants from villages like Moonshadow Pond and beyond. The foreman in the factory began to curse one of the young female workers by referring to her peasant identity and its connection with agricultural labor: "'What the hell are you doing? You are going to spoil this casing. Such a big scratch here . . . Did you learn something by heart? You know, you are not ploughing a furrow, don't you? These products are very expensive, you couldn't pay for it even if you worked in the fields for a year.'"[22]

"In the post-Mao cities," anthropologist Hairong Yan tells us, "it has become an epithet or a crude joke to call someone peasant (*nongmin*), a sign most potently suggesting ignorance (*yumei*), backwardness (*luohou*), and a dire lack of civility (*bu wenming*)."[23] Yan goes on to paint a picture of the role of the food producer in the rural areas from which young labor migrants come, pointing out that many people now farm only for "basic subsistence," rather than to earn money, and negatively portraying such subsistence activities: "Production land has become welfare land absorbing the ill, injured, and unemployed bodies and enabling a cheap reproduction of the next generation of migrant workers."[24]

Such negative ideas about the category of "peasant" are not necessarily rejected by the sons and daughters of peasants themselves in Moonshadow Pond. For instance, Songling's daughter Fengying once said to me, "If you just stay in the village and *gengtian,* if you don't get a job, it's sort of like you're embarrassed and people think it looks like you are not too bright." In Moonshadow Pond, when I participated only briefly in the rice harvest, and then in transplanting, several people took care to remind me that educated people (*you wenhua shuiping*) did not till the soil. The phrase used to refer to educated people in Chinese has certain connotations that it does not have in English. *Wenhua shuiping* technically means people with a certain cultural level, so the implication is that education gives one a higher level of cultural refinement, which does not comport with the muddy work of tilling fields and growing rice!

Indeed, Songling once told me that when her children were small, they would often help out with the harvest. "Are you afraid of this!?" she would say to them. "If you are, then you better study hard!" And Yinzhao's son, who was so tired after taking a few days off from his regular job to help his mother with the rice harvest, said to me, "A wage is much better than *gengtian,* because you can always buy the rice." But, he added, for people like his mother, who did not have a wage, it was a different matter. It made economic sense to grow rice, if you were not sacrificing a wage to do so, for the cost of inputs for growing rice was less than the cost of purchasing rice on the market.[25]

Looked at in all these ways, *gengtian* and gardening apparently have only residual value—as activities of those who cannot contribute any monetary value to the family. But it is not so simple. There is certainly no doubt that the government, in implementing rural reforms in the early 1980s, conceived of use rights in land as a safety hatch. If workers lose their jobs in the cities during an economic downturn, they can at least return home to work on family land, which they can depend upon for subsistence. It is certainly easy to see this in a cynical way—as a way of defusing urban unrest.

But, in fact, young people from Moonshadow Pond also view their access to land and agricultural subsistence work as real security. This can function in a number of ways. For instance, one young man, who worked in Guangzhou but returned to his home in Moonshadow Pond for holidays, told me that whenever he searched for employment, he did not feel compelled to take a job with a wage that was too low. The reason, he told me, was that, if his wages evaporated in living expenses such as food and dormitory fees, he could always quit and return home to Moonshadow Pond, where his parents are able to provide food for their family from their land.

Agricultural subsistence tasks can also supplement the paid work or business activities of the younger generation. For instance, the son of one of our neighbors in the village runs a small auto- and motorcycle-repair shop on the highway. His mother has a large garden, and uses it not only to feed her family but to provide food for the workers in her son's shop—as it would be expensive to purchase vegetables for these workers every day.

Additionally, as previously noted, Moonshadow Pond residents who live in the village but work in town may use their spare time to help their families with rice cultivation or vegetable gardening. This also means that rice cultivation and gardening, although not remunerated, play into family dynamics and obligations in many ways. A mother who provisions her sons with rice, or grows vegetables for the workers in his shop, is creating obligations that are not easy to ignore.

On the other side of this, tensions can arise over contradictory expectations. The "good" daughter-in-law is viewed as one who relieves, or at least helps, her mother-in-law with the work of growing rice and vegetables. For instance, Xiuling is a woman in her eighties. Her son and daughter-in-law both work in town, but on weekends, they help maintain the rice crop when necessary.

"Just because you work in an office [shangban] or engage in hard physical labor or factory work [zuogong] does not mean you can't help grow rice," Baoli complained to me one day in 2012, no doubt thinking of his own situation. Baoli's son was busy from the morning into the night with his shop in town, while Baoli's daughter-in-law worked in a factory in town. But in Baoli's mind their paid work need not have excluded growing food for the family. As he continued, "Xiuling's daughter-in-law and son do this [grow rice on their days off], so they can still eat their own rice. Everyone knows eating your own rice is better, and this is a matter of doing things for the family." Indeed, later that morning as we took our morning walk, Baoli pointed to a rice-paddy field that Xiuling's son and daughter-in-law worked on. (It was late September 2012 and almost time for the second harvest.) "Everyone knows that Xiuling's daughter-in-law is very *qinlao*" [diligent, hardworking], he said to me. He continued by explaining the hardships he and Songling had lived through over the last many decades and detailing their slow progress toward their current, and better, situation. In his mind, the younger generation had it much easier now, and the least they could do was pitch in and help grow rice and vegetables for the family!

The tension over "who will plant and harvest the rice" is complicated by childcare issues. Older women are often the main providers of childcare for their grandchildren, or even for their great-grandchildren. For instance, during the years when Songling was taking care of her preschool-aged grandchildren, she was unable to plant and harvest rice for the family. Aihua also took care of her grandchildren, but because her daughter-in-law did not work for a wage, they had a less stressful situation; Aihua's daughter-in-law took charge of rice cultivation, and Aihua took care of the grandchildren.

So for the elder generation, *gengtian* has an additional meaning. It is work for the family. We see here several contradictory threads. To till the soil is backbreaking work and is not the end goal of any parent for their children or grandchildren. Yet at present it is also a way of enacting commitment to the family. Those exceptional individuals who can make room for it, despite waged employment, are widely praised for their character. "Eating one's own rice," is still highly valued, even if the reality of the younger generation's work lives is making this goal more and more difficult.

Ironically, at least for the time being, these various modes of work—subsistence agriculture versus working for a wage or running a business—may be interdependent. Growing rice and vegetables cannot produce cash. But the cash that comes into families from wages and small businesses provides enough of a cushion to support the nonwage work of those who still *gengtian* and garden. Interestingly, this phenomenon has also been documented in parts of rural Mexico, where the remissions of young family members who have migrated to North America enable those who are left behind to cultivate corn for subsistence. This allows them to avoid being dependent on commercially produced GMO corn.[26] Furthermore, as we have seen in Moonshadow Pond, the agricultural work of some family members acts as a safety net for other family members, who work in the market economy. If wage work is unsatisfactory or evaporates for a time, there is always the possibility of temporarily returning home to be minimally supported by subsistence agriculture.

It is important to note, however, that this interdependence between wage work and agricultural production is presently based on different generational roles that are also in flux. When I asked residents of Moonshadow Pond what will happen when the older generation was no longer around to work the land, they often responded by saying that the next generation would end up purchasing their rice, since it was unlikely that any of them would *gengtian*. Some alternatively anticipated a time when they would pay others to grow their rice for them—migrants, perhaps, from less prosperous areas.

Indeed, large tracts of land in Moonshadow Pond that were formerly used for rice cultivation have already been turned to other uses. In 2011, a joint venture between the township government and private enterprise came to Moonshadow Pond and leased over a hundred mu of land. Leasing in this context means that an annual fee is divided among all those who have shares of land, and thus use rights, from the production team the land belongs to. In this case, the land was leased for the purpose of raising orchids for export. When I asked villagers about this, many responded by saying that, with so many young people now working for wages, and so little interest in rice cultivation, it was inevitable that the land would slowly be put to other uses. Whether rice cultivation will remain a feature of the Moonshadow Pond landscape in the future is not clear. The emotional attachment of residents to "our own rice" may be particularly keen as the ability to provide it becomes increasingly difficult.

On any given day in Moonshadow Pond, a lively informal gathering among women might suddenly come to an end. "*Shaohuo!*" someone will suddenly interject, and with this, everyone will head back home without ceremony. *Shaohuo* literally means "to tend the kitchen fires" or "to start up the flames." But it is shorthand for saying, "It's time to go back and prepare for the next meal!"

Food preparation is the flip side of subsistence agriculture in Moonshadow Pond, even more universal than growing food because it is part of every household's daily activities. But like tilling the fields, tending the fires structures time and is shaped by gender and generation. Similar to tilling the fields, cooking and food preparation have not taken place inside a time warp but, rather, have changed in significant ways over time, even as certain long-lasting symbolic elements remain strong.

The stove and kitchen in rural China have always been important as symbols of family unity. In traditional rural families, the cultural ideal entailed a joint family of five generations related through the patrilineal line, with wives marrying in and several generations of male descendants and their families eating together and sharing one kitchen. Sharing a stove and eating together indicated that the family held joint property and pooled income. This ideal was rarely achieved in practice. Poor families especially were marked by high rates of male emigration for work, lower survival rates of children, and many other factors that kept families far smaller than the ideal. When families did divide, however, it meant that brothers (who had already married) would separate their assets, and each of their families would cook and eat separately.

So "sharing a stove" meant a family was still together, whereas dividing the stove meant that family division had already taken place. Indeed, the symbolism of the stove is so important in Meixian that a family cannot move into a new house or flat without first lighting the flames on their stove and making offerings to the Stove God. We will have more to say about the Stove God in chapter 4, but it is relevant to point out here that the Stove God traditionally was seen as presiding over the family unit, which indicates the strong association between the stove and family boundaries.

In fact, in the past sharing a stove was even more important than coresidence in defining a family. Until the mid-1980s, when villagers began to build new houses, several different families would often share one old house.

Alternatively, members of a single family might be dispersed across several different structures. For instance, an older but unmarried son might sleep in a room in one house, while other members of his family might sleep somewhere else. However, even if a family had only one room to live in, or had a few rooms at their disposal that were dispersed through several different physical structures, their unity—and separation from other families—was marked by their shared stove.

For instance, until 1985, Songling and Baoli's kitchen had been in an old house with three other kitchens belonging to different families. Songling and Baoli and their three children all slept in just one room in a different house located across the courtyard from the house where they cooked. Ailing, whose family used another kitchen in that same house, remembered the mid-1970s. As most families were poor, and often lived in just one or two rooms, "There was no place in the house to eat, so [at mealtimes] everyone would just take their bowls and eat outside." She continued to recollect that it was a great deal of fun, especially for the children.

In this case, mealtimes involved little family privacy. However, families were still differentiated because their food came from separate stoves. Interestingly, in recollecting her childhood during those days, Ailing said that sometimes if she did not like her own family's meal, she would procure something different simply by carrying her bowl of rice or congee outside and adding trimmings prepared by another family. Of course, it is important to point out that Ailing was talking about the *cai,* or trimmings, not the staple, rice. Each family always had its own rice pot, and rice or congee as the basis of each meal would not have been shared between families. As Stuart Thompson, in reference to the southeastern Chinese context states, "Rice is also very much the key food substance shared by members of a family." Thompson quotes the anthropologist David Jordan, who writes, "A family is the unit attached to a rice pot. . . . Rice is ideally not exchanged between families, for it is 'substance shared.'"[27] And humorously, in Moonshadow Pond a premarital pregnancy that precipitates a marriage is often referred to by the phrase, "the rice is cooked."

As mentioned in the last chapter, rice is still the most common staple and is the centerpiece of daily family meals in Moonshadow Pond. Each person begins his or her meal with a bowl filled with rice or congee. Children have to be encouraged and prodded to finish their bowls, and parents may sit a long time with their children until they have eaten all their rice. Finishing one's rice bowl is still viewed as a good trait in a child, and refusing to eat rice is a sign of being spoiled. One day in 2007, I was sitting outside a small local shop where people frequently gathered to talk. Songling's sister-in-law Jinhua came by with her grandson. Songling's own grandson Jiabing was also there playing with some friends. Making sure that Jiabing could hear her, Jinhua looked toward him and said rather loudly, "He doesn't eat rice all day long." Then, looking at her own grandson, she continued, "*he* eats three bowls of rice a day." Jinhua then went on to draw a number of other conclusions from this observation about childhood rice eating. "Rich people's children," she told me, can be spoiled and "don't eat rice" (in reality, her own family was quite well off as her husband, Songling's brother, was a contractor). Nonetheless, she continued, "My son had to go to Hong Kong for five years to work and he had to spend thirteen hours every day killing chickens, so he was not spoiled. But children who are spoiled will not eat right."

The sharing of rice as an index of family unity applies to both cooked and uncooked rice. For instance, Yinzhao's two sons live in town. They have separate family economies and different jobs and do not pool their individual incomes. However, as Yinzhao provisions them with the rice she grows, and as they return with their families to eat together in Moonshadow Pond on weekends, residents of Moonshadow Pond say that their family has not officially divided.

Currently, three-generational families such as Songling and Baoli's are still common in Moonshadow Pond, though they are far from the size of the multigenerational joint families envisioned as the cultural ideal of the past.[28] Most three-generational families are now like Songling and Baoli's family, stem families consisting of parents and one married offspring—usually a son—who share economic resources. Only a small number of families (12%) include more than one married offspring sharing property and income.[29] However, in the current context, it is important to remember that sharing economic resources does not mean that families actually eat together or live together every day. Because of urban migration, the number of people who remain in their Moonshadow Pond households is less than the number of people who count themselves as family members.

Nonetheless, despite the phenomenon of urban migration, the symbolism of the stove and the sharing of food are still important to family definition. Villagers in Moonshadow Pond assured me that the family you return to, *and share food with on New Year's Eve,* indicates the boundaries of the undivided family (*jia*). One does not share a New Year's Eve meal with a family that has already divided economically.

The link between sharing a stove and family identity in Moonshadow Pond and elsewhere in rural China does not mean that family division ends all food sharing. Brothers who have divided and set up separate households continue to have obligations to their aging parents, and following the food trail is a good way of assessing the degree to which offspring feel the pull of these obligations. For instance, *lunliu,* or meal rotation, is a common way in which sons divide responsibility for feeding aging parents. An aging parent may take his or her meals one month with one son, the next month with a different son, and so forth. In Songling and Baoli's household, as described in chapter 1, food was constantly flowing back and forth, not only within what would be considered their formal household—which included their son's family—but also between their married daughters and themselves. (Chapters 4 and 5 examine familial food exchanges, as well as the contradictory discourses surrounding the moral obligations implied by such exchanges, in more detail.)

As with agricultural production, the preparation of food has also been shaped by the very different contexts of the pre-Liberation, collective, and reform eras. But in addition to being shaped by historical developments, cooking has undoubtedly been influenced by certain enduring and critically important cultural categories about what constitutes a meal. We therefore turn next to examining in more detail the contexts of food preparation in Moonshadow Pond, beginning with cooking for the family.

COOKING FOR THE FAMILY, FROM DAILY MEALS TO YEARLY FESTIVALS

Walking into Yinzhao's kitchen is almost like reading the strata of cooking history in Moonshadow Pond. The family's forebears were overseas Chinese, who had returned from Indonesia and built a beautiful stone house (not mud brick as was the norm in the 1930s). In the 1980s, most families in Moonshadow Pond moved out of their old mud-brick dwellings and began to build new homes. However, Yinzhao's old house has withstood the test of time. In her kitchen, a large old wok sits atop a brick stove, under which wood and kindling, the preferred fuel of the past, are placed to feed the fire. In addition, Yinzhao's kitchen, like most of the kitchens in Moonshadow Pond now, contains some burners attached to gas, which is currently the favored cooking fuel for daily cooking. In her case, the gas comes from methane generated from her neighbors' pig waste. The neighbor uses Yinzhao's shed to raise ten pigs, and in return Yinzhao is provided with the methane.

The old stove in Yinzhao's kitchen reminds us that in the past the work of cooking began with gathering fuel and water. Until the mid-1970s, wood and kindling for cooking were gathered in the hills surrounding Moonshadow Pond. Women and girls would go to the river running through the village to collect water and would carry it back to their homes in buckets hung from shoulder poles. Ailing, now a teacher's aide with two children in college, recalled her days then, commenting on both her hard work and her brothers' privilege: "I had five brothers, so I had a lot of work to do. I had to go several times a day to the stream to fetch water, and I had to go up the hills to get kindling for cooking."[30] After the mid-1970s, however, coal began to replace wood, eliminating the need to gather wood for cooking. By the mid-1990s, gas was more widely available and became the preferred source. Not all families use methane from pig manure, and many purchase their gas. By the end of the collective era, families also began to sink wells, eliminating the need to fetch water for everyday needs (although as mentioned earlier, there is now a quest to get purer water from natural aquifers).

In addition to having stoves, every kitchen in Moonshadow Pond is minimally equipped with a few very thick cutting boards; some sharp cleavers; woks; some pots for making soup; and, of course, a rice cooker. Some families have refrigerators, but these are typically used to store only specialty items. Refrigerators sometimes are used to store leftovers, although even these are usually put aside and eaten at the very next meal. Interestingly, refrigerators are rarely placed in the kitchen at all but may often be tucked away in another part of the house—hardly playing the central role we think about for the fridge in American families.

The separation between inside and outside is still not a firm one in most country homes. Food preparation may take place partially in public. For instance, one may take a cutting board or plastic washbasin outside the house, and sit on a low plastic stool while cutting, peeling, or rinsing vegetables. If a neighbor comes along, he or she may simply crouch down and join you in the activity while gossiping. Furthermore, the kitchen or cooking space is rarely an eating space as well, and it may adjoin a courtyard or backyard (see figs. 10–11). In Songling and Baoli's house, for instance, we normally took our daily meals in an enclosed area next to an internal courtyard. There was a round table and a collection of stools, which could be taken out and arranged as needed around the table. The courtyard could also function as a

FIGURE 10. Preparing vegetables outdoors.

work space for food preparation, such as for cutting vegetables or cleaning fish.

One might expect that the division of daily labor during food preparation in Moonshadow Pond families would parallel that of rice cultivation and vegetable gardening, in which middle-aged and elderly women predominate. Both involve immediate provisioning of the family. Both are about "use-values," as even food that has been purchased is converted to a use-value when cooked for the immediate family. However, the division of labor in cooking food does not quite parallel that of cultivating food. Women are responsible for cooking in many families but not all. The work of cooking is not only less exclusively female than subsistence agriculture but also somewhat more dispersed among generations than that of rice cultivation and gardening.

For instance, of thirty-five families questioned in 2007, all the cooking was done by one or more women in two-thirds of them. In four families, all the cooking was done by the father or grandfather, while in another four families, spouses cooked together. There was a variety of other arrangements, including that of one family in which both members of the senior generation prepared meals, with participation from their son and daughter-in-law, and even a granddaughter.

FIGURE 11. Home kitchen with view to courtyard.

Therefore, while the "default" option in Moonshadow Pond is still for women to be responsible for domestic food preparation, there are a number of other combinations. Further, there are other ways in which cooking and *gengtian* are not completely parallel. *Gengtian* is work that young people are taught to avoid as a life goal. But cooking for the family does not have any such negative connotations. Many youth actually become conversant at an early age with basic cooking skills. One young woman, who had a good job in the county capital with the local television station but lived at home in Moonshadow Pond with her parents, said this about learning to cook: "We learn from our grandparents mainly. More girls learn than boys, but some boys learn too. Our parents are usually working, so we learn from our grandparents. Or, if we don't have grandparents, we might help our parents. If you live in the city, and you don't live with your parents, then you might need a cookbook, though."

The requirements of a "meal," referred to in chapter 1, are also critical to the importance of cooking. As stated earlier, the combination of some kind of *fan,* or rice, and *cai* (meat and/or vegetable trimmings) has a long history in Chinese cuisine, and is a framework for ordinary meals among the Hakka as well. This combination, furthermore, needs to be cooked and hot. There is no Hakka equivalent of the American sandwich or cold meal (another reason why the refrigerator is usually placed in some far off corner of the house). If the family is small, meals will certainly be simple, but they will always be some combination of the *fan/cai* formula. For instance, Miaoli is a widow in her fifties, whose daughter is married. She now lives with only her adult son, who is still unmarried. She grows all the vegetables she eats and raises her own chickens. She buys meat, but that is really all she needs to buy. She harvests her own rice and cultivates a few pomelo trees as well. She does not eat elaborate meals, so she will usually cook one vegetable dish, one meat dish, and rice. Or she will cook a mixed vegetable and meat dish and eat that with rice and soup. Still, the basic *fan/cai* formula remains constant and entails at least some cooking for every meal.

The early age at which children become comfortable with cooking was illustrated to me when I took a short day trip with a group of about twenty sixth graders. I was the only adult on the trip, and we set out on our bicycles to a Buddhist temple that was about a one-hour bicycle ride from the village. The last part of the trip entailed a hike to the top of a small mountain. After arriving, the students unpacked their knapsacks. They had pots and pans, cooking oil, cooking implements, and basic ingredients—cut up pieces of meat and vegetables, a bit of soy sauce, and fish sauce. At the top of the mountain, these sixth graders, boys and girls together, started a fire and with a rice pot and wok proceeded to work together to cook lunch for the entire group. Imagining a similar situation in the United States, I was quite certain that the children would have taken sandwiches and bags of potato chips out of their backpacks instead.

Young people may also help out with cooking for holidays like the Lunar New Year. As with the rice harvest, which occurs only at certain times of year, older women may organize younger family members to help out with special preparations for these celebrations. For instance, *nianban* are deep fried or steamed, sweet or savory, treats composed of a number of local ingredients mixed into a batter made up of either glutinous rice flour or wheat flour.[31] Once they are prepared, *nianban* are served with tea during interfamilial visiting throughout the duration of the New Year's season, as they do not spoil for weeks. They are also enthusiastically consumed as an additional treat during breakfast, when they are reheated by steaming. This addition to the breakfast meal during New Year marks it as different from ordinary breakfasts of congee and basic trimmings.

The work of preparing *nianban* now entails generational exchanges. Because young parents are usually out working, an older or middle-aged woman may find herself making New Year's treats for several different families—those of her married daughters, as well as of her sons and daughters-in-law. During the preparation for the New Year, therefore, older women often take charge of the timely preparations of *nianban* and distribute the end results to several different family subgroups.

When I asked Songling about this, she said her daughters no longer had time to engage in this preparation, but it would also be unacceptable for them to simply purchase these treats in the county capital. First, she said, there was no comparison between homemade *nianban,* and the *nianban* that one buys at the market. The *nianban* available for sale, according to Songling, are made with substandard oil and are not good to digest. In addition to resolving issues related to food safety and taste, making these *nianban* is another way for Songling to fortify the bonds of obligation with her married daughters. Since elders in Moonshadow Pond believe that their grown children may not be as reliably filial as past generations, they endeavor to help both grown sons and daughters in any way they can, in order to create in them a feeling of indebtedness. (Chapter 5 will examine this topic in detail.)

Preparing *nianban* entails making different kinds of batter, rolling out the dough, and slicing and assembling the treats in different shapes. Often, as this is a holiday period, young people are home, so it is not uncommon for grandmothers and their grandchildren (especially granddaughters) to work on this together over several days (see figs. 12–13). As these treats are made in huge quantities, cooking with gas would be much too expensive. Thus, families amass a large supply of wood and cook the *nianban* in large woks set over a wood fire, often laid out in a yard or courtyard.

In the winters of 1996 and 2007, I was able to enjoy the New Year's celebrations in Moonshadow Pond, and to observe and take part in the preparations, including making *nianban*. One morning about a week before the New Year in 2007, I visited with Yinzhao. She was joined in making *nianban*

FIGURE 12. Preparing New Year's treats in the courtyard.

FIGURE 13. Grandmother and granddaughter prepare New Year's treats together.

by both of her married daughters, her eldest son's wife, and two of her grand-daughters, who were home from college. This was just the first day, and they spent hours making one of the more popular treats, deep-fried sesame seed balls (*jianban*). The preparations continued for several more days, until most of the varieties of *nianban* had been made. In the end, Yinzhao had used over 50 jin (67 pounds) of glutinous rice flour, and had overseen the preparation of New Year's treats for seven families: those of four married children (two daughters and two sons), a married granddaughter, and two of her own younger sisters. She had also made some treats for herself, so she would have her own supply to bring out when people visited her family's country home in Moonshadow Pond.

Songling also spent a few days preparing her own New Year's treats, recruiting her daughter-in-law, a granddaughter, and a neighbor (whom she paid) to help. Baoli participated as well, although he was "cursed out" by Songling for making batter that was too watery!

The range of people in Moonshadow Pond who have skills at cooking is expanded further if one includes those who cook for paid employment. Many young men in Moonshadow Pond work as cooks, either in the county capital or further afield in large cities. When these young men return home, how-ever, they do not shun the work of cooking for their families.

During the Mid-Autumn Festival in 2012, for instance, Songling's son Yanhong cooked an impressive meal for the family. Yanhong's command of cooking was, of course, greater than the average, as he had trained as a cook and had worked as a cook for twelve years in the two largest metropolises, Guangzhou and Shenzen, of Guangdong Province. (On that day, he put together an impressive meal in about ninety minutes!) The notes I wrote while watching Yanhong, who prepared the meal with the help of his sisters and mother, impart a sense of the process of preparing a special family meal for a holiday (see appendix B, "Preparing a Holiday Meal").

It is important to point out that, despite the elaborate preparation, this was very much a family-oriented meal—for Songling, Baoli, their three mar-ried children, and their children's families. It was not a banquet framed around the categories of host and guest (more on this below). The one non-familial participant in the meal was the son of Songling's "sworn sister," and his family had been close to Songling and Baoli's for many decades. Interestingly, however, as the only participant who was not a family member, he also was the only one who brought an appropriate gift for a banquet—a large box of fancy moon cakes from Hong Kong.

Yanhong's sisters, on the other hand, brought food items to the event that could be put to immediate use in the work of preparing the meal. And indeed, after arriving they also pitched into the cooking. Furthermore, unlike a formal banquet, this meal was not marked by elaborate and competitive toasting. Baoli took out some wine, and there was brief toasting to everyone's health, but certainly not the extended and ongoing bouts of toasting that can lead to men becoming inebriated, as happens at many banquets.

So despite its great complexity, the cooking for this meal can still be understood as family-oriented labor, much like the work of gardening, or *gengtian*. But what of the labor of cooking in regard to banquets? As we will see below, when it comes to preparing a banquet, there has been a gradual shift away from relying on mutual assistance from other villagers, who are compensated with gifts in kind or monetary gifts enclosed in traditional red envelopes, toward contracting the work out to professional catering teams, who pay wages to their workers. Nonetheless, the commodification of the labor of cooking for banquets has not displaced earlier forms of cooking labor; it has just added new ones.

For the purposes of this analysis, I consider a banquet to be any meal that is categorized by people in Moonshadow Pond as *shijiu*, which means "to consume spirts or liquor." As mentioned earlier, this is opposed to *shifan*, which refers to eating rice, a way of categorizing ordinary meals. Furthermore, banquets must involve guests beyond either the immediate family or daughters returning to their natal family. A large family get together, such as the Mid-Autumn Festival meal prepared by Yanhong with the help of his sisters and mother, is referred to as a "happy occasion" (*hao shi*). However, it is not categorized as *shijiu*, even if spirits are consumed. Similarly, another important family gathering is the dinner that a family eats together on the eve of the Lunar New Year. This is, significantly, referred to as a "reunion dinner" (*tuanyuan fan*). The emphasis for this meal is on the family coming together; therefore the substance indicated in its name is *fan,* or rice, rather than *jiu,* or spirits.

A TALE OF PREPARING TWO BANQUETS

In September 2012, I returned to Moonshadow Pond to participate in an important local festival that is held around the same time of year as the Mid-Autumn Festival. The Mid-Autumn Festival occurs on the fifteenth day of the eighth month in the lunar calendar, and, since 2007, it has been declared a national holiday.[32] Like the Lunar New Year, it is now a time when universities close down, government offices are shut, and traffic on national highways becomes congested as students and other workers return to their homes. But in Moonshadow Pond, this time of year is a period in which Zuofu, an important local festival, is also celebrated.

Zuofu literally means to create blessings, or celebrate one's good fortune, and might best be understood as a local thanksgiving (we will have more to say about the meanings of Zuofu in chapter 4). It is celebrated any time between the first and fifteenth of the eighth lunar month, but each village in the township traditionally chooses a different date for the celebration; in this way, the festivities circulate for over two weeks. This circulating schedule also enables people to alternate between the roles of hosts and guests. The guest list may include friends, affines (relatives through marriage), or matrilateral relatives (those connected through maternal ties).The holiday, therefore, emphasizes a family's connections outside the patriline (the descent group traced through the male line). We will say more about issues of exchange, connections, and sociability in later chapters and will concentrate here on the actual labor of preparing food for these events.

Village elders recollected that, in the past, Zuofu involved at least two weeks of food preparation. People made their own sweet fermented glutinous rice cakes (*fajiao ban*) to give away to guests, and they slaughtered their own ducks and chickens (which could be raised by individual families after the Great Leap Forward). Elders remembered this holiday, along with the Lunar New Year, as one of the few times during the collective era when they also received rations of pork. Another special, former Zuofu holiday preparation was grinding one's own soybeans to make bean curd. But as mentioned earlier, bean curd is now considered a common food that can be bought daily from local vendors, and as such it is not even included in special feasts anymore.

I had heard much about Zuofu, but it was one festivity that I had missed on all my previous trips to Moonshadow Pond because I either arrived after it had taken place or left before it occurred. Fortunately, two of the Zuofu banquets I attended in 2012 were illustrative of different modes of coordinating the work of cooking for a banquet. One was organized around the mutual-help model and the other used the services of a professional caterer.

Songling and Baoli's Zuofu banquet included four tables of ten persons each. (The size of banquets in China is usually conveyed by referring to the number of tables rather than to the number of guests invited; tables generally seat eight or ten guests, depending on whether they are round or square.) In this case, rather than cooking all the food themselves, as they had in the past, Songling and Baoli cooperated with three other neighbors and contracted the services of a caterer.

This was the first time I had actually seen professional caterers come to Moonshadow Pond. In the past, catering was not provided by businesses from outside the village. Rather, particular village residents specialized in organizing banquets as a side activity. They bought the ingredients, solicited help from other locals, and compensated that help with money or material gifts. For instance, in the 1990s, Uncle Wei, who had already retired from his job as general secretary of the production brigade, often took charge of organizing local banquets. He planned the menus, ordered the ingredients, and thanked the helpers (local village women) with monetary gifts enclosed in traditional red envelopes. In some cases, even cash gifts were unnecessary. If village women assisted with the cooking, payment might have been simply a thank you in the form of packets of biscuits. By the mid-1990s, the most prosperous villagers could afford to stage large banquets for several hundred guests. However, even then, banquets were organized within the village itself. The services of professional caterers were still unheard of. But now caterers are becoming much more common.

Additionally, local restaurant businesses have expanded greatly over the last few years and are increasingly used for banqueting and special meals. As mentioned in the previous chapter, two formerly modest roadside restaurants in Moonshadow Pond have now become large establishments, with many individual dining rooms. Each room is not only outfitted with dining tables but also with low tea tables, around which guests can sit to eat snacks, drink tea, and socialize both before and after the meal, as well as mahjong tables for guests who want to gamble—mainly after the meal. These local restaurants are all family-owned businesses. The largest one is operated by three generations of one family, and, on any given day, one can find family members working at the restaurant, taking reservations, sitting out front shelling peanuts, and overseeing deliveries. However, as the operation has grown it has needed to extend beyond family labor. In all, the restaurant has thirty staff members, including the chef, cooks, and kitchen help.

The use of professional catering services hired from outside the village is the latest addition to the gradual professionalization and commodification of cooking in Moonshadow Pond. For the Zuofu banquet in 2012, the caterer prepared food for a total of 190 people, including Songling and Baoli's forty guests. By nine on the morning of the banquet day, the caterer had already arrived with four truckloads of supplies. Setting up mostly outdoors, and also in an empty garage, the caterers assembled their huge woks atop large tin drums placed over fires fueled with stacks of wood. The caterer's employees were all middle-aged women. But unlike the village women who helped out at village banquets in the 1990s, they had no kin connections to the hosts, and they were paid in cash wages, not presented with thank you gifts, such as biscuits or money (in a red envelope). As the workers prepared the meal, guests began to arrive in the village by motorcycle and car. At Songling and Baoli's house, the atmosphere was extremely festive as guests entered with gifts, including wine, liquor, apples, and bags of cookies and biscuits. (Chapter 4 will look more closely at food and exchange in the Zuofu holiday.) Within three hours, the caterers had produced a sumptuous banquet consisting of twelve dishes.

Still, despite the new option of using a catering service, many Zuofu celebrations still rely on the old system of family help and cooperation to prepare the banquet meal. Two days after Songling and Baoli's banquet, I attended another Zuofu banquet at the home of Songling's nephew Wenping (see fig. 14). This banquet for about thirty guests was prepared entirely by family members; Wenping's wife, Daihua, worked with her aunt, and with the mother of her son's fiancé, to prepare a banquet of fourteen dishes. As guests arrived, Daihua alternately helped with the cooking and took charge of her one-and-a-half-year-old granddaughter, while in the upstairs living room, Wenping entertained the guests with tea, pomelo, biscuits, and stories. Meanwhile, Daihua's other female relations pitched in to complete the food preparation.

When I asked Wenping about their sumptuous fourteen-course banquet the following day, he told me, "Last year we prepared twenty-one dishes, but it was too wasteful, so this year we prepared fewer ones!"

We will discuss the role of banqueting as exchange and sociability in greater detail in later chapters. For now, it is important to point out that, whether the meal is prepared by a caterer or by family members, the need to provide a generous preparation for Zuofu is difficult to shirk. As one villager said to me, "If you don't have all these dishes, then you just don't respect your guests."

Following are lists of the foods cooked by the family members and caterers, respectively:

Wenping and Daihua's banquet (cooked by family members)

sea cucumber/sea slug

chicken and duck feet

squid with chive flowers (*jiucai hua*)

pig stomach and celery

lotus root soup (*lien e*)

braised dog meat

whole chickens in soup with ginseng

steamed fish, silvery pomfret (*cheng eu*)

braised duck

steamed shrimp

red braised pork with mushrooms

frog and green peppers

fragrant veined vegetable, a local green (*xiangmai cai*)

fish and meatball soup

Songling and Baoli's banquet (cooked by caterers)

sea cucumber

pigeon

sweet and sour pork

shrimp with pea pods

duck feet

greens

sweet dumplings filled with custard

steamed chicken with ginger

red braised pork

chicken and ginseng in soup

fried rice flour balls

steamed fish

FROM FIELD TO TABLE IN MOONSHADOW
POND: LABORS OF FOOD

In assessing the labor of agricultural production, as well as food preparation, in Moonshadow Pond, from field to table, and from the production of staple

FIGURE 14. An intergenerational table enjoys a homemade Zuofu banquet.

foods to banquets, the question is how are we to understand it? Certainly, it would be impossible to ignore the way it is shaped by gender and generation. Women are involved in the production-of-use values in subsistence rice production; in vegetable gardening; and certainly to a very large extent, though not exclusively, in the daily preparation of food for family meals. When looking at the way the labor of cooking is commodified, we also see gendered patterns. Women may work as local helpers or day laborers to prepare food for a banquet. Men, on the other hand, may manage catering as Uncle Wei did, or they may study cooking like Yanhong and be employed professionally as cooks or chefs. (Certainly this particular division, between female "home cook" and male "chef" is hardly unique to rural China.)

It might seem, therefore, that we can delineate between a use-value realm of food production and preparation, in which women's work predominates, and a market realm, in which both men and women participate but which is stratified by gender. (This is illustrated in comparing male chefs and banquet managers to female daily workers in the catering field.) But the situation is a bit more complex. First, as previously explained, in Moonshadow Pond young people of both sexes are comfortable with cooking but play no role in agricultural production. Women as well as men are also significantly involved in food production for the market—whether it is raising livestock, producing cash crops like pomelo, or producing value-added food products, bean curd.

Further, the labor of food production from agriculture to cooking, as already noted, cannot really be understood apart from a host of social relationships and responsibilities that lie both within and outside the family. The anthropologist David Sutton has pointed out that in a world of commodity production and exchange, or "commodity fetishism" as Marx referred to it, "Objects are compared based on a price derived from their market value rather than on the history of labor relations that went into producing them. . . . a purposeful forgetting of the past that went into the making of the present."[33] However, most of the labor discussed in this chapter does not fit into such a framework of forgetfulness. It cannot be forgotten, because whether it is remunerated or not, the labor of food production within the village is still mainly incorporated into ongoing relationships based on social obligations, memories, and notions of moral debt. In the next chapters, we turn to these aspects of labor for a broader view.

THREE

Memory

"WHEN WE WERE GROWING UP, we always used to look forward to the Lunar New Year and to the time when we would have *nianban*. The children loved to eat them, but now the children don't want them."

Baoli reminisced about the past. He then continued with a complaint about the packages of factory-made cookies that his grandson was so fond of.

When it comes to both food and memory, some have argued that industrialized food consumption creates mass amnesia. For instance, Sidney Mintz compared modern food consumption in North America to "the hunting-and-gathering existence of our species, when food was eaten as it became available, without much reference to situation or circumstance." He concluded that, when food is consumed in such unstructured nonevents, then both the food and the event are quickly forgotten.[1] For Mintz, phonomena such as fast food and manufactured food create uniformity over many different spaces and time zones, and turn eating into a process of "refueling" emptied of local significance. Such culinary amnesia has also been linked by some analysts to a counter-reaction, indicated by growing interest in "ethnic" food in North America and Europe. However, David Sutton contends that even these eating events can take the form of a search for "novel consumptive experiences,"[2] rather than serving to denote a particular time in a particular place.

Eating events unrelated to specific times and places are just one illustration of the relationship between modernity and time as characterized by Anthony Giddens. Modern time, states Giddens, is "empty time."[3] Hence it is not marked by festivals, customs, and practices that indicate that it is time as experienced in a specific locale.[4] The notion of "disembedding" is critical here,[5] that is, the idea that modern life separates time from particular spaces, and has ripped apart the connections or "embedding" of social activities in particular contexts.[6] In the context of food and diet, such "empty time" might be contrasted with what Sutton describes as time that is marked by "local culinary traditions," which "reenact belonging and identity at every meal."[7] Such culinary traditions, says Sutton, are part of "cultural memory" because "one cannot enact what one cannot remember."[8]

In real life, of course, societies are not dichotomized quite so simply between those with strong local culinary traditions, closely tied to cultural memory, and those with industrialized food, emptied of all meaning. But one can use these analytical distinctions to evaluate food practices and meaning systems in a range of societies. For instance, while "ethnic" restaurants in North America may function as novel consumptive experiences for cultural outsiders, they may also serve to connect immigrants and their descendants to memories or traditions from a cultural homeland.[9] Furthermore, symbolically meaningful eating practices are not entirely absent from societies with industrialized food systems and fast food. They may be tied to local traditions, like regional festivals, or to national ones, like American Thanksgiving.

Nonetheless, this contrast between local culinary traditions, rich in cultural memory, and industrialized food, characterized as lacking in layers of meaning and memories, is a useful perspective by which to begin thinking about the connections between food and memory in Moonshadow Pond. Certainly, on a scale of unmemorable refueling experiences versus symbolically loaded locally embedded ones, Moonshadow Pond eating practices lean much more heavily in the latter direction. The food practices in Moonshadow Pond undoubtedly bear much more resemblance to Sutton's description of a strong "local culinary tradition" than to the mere "refueling events" described by Mintz.

In examining connections between food and memory in Moonshadow Pond, several different elements immediately come to mind. First, and most obvious, we might think about the way food can create real or imagined links to the past. This is partially through the simple process of reenacting food traditions in the ways Sutton points to. By eating foods characterized as Hakka foods, one is presumably connecting to a set of past practices. Furthermore, celebrations and rituals create a space of time to think even more specifically about tradition. As Sutton phrases it, calendrical rituals are "'out of ordinary time' and thus a chance for people to reflect on the passing of time: how their lives have changed while the rituals presumably have not."[10] This certainly occurs in Moonshadow Pond during major holidays such as the Lunar New Year's celebrations, or the Zuofu holiday (described in the previous chapter), as well as during several other minor holidays.

However, even here, there is a complication. Given the transformations in standards of living in Moonshadow Pond over the last several decades, calendrical and life-cycle celebrations are as much a reminder of breaks in continuity as they are about connecting to unchanging tradition. Thus, food in Moonshadow Pond can function very much as a "socially charged marker of ephochal shifts."[11] It is a primary vehicle through which villagers understand the historical transformations of the last half century, and thus "remember" the past through comparison with the much different present.

Furthermore, in thinking of the food/memory nexus, one has to take account of what Jon Holtzman has characterized as the unconscious elements of memory in regard to food. As he reminds us, many elements of food culture are to be found in "practices that may, or may not be clearly reflected in conscious memory."[12] These practices can be understood most cogently through the use of Bourdieu's notion of "habitus"—internalized and taken for granted practices related to a given social context, which are connected to one's class position or to other elements of one's identity. Some elements of memory, therefore, can be "verbally narrativized," while other elements of memory "are rooted in unreflected-upon bodily practices."[13] For instance, everyday cooking practices and the ways in which meals are constituted can be seen as falling into the category of internalized and taken-for-granted practices that can be framed as habitus.

A further category of relation between memory and food is the one Robert Thaxton categorizes as "embodied memories." Examples of this would include damage to the body caused by past food shortages. These include chronic stomach problems set off by the inpact of consuming coarse ingredients to stem hunger during a famine. Such unconscious embodied memories are juxtaposed by Thaxton with consciously articulated "semantic memories."[14]

However, even when memory is conciously articulated, we need to keep in mind that food, even in sparking conscious memory, often operates at unconscious levels because of its power to operate on so many senses. Sutton uses the word "synesthesia" to invoke food's power to arouse memory. As he says, "Food's memory power derives in part from synesthesia. . . . the synthesis or crossing of experiences from different sensory registers (i.e., taste, smell, hearing). . . . Taste and smell . . . become evocative of social situations with which they are associated."[15]

With these caveats in mind, this chapter will examine the connections between memory and food in Moonshadow Pond. Our main focus will be on the conscious elements of memory articulated by individuals, rather than on those unconscious ones highlighted by the concept of habitus or embodied memory. Primarily, these conscious memories relate to an historical conciousness, as food evokes and reminds people of social, cultural, and political continuities or changes. But, in addition, conscious memories evoked by food can also connect people to personal histories, as well as to societal ones. In this sense, food memories play a role in ongoing exchanges and moral obligations both to the living and to ancestors and gods. (This is an element of memory that subsequent chapters take up in more detail.)

We also need to keep in mind that memories in Moonshadow Pond, like any place, differ in terms of individual and generational experiences. Foods, such as the sweet potato, that evoke memories of lean times for older and middle-aged people may not have the same impact on younger people, who receive these memories secondhand when they hear their elders speak of times they did not live through.

Contrary to what one might assume, not all memories of food during the collective era are associated with dearth and bad times. Food, after all, can also evoke feelings of nostalgia. Villagers' discussions of food during the collective era are thus not without contradictions. In describing their memories of the collective era, people may talk about the Great Leap famine or the dearth of food throughout the collective era in general. But they may simultaneously recount wistfully that meals and mealtimes were characterized by a greater sense of social solidarity than they are in the present. For instance, chapter 2 noted the memories of Ailing, a middle-aged woman who was an adolescent in the 1960s. She remembered the communal nature of mealtimes during the collective era, and recalled how everyone would pile some food on top of their rice or congee, take their bowls outside, and eat together while perched on their knees, on door thresholds, or while sitting on benches. As she recollected further, she noted that the food was not abundant, but the experience was a shared one. "Not like now," she griped, "when everyone is just inside watching television."

We begin our analysis with a discussion of the relationship of food to memory as pertains to holidays and life-cycle rituals, followed by a discussion of several common foodstuffs, and the ways in which they not only evoke consciousness of historical transformations but also provide a framework for thinking about such transformations. We will also consider dishes that are strongly connected to Hakka identity and, therefore, connect people to the past through an emphasis on continuity. By concentrating on the ways food evokes memories and links people to the past, while also reminding them of disruptions and thus discontinuities of that past, we can begin to think of food in Moonshadow Pond as part of an overarching semiotic system. But it is certainly not a static one.

MEMORY, FOOD, AND CALENDRICAL RITUALS

Moonshadow Pond residents say that the three grandest (*longzhong*) yearly holidays are the Lunar New Year, the Mid-Autumn Festival, and Zuofu (the local Moonshadow Pond celebration described in chapter 2). These celebrations involve large family meals, or banqueting, and interfamily visiting. Each sparks a variety of memories and discourses about the past, some of which are contradictory or ambivalent and many of which are sparked by the role of food.[16] Furthermore, changes in national policies, as China has moved from the collective to the reform era, have been inextricably linked, in either overt or more subtle ways, with people's memories of these holidays.

On the one hand, today's festivities are often a springboard to memories of hunger and food scarcity for those who lived through those times. On the other hand, there is another, more nostalgic, narrative that bemoans the gradual loss of some foods or food customs because of peoples' busy lives, and because substitutes for food once laboriously produced at home can now be found in the market. Both narratives—the scarcity narrative and the narrative that expresses nostalgia for earlier foods and food customs—provide important contrasts with images of food's role now. They are a way of talking about the present by drawing a contrast with the past through the lens of food. However, neither narrative can be taken at face value as an historical account.

For instance, Teacher Liu's recounting of food's connection to calendrical festivals was typical of those narratives that used holidays as a springboard to talk about past food scarcity: "In the past, we never had much to eat," Teacher Liu wrote to me in a letter in 2007. Teacher Liu taught for many years in the primary school in Moonshadow Pond and was in her early thirties when she wrote this. She was old enough, having grown up in the early eighties, to remember times when food was less abundant. But, certainly, she was not old enough to personally remember the most trying times. Still, through her lens on the holidays, she viewed them in terms of how they shed light on the less secure times of the past—either those that she experienced herself, or those she heard others speak about. As she put it, "We usually just relied on our own vegetables, and we lived frugally [*sheng chi jian yong*]. It was only during holidays that we would get meat, make some *ban* [treats such as the *nianban*, made from either glutinous rice flour or wheat flour], and comfort our stomachs. Therefore, until the present, 'What holiday?' means 'What will we eat?'"

One elderly woman in Moonshadow Pond also used her memory of holidays to remark on culinary change. She noted that even the holidays of the past were celebrated in much less grandiose fashion when it came to food. Comparing the rather elaborate Mid-Autumn Festival meals of the present with the simple celebrations she remembered from the past, she said, "All we used to do during the Mid-Autumn Festival was make some deep-fried taro ball (*Jian yuyuan*) and savory deep-fried wheat thins (*chanzi*), and we would also eat peanuts and moon cakes. In the evening we would worship the deities and wait for the moon's sister to come down and eat the moon cake. The kids would play with the vegetable basket and put a man's clothes in it. They would ask the moon's sister to come down and, if the clothes moved, we would be really scared and all run away! This happened in the old society and in the collective era as well. Now these things like candies and peanuts and even moon cakes are not that special for kids anymore."

It is interesting that, like Baoli's remarks at the beginning of this chapter about the decline in appreciation for *nianban*, this villager's reminiscence was not so much a celebration of contemporary abundance but a commentary on the inability of today's youth to appreciate the simpler treats of the past. Indeed, Baoli once said that even the work involved in making *nianban* in the present was not equivalent to the amount of work that used to be required. Baoli noted that children used to love and anticipate *nianban*. But now, because of their desire for factory-made cookies, "We make many fewer *nianban* than we used to." In this case, he looked back nostalgically at the past, and used his memories to critique present-day trends.

Despite Baoli's complaints about the current lack of appreciation for traditional treats, much about the contemporary celebration of the Lunar New Year in Moonshadow Pond does remain connected to tradition. The preparation of customary foods such as *nianban,* braised ducks, and sausages still consumes people for days. Food is also offered as prestations to ancestors and local deities (see fig. 15). In each house, on the morning before the New Year,

FIGURE 15. Making offerings to lineage-branch ancestors on Lunar New Year's Eve.

offerings of food are presented to heaven, to the Stove God, and to one's ancestors; villagers then carry these offerings in baskets strung from bamboo poles balanced over their shoulders. They walk to the village entrance, where they lay out their offerings to the village guardian guards (*Sheguan Laoye* and *Gongwang*), and then proceed to the lineage temple and lineage-branch temples to honor their ancestors, laying the same offerings out again. These prestations include the three sacrifical meats (*san sheng*), chicken, pork, and fish, and "vegetarian offerings" (*zhai pan*), which include *nianban,* citrus fruits and apples, candies, and, finally, tea and glutinous rice wine.

On New Year's Eve, the family sits together for their unity or reunion meal (*tuanyuan fan*). Then, at midnight, the God of Wealth (*Caishen*) is welcomed at the front door. Because he is being asked in for tea, and not a meal, he is presented with vegetarian offerings, and thus the three sacrificial meats are excluded. The next morning, the family eats breakfast together in another reaffirmation of unity.

Throughout the holiday, food homonyms for prosperity, harmony, and family unity are used, as they are on other auspicious occasions such as marriages, house-moving celebrations, and new business openings. For instance, the reunion meal should include fish because the word for "fish" (*yu*) is a homonym for the word for "plentiful," and therefore connotes prosperity or abundance (*yu*). On New Year's morning, celery is added to the morning congee because the word for "celery" (*qincai*) contains the same sound as the word for "industrious" and "hardworking," and one needs to work hard to prosper. Also, garlic stems are stir fried that same morning because the word for "garlic" (*suan*) sounds like the word for "calculate," and in order to prosper one most certainly needs to calculate properly! Many of the varieties of *nianban* are round, to emphasize unity, and they may also have ingredients or names that are homonyms for other words that mean "to prosper"(see tables 1–2).

The two weeks of the Lunar New Year's holiday include visits from and meals with married daughters and their families, and much back-and-forth movement as friends and relatives visit each others' homes, and are plied with tea, *nianban,* biscuits, pomelos, peanuts, and other treats. Nonetheless, villagers often reflect on these holiday practices as something new because they never before had the material abundance to celebrate the New Year with such a cornucopia of foods. A few villagers also pointed out to me that this contemporary feasting is not only different because of the profusion of foods but also because its meaning has changed. During more radical periods of the collective era, the government attempted to insert new symbols into the New Year's celebrations, particularly into the family unity meal. These "new" symbols were jettisoned during the reform era in favor of more traditional meanings.

For instance, although no one would admit to practicing it themselves, a number of people told me about the "recall bitterness meal" (*yi ku fan*) that the authorities urged them to eat before consuming their family unity meal during the Cultural Revolution (1966–69). The idea was to boil wild vegetables together with rice chaff and make a paste—certainly an extremely unappetizing gruel. Each family member was supposed to be given a bowl of this recall bitterness dish, and while eating it they would be prompted to recall the bitterness of their past lives in the preliberation era, referred to as the "old society" (*jiu shehui*). These memories were also supposed to prompt thoughts and gratitude about the relative "sweetness" of the present. This was all prompted by Mao's call to "recall the bitter before thinking of the sweet" (*yiku sitian*). The aim, of course, was to build support for Communist rule and especially for the radical path of the Cultural Revolution. The use of food to spark memories of the bitter past of the old society was one way to do this. However, a number of older villagers told me that while this practice *did* make them remember the bitter, it was not the bitter of the old society but precisely the harsh times during the Great Leap Forward (1958–61), when they were reduced to surviving on such things as buns made from rice chaff.[17]

The Lunar New Year's reunion meal now plays into memories in quite different ways. The large number of people who have migrated to urban areas to work during the reform era have had an important impact on the context of the Lunar New Year's celebrations in rural areas. During the days preceding the Lunar New Year, tens of millions of China's urban workers, including many unmarried youth, take part in a mad scramble as they board buses and trains to return to their village homes. The return of so many labor migrants to their homes in Moonshadow Pond creates a new context for the unity meal on New Year's Eve. As pointed out in chapter 2, the unity meal spells out the boundaries of the family as an income-sharing unit. While these boundaries might have seemed obvious in the past, the exodus of so many youth and even married family members to the cities for work means that the family does not eat together every day. The unity meal, as a consequence, is an even more important reminder of family membership now than it was in the past.

Other food-related activities surrounding calendrical festivals take on similar significance as memory enhancers in light of student and migrant returns. For instance, Yinzhao's daughter Small Gao still farms land in Moonshadow Pond, while her husband is a bus driver for one of the high schools in the county capital. However, both her children are in college in Guangzhou. In February 2007, they came home and participated in the entire array of New Year's activities. I accompanied them as they helped their grandmother make *nianban* and climbed the hills above the village with their relatives to clean the graves and make offerings to both immediate and more distant lineage ancestors. After laying out the "three sacrificial meats" and the vegetarian offerings, burning spirit money, and setting off fireworks, we descended the hills and gathered for an informal meal at Yinzhao's house. These rituals and the accompanying meals reinscribe the connections of young migrants to their native place. They therefore counter the memory loss that might otherwise occur as Moonshadow Pond's young emigrants disperse for most of the year to many different urban locations.

We now turn from the issue of memories awakened by food during the celebration of calendrical festivals, to examine the ways in which specific regularly consumed foods have come to embody memories. Unlike the unconscious "embodied memories" that Ralph Thaxton refers to in his discussion
of famines and long-lasting bodily harm, the conscious memories evoked by
these foodstuffs are of the historical past, and "stand for" particular elements
of that past for many residents of Moonshadow Pond. At the same time,
these food items may now be consumed in new contexts, and they may not
necessarily index the same meanings to younger people, who are unaware of
their former uses and settings.

Kumai *and Other Ordinary Vegetables*

A ubiquitous leafy green vegetable, the "bitter veined" vegetable (*kumai cai*)
is available from winter through August.[18] As implied by its name, it has a
bitter taste, particularly when boiled or steamed. Villagers say that, during
the old society and collective era, it was especially bitter tasting because people had little or no oil to cook with, which could have improved its flavor.

With prosperity, however, there is an ever-expanding number of vegetables cultivated in Moonshadow Pond. Indeed, according to the *Meixian
Gazetteer,* the number of commonly grown vegetables increased from twenty
to thirty varieties at the time of Liberation, to seventy to eighty varieties
now.[19] As the diversity and total volume of vegetables that are planted have
greatly increased, one might wonder why vegetables of the past would spark
nostalgia. As mentioned earlier, however, while no one ever articulates nostalgia for the economic hardships, or the meager diet, of the past, people
sometimes express nostalgia for what they portray as the simpler and less
corrupt social relationships of the past, as well as its greater security. As such,
kumai cai also has positive connotations, even though it is associated with the
greater poverty of both the old society and the collective era, when compared
to the present.

For instance, several folktales villagers like to tell show how *kumai cai,*
despite its bitter taste, has a high nutritional value, while higher-status vegetables with sweeter tastes may, in fact, be nutritionally worthless. In one such
story, a man with one adopted son and another son by birth decided to

discriminate against the adopted son. He fed *kumai cai* to the adopted son, while the birth son was given a sweet-tasting green (amaranth).[20] The father thought he was favoring his own son by giving him the tastier green, but instead the adopted son grew strong and the birth son grew weak because *kumai cai* has a higher nutritional value than the sweet green.

Kumai is also used to accompany congee (rice porridge). As congee is more watery than cooked rice (dry rice), it used the rice grains at a slower pace, and thus was eaten more frequently, than dry rice prior to the reform period. While congee is still a fairly common breakfast dish in Moonshadow Pond, it has been replaced during lunch and dinner with dry rice. *Kumai kao zhou,* which means that *kumai* accompanies congee, is a common adage that villagers often quoted to me. *Kumai*'s relationship with congee is thus another aspect of its ordinariness, and yet it is also an aspect of its appeal.

Still, *kumai,* like many other foods, has other nonordinary aspects, especially in its having made a recent comeback in the specialty restaurant business. It is now combined with items like foraged foods that were once widely available but have become highly priced specialty commodities. In this sense, *kumai*'s meanings have changed along with the economic transformations that have occurred from the old society through the collective and reform eras. An example of this is an eel that can be stir fried with *kumai cai.* The swamp eel (*huangshan*) used to be found in abundance in flooded rice paddies. It was originally mixed with *kumai cai* to give it a better taste and to counter its bitter flavor. Baoli remembered gathering swamp eel, especially during the Great Leap Forward, when hunger was widespread, as it was also a significant source of protein. Elders also spoke of their memories of mixing swamp eel and *kumai cai* during the old society. As pesticide use in rice paddies has become more widespread, swamp eels have become rarer, although one can still occasionally find them in the flooded paddies. However, swamp eel has now made a new appearance in restaurants, where it is stir fried with *kumai* as a banquet specialty.[21] Thus, while *kumai cai* reminds old people of both the bitter adversities of the past and its simple pleasures, it represents something different to younger generations—who may now also consume it as part of a specialty dish in restaurants and banquet halls.

Sweet Potatoes

When elders speak about the past, and about the ways their lives have changed, they usually begin by talking about sweet potatoes. "All we ate was sweet potatoes," is a frequent refrain. The sweet potato is called *fanshu*, which means "foreign potato," presumably because it was introduced to southeastern China from abroad.[22] The governor of Fujian Province has been credited with importing the sweet potato in 1594 from the Philippines, where there was already a Fujianese community, in order to give local peasants a staple they could subsist on in case their grain crops failed.[23] By the late eighteenth century, the sweet potato had "become a staple food for the poor in the coastal southeastern provinces."[24] The tuber spread rapidly to other parts of China, and, even in the north, it became an important part of the diet, allowing a larger population to subsist than would have been possible without it.[25]

Farmers would have to part with some of their grain harvest as taxes or rent, or might even have to sell some of their grains. In contrast, the perishable nature of sweet potatoes meant that most sweet potatoes were grown for immediate consumption. In his 1937 study of farm families in China, John Lossing Buck notes that, in the double rice-cropping area of China, families consumed up to 92% of the sweet potatoes they cultivated. Contrastingly they consumed just 66% of the grains they produced.[26] The widespread use of the sweet potato to stave off hunger in rural China is vividly illustrated in Martin Yang's 1945 ethnography of the village of Taitou in Shandong Province. Yang categorized the entire village into classes based on food consumption, and identified the very poorest as those "for whom sweet potatoes are the main item of the diet . . . at every meal every day throughout the year."[27]

As mentioned in chapter 2, another of the sweet potato's advantages is that it grows on dry land and thus does not use up paddy land. It is also extremely hardy and can grow in adverse conditions. Although it was characterized as one of the "miscellaneous foods" or provisions (*zaliang*) by ordinary people in the Meixian area, the sweet potato was also an important staple in the past, as it was particularly versatile and dependable.[28] Sweet potatoes were boiled, steamed, or roasted, and then cut up and added to congee or soup. They could be dried, or turned into starch to be made into steamed buns or used as a thickener. In the past, people were especially dependent on sweet potatoes when the autumn crop of rice had run out, and the next crop had not yet been harvested. Additionally, sweet potato leaves could be stir fried and the stems could be fed to pigs.

As they were filling and common, sweet potatoes figure prominently in recollections about food scarcity, regardless of whether the individual talking about them is remembering the old society or the collective era. For instance, in 2007, a school teacher remembered his childhood in the 1960s and compared it to that of his son. "My son doesn't even know the meaning of being hungry," he complained one night. "At that time, all we ate was sweet potato, and the starch of the cassava [shufanshu] mixed with water to make us feel full. If we even had a bit of pork, we thought it was a special treat." When I asked older people what they ate during childhood, they almost always included sweet potatoes in their memories. Many simply said to me, "All we ate was sweet potatoes!" Others also mentioned rice gruel as an accompaniment for sweet potatoes. For instance, one old woman told me that, when her son was born in 1948, all she gave him to eat after weaning was watery congee and sweet potato.

The sweet potato also figures in published accounts and memoirs of the Great Leap Forward famine, where it is often referred to as a last resort survival food. For instance, in Yang Jisheng's monumental study of the famine, he quotes a party secretary from a prefecture in Henan, who remembered how, in Sichuan, people were so hungry that they ate sweet potatoes as they pulled them from the soil.[29] And, in Moonshadow Pond, many people remember that areas, such as the Chaozhou area of Guangdong, where the food situation was not as bad during the Great Leap Forward were often ones where sweet potato was still available, even if nothing else was.

Sweet potato also had a decidedly "rural" connotation. When I traveled to Hong Kong with some dried sweet potatoes, some of my friends commented that this was the kind of thing people in the countryside ate. One of my neighbors in the village, Red Chong, told me a story about Ruolan, my Hong Kong friend, who introduced me to Moonshadow Pond. Her family roots were in Moonshadow Pond, but her family lived in India, and only returned to China after the Sino-Indian conflict of 1962, when many Indian Chinese were deported from India. Ruolan's family settled in Guangzhou after leaving India, but during the Cultural Revolution, Ruolan was required to move to a rural area. She moved to Moonshadow Pond, because of her kinship connections there, and stayed for four years before finally emigrating to Hong Kong (where her husband already resided). "When Ruolan was in the village," Red Chong told me, "her husband would send her things from Hong Kong, which she considered more nutritious. She thought that sweet potatoes were not good for you, and could not be digested well, so she would not let her son, who was about four then, eat them. He loved them, though, and would steal them when she wasn't looking!"

Like the fictional parable about the man who feeds his adopted son *kumai cai* because he thinks it is common and not special, this story indicates that the teller thinks he can appreciate something about this decidedly simple foodstuff that cannot be understood by someone from an urban background. This story affiliates the speaker positively with his rural roots through his appreciation of the sweet potato. But rural speakers also use the metaphor of a "sweet potato" to convey pejorative meanings. To call someone a "big sweet potato"[30] is to speak about him or her as being too simple, or even stupid.

Indeed, it may be precisely because of the rural connotation of the sweet potato that it figures so importantly in the memories of older village residents as a hunger killer. As Frank Dikötter tells us in his study of the Great Leap, one of the reasons that the state was not interested in procuring sweet potatoes from the rural areas at that time was because urban residents, who were not interested in eating them, regarded them as peasant food. Of course, as mentioned earlier, there was also a practical reason, since sweet potatoes spoil much more rapidly than grains.[31] For this reason, while any grains that were produced during the famine were often extracted for consumption in the cities, sweet potatoes remained for villagers to eat. Indeed, as a result of this, "Cadres responded to pressure to increase the yield by switching to the tuber, which was easy to cultivate. More often than not, farmers were left with potatoes only."[32]

During the reform period, the fate of the sweet potato in Moonshadow Pond has also changed. With the abundance of meat, fruit, and numerous varieties of vegetables, sweet potato is no longer needed to create a feeling of fullness, and it is no longer mixed with congee or made into flour. Indeed, the *Meixian Gazetteer* reports that the amount of land dedicated to growing sweet potatoes in Meixian was reduced by two-thirds between 1955 and 1987.[33] In fact, sweet potatoes are now often used as feed for pigs. They are also boiled and consumed as a between-meal snack, particularly by children. Yinzhao, whose cultivation of rice and vegetables into her late seventies was discussed in the previous chapter, summarized the drastic change in the role of the sweet potato by saying that she grew only a few sweet potatoes now, "because people only eat one or two, and then no one eats the rest."

When sweet potato is used in cooking now, it is sometimes part of expensive combinations that would not have been possible during the lean years: for instance, to make soup with sweet potato, ginger, and sugar in the event of an upset stomach. One day when my stomach was upset, Songling made some of this soup for me. She immediately noted that sweet potatoes would never have been used in this fashion in the past because the sugar would have made it too expensive. Many of Moonshadow Pond's older residents now contrast the sweet potato with new vegetables, especially greens such as spinach, cilantro, or green cabbage (*bao cai*). These items either need lots of oil to cook (like cabbage), or they don't fill the stomach (like spinach and cilantro), whereas sweet potato is filling. Interestingly, I heard some village residents speculate that sweet potato may one day go the way of other common foods of the past; as fewer farmers plant sweet potato and it becomes a less important part of the diet, its rarity will cause its prestige value to rise. They muse, therefore, that sweet potato may one day turn into a special culinary item in banquet halls, filling the role of a prized heritage food.

Congee versus Rice

Like sweet potatoes, congee (rice porridge) is associated with the past in the minds of older villagers. Congee can be served as a thick porridge, or watered down to a thin gruel with almost no nutritional value. Memories of trying to subsist on such a watery gruel are, of course, often told about the collective canteens during the Great Leap Forward. As mentioned above, congee, as opposed to dry rice, is associated with the collective era in general. I heard a number of stories about trying to subsist in the past on a diet of watered-down congee paired with sweet potatoes or dried vegetables. Congee was contrasted with rice in these stories—with dry rice seen as a luxury of the reform era.

However, unlike sweet potatoes, congee is still a daily feature of the diets of most villagers. While villagers no longer subsist on a diet of watery rice gruel, they do eat congee almost every day, usually for breakfast. With the addition of items such as pork, dried mushrooms, celery, squid, dried radish, or greens, congee can also be prepared as an extremely tasty and savory dish. In other areas of Guangdong, in fact, such rich kinds of congee are actually savored, and in the Chaoshan area it is favored so much that it is even served for banquets.[34]

Because of its elasticity and use in the current diet, congee—unlike the sweet potato—sparks different associations in peoples' minds, and does not always connote the scarcity of the past. It is sometimes seen as the food of the very old and the very young because it is easier on the digestive system than dry rice. For instance, grandparents are often left in charge of their grandchildren because the middle generation is out working. When I asked them what they fed their grandchildren, I would inevitably get a mixture of answers. Some said they saw no necessity for the relatively newer trend of giving children milk, either powdered milk or the fresh goat milk available in the village. Instead, they opted for the traditional *geng,* a porridge made from rice flour. Or they would give slightly older toddlers congee, with other items, typically greens, added gradually as the child was able to digest them. Some elders said they did prepare powdered milk for their grandchildren as a special treat, but that *geng* and congee with leafy green vegetables were the main staples for a toddler's diet. (They also commented that, because of the scandals in recent years that involved adulterated milk powder, they would buy only "foreign" milk powder if they used it, even though some of the scandals also involved foreign companies.)

Because of its continuing role in the contemporary diet, therefore, congee did not conjure up solely those circumstances—poverty and rural identity—most often connected to the sweet potato. Still, the contrast between congee versus rice is still one way to evoke the difference between past and present, poverty versus relative plenty.

Eggs

Some rather common items figure prominently in memories of the past, not because they were "hunger killers," like the sweet potato, but because they were, like meat, prized, nutritious, and relatively scarce. Two valuable sources of protein are eggs and bean curd. Although they were not as difficult to obtain as meat, they were still seen as special treats, and their current abundance is compared to their previous rareness.

Symbolically, eggs not unexpectedly stand for fertility, and they play an important role in Hakka weddings. The most critical moment in the Hakka marriage ceremony is when the bride serves the groom two hard-boiled eggs. Taking two chopsticks, she puts each egg whole into his mouth, which usually results in a great deal of hilarity among onlookers as he tries to swallow them.

Eggs feature rather prominently in people's memories of past sharing and scarcity. While for North Americans, eggs are common, they were a special treat in traditional China and during the collective era. The evidence we have from pre-Liberation China indicates that ordinary farmers usually sold most of their eggs for cash, and saved just a few to be consumed as a luxury for special celebrations.[35] During the Great Leap Forward, throughout China, most eggs were requisitioned to cities, thus depriving peasants of any access to this valuable protein source.[36] Even after the famine years, however, eggs remained a special treat. In Meixian, families were allowed to keep their own chickens after the Great Leap ended in 1961, but they were limited to three-to-five birds until the beginning of the reform era in 1978.[37]

For older people, eggs are particularly emblematic of family power dynamics in times of scarcity. For instance, one older woman, remembering the days before Liberation, said to me, "Men got more food, if there was an egg, then the household head would give it to his grandson." And Songling, describing Miaoli's sour relationship with her mother-in-law, explained that it turned sour with arguments over food during the collective era. As she recounted to me, "Miaoli's husband's brother was sickly. Very often if there was one egg, he would get the egg, and then Miaoli would resent this and start fighting."

Many villagers' stories about eggs evoked sharing within families, rather than conflict. For instance, one couple in Moonshadow Pond had seven daughters and no sons during the collective era (this was in the days before the birth-limitation policy). Describing the mother's efforts to feed her children, one villager told me, "She was so poor that she could only buy two chicken heads to serve her family. And, she would take one egg and divide it up seven ways for her children!"

Stories about giving away an egg, and offering it to a family elder, were used to illustrate generosity, or possibly smart family politics. For instance, Guizhen's mother-in-law was characterized by some villagers as difficult to please. During the collective era, however, Guizhen would respond to her mother-in-law's complaints by asking if she wanted an egg. By turning the other cheek, so to speak, and offering her mother-in-law a delicacy, she was able to smooth family relations.

Rare as eggs were, they were not as rare as meat, and sometimes acted as a substitute for meat. For instance, as mentioned in chapter 1, it is customary for a mother-in-law to make a special chicken dish for her daughter-in-law to eat daily for thirty days after she gives birth (*ji jiu,* the dish made of chicken braised in fermented rice wine and ginger). The custom of preparing this dish for new mothers is practiced now in Moonshadow Pond, but the ideal was impossible to attain in the past. Instead, I was told that new mothers during the collective years, and also during the old society, would eat the dish only a few times over the entire month, after they gave birth, and an egg would often be substituted for a chicken.

Another villager used the image of the egg's former value to compare officials' corruption in the past with that in the present. She told me about an old man now living in Moonshadow Pond, who had been a cadre in the 1960s and had used his position to try to get women to sleep with him. A village woman who had sexual relations with him just to get food, is still living in the village and viewed empathetically. However, he is looked at disdainfully and does not come out for many events, such as meetings of the local council of elders. In light of the many current scandals in China, with cadres taking advantage of their positions and squandering money on mistresses, one villager used the egg to make an interesting comparison with the corruption of the past and the present in terms of food. Cadres are just as bad now, she said, but they no longer pay their mistresses with a mere egg. Instead, they must furnish them with entire apartments!

Bean Curd

Unlike sweet potatoes, which were a foreign import in the sixteenth century, bean curd has a long history in China, and its use has been traced back over two thousand years, to the Han dynasty.[38] In Moonshadow Pond, bean curd is now so common that it is neither included in banquet menus nor served on special occasions, except for house-moving celebrations, where it is always included because of its symbolic value. This is because the word for "bean curd" (*doufu*) contains a homonym for a word that means "blessing and good fortune" (*fu*), which is considered auspicious for those about to move to a new home. However, as mentioned in the last chapter, during the collective era, bean curd served in any form was considered a special treat suitable for celebratory meals.

Bean curd also connects past to present through its strong associations with Hakka identity. The Hakka make a special dumpling in which chopped meat is pressed into bean curd instead of into a rice or wheat flour wrapper. The resulting dumpling (*niang doufu*) is then steamed or served in a braised stew. Many local theories about this dish emphasize its connection to a unique Hakka identity as "guest people," who migrated from northern China hundreds of years ago and therefore blended elements of northern and southern cultures. One theory, for instance, is that, in migrating from the north to the south, the Hakka switched from flour to rice. Rather than making dumplings from wheat flour wrappers and filling, they placed the filling into bean curd.[39] Whether this explanation is actually true is less important than the association of the dish with a specific Hakka identity and historical narrative.

A final byproduct of making bean curd is a paste called *doufu tou*, which is a leftover produced by the fermenting process that makes bean curd. The changing use of *doufu tou* illustrates that not all foods of the past are rich in evoking memories. Residents always mentioned sweet potato to me, but some of the other "poverty foods" never came up in conversation; they had just become irrelevant. *Doufu tou* was one such food. Aihua told me *doufu tou* used to be dried in the sun, then fried and consumed during feasts as a meat substitute. But now, she said, it is mostly given to pigs, ducks, and chickens as feed. Indeed, in my many visits to Moonshadow Pond, and in many years of writing down my daily and special meals, I had never consumed the bean curd paste. When I watched Liqiao produce bean curd, I finally learned about the paste and brought it home to sample. It was only then that I found out about its past role in the diet.

Nianban *versus Factory Treats*

The evoking of memory is relevant to the role of *nianban,* the New Year's treats that are prepared so laboriously (as discussed in the previous chapter). While the Hakka distinguish among several categories of buns, cakes, and sweets, the category of *ban* can be distinguished from others because it is usually made at home. Interestingly, *nianban* play a somewhat similar role among the Hakka to the role that dumplings play in northern China. Observing family reunions during the Lunar New Year in North China, Charles Stafford noted that dumplings are often made at that time by "groups of friends and relatives in a time-consuming process which repeatedly suggests 'roundness' and 'completion'— and by extension, 'reunion.'"[40] Since many *nianban* are round like dumplings, they similarly evoke the symbolism of family reunions, and like dumplings, as we have seen, they are made together by family members in Hakka villages over the Lunar New Year. While Hakka also make dumplings, doing so does not play a central role in their calendrical rituals as making the *nianban* does.

In Meixian, in addition to the *nianban,* there are *ban* made specifically for the Qingming Festival and *ban* that are suitable for any happy celebration.

For Baoli, *nianban* once symbolized a specifically Hakka way of enjoying a traditional New Year, but now, the New Year's and other celebrations also entail the exchange of factory-made cookies, referred to as *binggan,* or literally "dry cakes." *Binggan* are, in fact, distinguished from *ban* precisely in that they cannot be made at home. Their virtue lies in their being easy to carry and exchange. One can readily bring packages of biscuits along with fruits when making a formal visit. And packages of biscuits can also be handed out as small tokens of thanks to relatives and important friends who attend celebrations such as Zuofu or house moving. In the past, *binggan* were even used as thanks for local women, who helped cook at funerals or wedding banquets. If a visitor comes to the house, *binggan* may be placed on a serving tray along with *nianban,* candies, and peanuts to accompany tea. (I never saw any adults actually *eat* a factory-made cookie, only children). These cookies, along with fruit, *nianban,* the three sacrificial meats, and other more traditional items, are also perfectly appropriate as part of a table of sacrificial offerings to gods or ancestors.

Offerings to gods are often invested with meanings because of a play on words; therefore, whether the offerings are factory produced or homemade and homegrown is less important (see fig. 16). For instance, another sweet or savory item that is produced outside the home is *gaobing.* The word *gaobing* usually refers to cakes or pastries that are either factory made or made commercially, even if in a small bakery. One example are moon cakes, which consist of dough filled with a slightly sweet filling made from lotus seed or red bean paste. In addition to moon cakes, there are hundreds of other varieties of *gaobing.*

Since, the character *gao* in *gaobing* is a homonym for a different character that means "tall," *gaobing* connotes "rising high" in status and wealth. Thus, *gaobing* are particularly appropriate as offerings because of the meanings they encode. Similarly, commercially produced candies can imply sweetness in the future. Factory- or bakery-produced buns are also good offerings because of their meanings; the word for buns is *baozi,* and *bao* is the first character in the idiom *baoying bushu,* which means "to ensure victory rather than loss."

Despite the appropriateness of all these items as gifts to humans, ancestors, and gods (a topic we will look at in more depth in the next chapter on exchange), biscuits and other factory-made treats still cannot replace *nianban* in terms of their ability to embody memory. For one of the characteristics that differentiate such commercially produced items from *nianban* is the memory of the labor

FIGURE 16. Display of ancestral offerings, including fruit, biscuits, wine, tea, and the three sacrificial meats.

entailed in producing *nianban*. Labor is needed to produce the biscuits, of course, but the biscuits are commodities and therefore have been made by hidden labor—unknown people who are not obligated to the consumer. Factory-made treats are not distinctly tied to time, place, or specific individuals—that is, their production is not associated with a specific place at a special time, nor is it tied to memories of their producers. Such treats are easily transportable and useful for a variety of occasions but are also less memorable.

These considerations show us that the issue of memory is ultimately tied to labor, exchange, social relations, and moral obligations. What Baoli said to me in his complaint about contemporary youth, and their attraction to *binggan* and candy, was, "When we were growing up, we always used to look forward to the New Year and to the time when we would have *nianban*." While some authors have called this kind of recollection "gustatory nostalgia,"[41] there is no doubt that, unlike factory food, the *nianban* are memorable, not only because they are tied to a specific time in a specific place and create nostalgic longing, but also because the labor that goes into making them strengthens lasting family relationships and obligations. Such labor is, therefore, also memorable.

TABLE I Food homonyms in sacrificial offerings in Meixian

Food	Mandarin pronunciation	Homophone	Meaning of homophone	Additional comments
Biscuits	*gaobing* 糕饼	*shenggao* 升高	To rise up	—
Buns	*baozi* 包子	*baoying bushu* 包赢不输	To ensure victory and not to lose	—
Peanuts	*fandou* 番豆	*fan hui lai* 返回来	To come back	—
Fermented rice cakes	*faban* 发粄	*facai* 发财	To prosper	Red color is auspicious
Apples	*pingguo* 苹果	*pingan* 平安 *heping* 和平	Safety, peace	—
Oranges	*juzi* 桔子	*jili* 吉利	Auspicious	—
Circular food items (fish and pork balls, New Year's treats/ *nianban*)	*yuan* 圆	*tuanyuan* 团圆	Reunion, which suggests wholeness and harmony of the family	—
Sugar cane	—	—	Notches are like those of a ladder, and signify gradually rising	—

CONCLUSION

As we saw in the discussion of *nianban* versus commercially made treats, the issue of memory inevitably merges with the issue of exchange. In his book on food and memory in Greece, David Sutton asks if commodities are unmemorable. He gives the example of Easter cookies on the Greek island of Kalymnos, where he did his fieldwork, and points out that by 1993, "A number of women commented on the fact that it is rare for women to bake Easter cookies any more, that they are now available ready-made at the store. As one woman in her 30s commented, because of this, Easter will pass by this year and we won't realize it."[42]

Certainly, the stereotypical "fast food" is unattached to a particular space and has no history, while foods that are attached to particular places will be remembered and also understood as having a history. If we understand memory as "the notion of experience or meaning in reference to the past,"[43] then bitter greens, sweet potato, *nianban,* eggs, and bean curd are all remembered and historicized foods in Moonshadow Pond. Their current use is

TABLE 2 Food homonyms in festivals in Moonshadow Pond

Food	Mandarin pronunciation	Homophone	Meaning of homophone	Additional comments
LUNAR NEW YEAR 春节: FIRST 15 DAYS OF THE YEAR IN THE LUNISOLAR CALENDAR				
Kumquats	*jinju* 金桔	*jinzi* 金子	Money, fortune	The bright orange color is auspicious
Fish	*Yu* 鱼	*yu* 余 *yu* 裕	Surplus, plenty	New Year's saying: "May there be fish/surplus every year."
Candy (sweet)	*tian* 甜	*tianmi* 甜蜜	Sweet or happy	The candy plates are usually round or hexagonal; a circle (*yuan* 圆), represents reunion (*tuanyuan* 团圆).
Celery	*qincai* 芹菜	*qinlao* 勤劳	Industrious	Common foods in the dish of seven vegetables (七样菜) that the Hakka serve on the seventh day of the New Year
Garlic	*suan* 蒜	*suan* 算	Calculate, plan for future	
Scallions	*cong* 葱	*congming* 聪明	Smart	
Mustard greens	*da cai* 大菜	*da cai* 大财	Big fortune	
Bean curd	*doufu* 豆腐	*fu* 富	Wealth	
LANTERN FESTIVAL 元宵节: FIFTEENTH DAY OF THE NEW YEAR, MARKING END TO THE LUNAR NEW YEAR'S FESTIVITIES				
Glutinous rice dumplings served in soup	*tangyuan* 汤圆	*tuanyuan* 团圆	Reunion, which suggests wholeness and harmony of the family	—
QINGMING FESTIVAL 清明节 : FIFTEENTH DAY AFTER THE SPRING EQUINOX				
Steamed qingming cakes (made of wild greens boiled and mixed with glutinous rice flour)	*qing* 青	*qing* 清	To cleanup, to exorcise evil spirits and get rid of excessive heat	—

never understood solely in terms of the here and now but always with reference to historical changes and social transformations. For this reason, they are a lens through which to access historical consciousness in rural China. However, of necessity, this historical consciousness is more acute for those who lived through either the old society or, minimally, have some memories of the collective era. Young people did not, as a rule, tell me stories about sweet potatoes or *kumai cai,* as these foods did not evoke any particular memories for those born during the reform era.

Beyond historical consciousness, however, is another issue of memory—how food is linked to the memory of the labor of producing it, or to the memory of the person who gifted or provided it. The memory of labor and the ensuing obligations are ongoing. On the face of it, this kind of memory might seem to separate more "traditional" homemade foods, such as *nianban,* which are associated with the past, from factory- and ready-made foods such as *binggan.* After all, the effort of making *nianban* might seem to dwarf that of buying a package of ready-made biscuits.

We must not be too quick, however, to dismiss all commodities as unmemorable because much depends on the local meanings and uses attached to them. As we saw, for instance, even factory-made food items can be used as items of exchange in social relationships, and these ongoing relations depend on memory. To really understand how labor and food are conjoined in memory, therefore, we need a more detailed analysis of food in exchange, as well as an analysis of the role of food in moral obligation. It is to these issues that we turn in the next two chapters.

———

FOUR

Exchange

JUST AS FRIENDS AND NEIGHBORS would greet me with special food treats whenever I arrived in Moonshadow Pond, so, too, when I was preparing to depart, would they bring local food specialties and tea for me to carry home. On one such occasion, I offhandedly remarked to Songling that I now had enough tea to last several years, besides which, I would soon make a return visit to Meixian.

"Of course," she reminded me, "when you return, everyone will give you still more [to bring home with you], because this tea is for you to give your friends, your mother, and your relatives."

I wondered how I could have momentarily forgotten that, in bestowing these food gifts, villagers never understood them as going only to me. Rather I was viewed as one node in an ongoing series of exchanges. I was expected, of course, to enjoy some of the tea and food treats, but it was also understood that these items would continue to circulate beyond me, and that they would connect people in Moonshadow Pond to my own friends and relatives back home.

This chapter focuses on the exchange and circulation of food in Moonshadow Pond. Food is part of a gift economy, as illustrated in the anecdote above. It is also part of a subsistence economy (to the extent that people self-provision) and a commodified market economy. Food is additionally exchanged in a system of direct payment or barter, in which foodstuffs themselves are traded for goods, services, or property.

In gift exchange, food circulates in a wide range of venues, from informal everyday give and take among close family members, to more formal exchanges during life-cycle rituals and yearly festivals. Finally, food circulates not only among humans but is used as an offering in a cosmic exchange with gods, ghosts, and ancestors. The exchange and circulation of food, therefore, structures a myriad of social and even cosmological relations and identities. We begin by looking at food as both a commodity and a simple item of barter.

FOOD IN MARKET EXCHANGE

As mentioned in chapter 1, Moonshadow Pond residents now provision food for themselves through a combination of their own subsistence-based agriculture and purchases from the market. A number of Moonshadow Pond residents also specialize in market-based agricultural activities, such as animal husbandry, or tend fruit orchards and fishponds.

It is important to recognize that integration into the market with respect to food is not a new phonomenon in rural China. From the late nineteenth century onward, peasants in China were increasingly incorporated into a market economy.[1] John Buck's 1929–33 survey of farm families in twenty-two provinces of China found that villagers provided 75 percent of their food from their own farms, purchased most of the rest, and relied on wild plants for 1 percent of their intake.[2] Purchased foods included such things as vegetable oil and animal products.[3] Buck noted that farmers would frequently sell animal products, such as meat and eggs, which were produced on the farm, and save the money earned from these transactions for holidays, when they would purchase small amounts of the same products with the cash procured from prior sales.[4] There were also a number of crops, such as tobacco, opium, peanuts, and rape seed,[5] that were grown exclusively for cash; rice was often used as a rent payment.[6]

Peasants in early twentieth-century China also frequently borrowed money, the primary reason being to purchase food so as to subsist until the next harvest.[7] Additionally, peasants borrowed cash to pay for important life-cycle events, such as weddings and funerals.[8] Borrowing often contributed to a cycle of debt, in which peasants who were unable to repay would lose their only productive asset, their land.[9] Such stories of borrowing money and losing land were routinely told to me by Moonshadow Pond elders.

Work in rural industry or trade was also used as a means of supplementing rural income in early twentieth-century China.[10] There was certainly a craft and small-industry economy in Meixian at this time. For instance, in the years before Liberation in Moonshadow Pond, the local tannery employed as many as seventy workers.[11] Still, while peasants often needed to borrow or earn money in order to eat, they also sometimes used food itself as payment. Villagers in Moonshadow Pond recall that during the pre-Liberation era they were paid primarily in grain for their work in the village tannery, as well as for manual labor, such as transporting goods and supplies on shoulder poles.

Our neighbor Aihua often recalled her days before Liberation carrying loads of salt and tobacco from Pingyuan, a county to the northwest of Meixian. Sometimes she went as far as Jiangxi Province, a ten-day journey on foot. At other times she carried finished leather, from the village tannery to the county capital, and returned with raw hides for processing in the tannery. At the time, Aihua was only a teenager, and she remembered being paid in grain (rice), not cash.

Other older villagers recalled being paid in grain for their work in the local tannery, in the 1930s, and receiving only a small amount of cash at the end of the year. Of course, this was a period of great political and economic instability, and, because of severe inflation, food would have been worth more than cash to them. Not only were laborers paid with grain, but the cost of renting land was calculated in terms of a portion of the grain produced, rather than in cash (as Buck found was also the case for much of the rest of China in the 1920s and 1930s).

The collective era, as discussed in chapter 2, instituted a totally new way of organizing the production of food and payment for it. But one might argue that, to a large degree, grain still came to the fore during the collective era as a mode of payment, means of exchange, and measure of value. Every member of a production team was entitled to a basic grain ration. Payment beyond the basic grain ration was made in grain, and some cash. It was distributed by the brigade to team members, according to the workpoints each one earned, calculated as a proportion of the team's total productivity. Taxes were also paid in grain and were collected by the brigade and passed on to higher authorities. For this reason, grain payments, as opposed to cash payments, assumed an important role for villagers during the collective era. These flowed in both directions—up from the team, to the brigade and beyond, and back again, as payment from the brigade to individual team members.

During the most difficult years of the collective era, social relationships were often better than cash as a way to gain access to food. Indeed, during the Great Leap Forward, social relationships might have been the only hedge between starvation and survival. Yunxiang Yan reports that, in the village he studied in North China, those with *guanxi* networks (social relationships and connections) outside the village were better able to survive the Great Leap Forward famine.[12] In Moonshadow Pond, those people who had overseas connections were able to receive care packages from relatives, which helped them to survive the worst depredations of the famine.[13]

Even now, in a greatly expanded and commodified economy, food continues in some cases to function as a mode of payment in Moonshadow Pond. Thus, Miaoli now works as a day laborer for a pomelo orchard. Her wage is low (65 yuan per day in 2012), but her boss provides her with lunch. Villagers explained to me that, if you have a low-wage job in the area, then your boss is considered to be responsible for providing your meals. For instance, as mentioned in chapter 2, one of our neighbors uses her garden's bounty not only for herself and her family but also to supply her son with vegetables to cook for the workers in his shop. Contrastingly, villagers do not expect higher-wage jobs to include any compensation in the form of food.

The use of grain as a rent payment continues on a limited scale as well. For instance, Aihua's son tends a fishpond on land that constitutes the rice paddy shares of six different families. He pays some of them a small money rent for use of the land, but he pays Songling and Baoli enough of his rice crop to supply half of their yearly rice consumption. Since neither Songling and Baoli nor their son and daughter-in-law still grow their own rice, this arrangement gives them a way to continue eating rice from the village, something which they value highly.

Of course, commoditization has now spread rapidly to many corners of the economy, and with this certain trends are unavoidable. Commodities are usually noted for their ability to mask the conditions of their production (including labor and environmental conditions). However, in Moonshadow Pond, such masking does not necessarily apply to the local market for food. Indeed, the transparency of the local market is what makes it so desirable compared with the relative opaqueness of markets in the city (where customers fear food adulteration). As mentioned earlier, villagers like to purchase local food, not only because of its freshness, but precisely because they know about the conditions of its production.

Nonetheless, even such a relatively transparent local market is still a market. It does not entail the kinds of ongoing social obligations that are inherent in gift exchange. As the anthropology of gift exchange has made abundantly clear, gifts, if nothing else, are both inalienable and interdependent.[14] In receiving a gift, one becomes indebted to the donor, and, certainly in the case of food gifts, one literally absorbs something from the donor into oneself.

In the remainder of this chapter, we turn our attention to the circulation of food through gift exchange in Moonshadow Pond. This is a broad category, which, as we shall see, encompasses everything from the simplest and most informal everyday exchanges of ordinary foods, to formal gift giving and banqueting, to elaborate food offerings to gods and ancestors.

EVERYDAY RELATIONSHIPS AND THE CIRCULATION OF FOOD

In thinking of the exchange of food in everyday life in Moonshadow Pond, I was always struck by its role as the continuous grease of all social relationships. Keeping track of the flow of food among people in the conduct of ordinary life was almost dizzying.

Even the most informal of visits minimally involve an offer to drink tea. People with stores or small shops usually dedicate space in their shop for tea drinking, and they are always ready to offer a cup of tea, either to an acquaintance or, potentially, to an important customer. Sometimes an open shop may be as much a place to congregate, talk, and drink tea as it is a place of commerce. A typical example occurred on an evening in October 2012. I went on an after-dinner stroll with Songling, past the roadside restaurant that sat at the intersection of the village and the highway. Next to the restaurant was a wholesale pomelo business run by Jisheng, the restaurant owner's brother. Jisheng would sit at night in his store, where he had set up a tea table, chairs, and a television. Pomelos were piled high in corners of the large room and the adjacent storeroom. Family members and passersby would frequently stop, drink tea, talk, and then go on their ways.

On this night, Jisheng's cousin entered the store holding her brother's baby in her arms. Songling and I stopped by, and Jisheng's grandmother also strolled in. Later on, our neighbor's wife walked past on her way back from group dancing (an evening activity popular with many middle-aged women). Finally, Jisheng broke open a pomelo. We all took pieces of pomelo, and he offered tea to everyone. Conversation continued and gradually people departed as informally as they had come in.

The informal exchange of food also occurs frequently among family members who are no longer coresident. If one thinks about the family as not only the formally defined patrilineal family but also as the continuing connections among women, such as a mother and her married daughters, then the circulation of food among family members extends beyond sharing meals. As mentioned in chapter 1, such connections are solidified and reaffirmed through an almost constant flow of very ordinary foodstuffs.

Exchanging raw vegetables and sometimes uncooked meat is actually quite common in day-to-day interactions among family members who no longer live in the same household. Raw vegetables would be completely inappropriate items to bring as gifts on a formal visit or to mark life-cycle or seasonal rites of passage. But vegetables flow back and forth between married daughters and their mothers, among other close kin, and among neighbors. Whenever Songling or Baoli traveled into town to visit their daughters, they placed some fresh vegetables into their bags to take with them. Sometimes they would also bring fresh pork from the village. If their daughters visited, Songling and Baoli would give them something to carry back. For instance, on one visit, Fengying returned to the county capital from her parents' home with a huge bag of rice from the village, as well as some fresh pork and towel gourd (*sigua*) from her mother's garden.

Yinzhao, who is now a great grandmother, often spends her weekends at the family's home in Moonshadow Pond. But on weekdays, she returns to the township center and cares for her great grandchildren, as her son and his wife are still employed and cannot look after their grandchildren themselves. One Sunday afternoon I was visiting Yinzhao, when her eldest son came to give her a lift back to town. (As a well-connected township officeholder, he was one of a small but growing minority of villagers who owned a car.) For her trip back to town, Yinzhao had prepared bundles of mustard greens to bring to each of her grown children.

Another typical familial exchange, which I actually took part in, occurred when I was about to return to the village from Fengying's store in the county capital. As I was leaving, Fengying handed me a huge daikon radish to take back for her mother to cook. This simple give and take of vegetables among village women need not be limited to immediate family. Like the exchange among family members described above, such interactions are almost always informal and do not mark any particular occasion. For instance, a neighbor may simply stop by with some greens that she has harvested but cannot immediately use.

For urban residents, procuring good foods from family and relatives in one's home village also fuels a continuous informal circulation, especially as those foodstuffs are viewed as higher quality than those in the urban market. For instance, during the Mid-Autumn Festival break in 2012, I accompanied the family of Teacher Li as they traveled to visit her brother in Dabu, another Hakka county located to the west of Meixian. As we prepared for the trip, Teacher Li and her husband, Teacher Wang, poured some glutinous rice wine into bottles to bring as gifts. They emphasized that this wine had been made at home by Teacher Wang's village relatives.

Before we set out on our journey, Teacher Li's sister and brother-in-law arrived from Shenzhen, the bustling industrial and commercial center near Hong Kong. We ate a small lunch, and Teacher Wang emphasized that the chicken we ate also came from his village. Teacher Li's sister commented, "You just have to have a friend or relative in the village so that you can get these things."

These village ingredients are not only viewed as higher quality because of their taste but because they are considered healthier—the vegetables are not adulterated with chemicals, and village pigs and chickens eat natural ingredients. For instance, when I visited a colleague at the local university, he invited me to his home for lunch, where his wife emphasized that many of the ingredients she used did not have farm chemicals. She proudly pointed out that the string beans, medicinal herb soup ingredients, papaya that was stir fried with pork, and chicken we ate that day came from her parents' village.

"You just shop in the market if you have no alternative," she told me.

This everyday exchange of items, such as village-originated vegetables and meat, is an indication of the close informality of those who share these items. In his work on exchange in rural North China, Yan Yunxiang also notes that "garden products, mainly vegetables" may be shared by women with "those who are in one's social network."[15] He continues, "Since the items exchanged are neither purchased nor cooked, these activities are the most common, and therefore the least significant in relation to the expectations of a proper return."[16] It makes sense, therefore, that such very ordinary food items would be exchanged by those within one's personal circle, and shared among those who are familiar, who are intimate, and with whom generalized reciprocity prevails.

In particular, the exchange of fresh produce and meat between close family members can be understood as a way of continuing the intimacy of the family, especially with daughters who have technically married "out" of the family. This exchange may also apply to meat or produce consumed during seasonal rituals. For instance, during the Lunar New Year, Songling would braise nine ducks, some of which she raised herself and some of which she procured from others who raised them at home. After braising the ducks, Songling would keep some of them for her own family and give others to her daughters, to her daughter-in-law's family, and to the family of her sworn sister.

Just as the giving of food can convey warmth, refusing to engage in such everyday exchanges can be a cause of complaint, or can indicate a bad relationship. One villager complained to me, "My daughter really cares about her parents, and brings us all kind of nourishing things from town. My daughter-in-law, however, never brings anything back!"

Comparing a daughter-in-law unfavorably with one's own daughter is hardly uncommon in rural China, where the daughter-in-law marries into her husband's family and has to struggle to establish herself within it. Whether this quote was a fair assessment, or too harsh a dismissal of the daughter-in-law, it nonetheless indicates the importance of the continuous sharing of food items as an indicator of good family relations.

FOOD AND FORMAL GIFT EXCHANGE

The anthropologist Charles Stafford points out that food is central to a system of reciprocity, both within and outside the family, what he calls "the cycles of *yang* and *laiwang*."[17] As he explains, the word *yang* refers to raising, supporting, and providing for. And the cycle of *yang* "centres primarily on the relationship between parents and children. . . . A very involving system of mutual obligations . . . it centrally entrails the provision of money and food."[18] On the other hand, the word *laiwang* means "comings and goings," and the cycle of *laiwang* "is used to describe the movement back and forth of people who have a non-kin relationship of mutual assistance and (usually) friendship."[19] With regard to food exchange, we can see the cycle of *yang* at work in Moonshadow Pond, not only within the coresident patrilineal family, but also in the informal flow of food items between married daughters and their natal families. (I will have much more to say about this cycle of *yang* in the next chapter, as it relates especially to food and issues of moral obligation.)

The role of food in the cycle of *laiwang* is evident in gift exchanges beyond the immediate family circle. Some of this can be seen in such things as the informal exchange of vegetables among neighbors, but it is also part of a more formal kind of gift exchange. There is a large literature on gift exchange in China, and concepts of reciprocity extend from moral notions of obligation to much more instrumental notions of networking and using gifts to gain access to favors or jobs.[20] Speaking about a rural setting, the anthropologist Yunxiang Yan distinguishes between "instrumental" and "expressive" gifts[21] and between "ritualized" and "nonritualized" gifts.[22] As he states, "Ritualized gift giving on occasions of great events is characterized by the host's offering of a banquet, formal invitations to selected (important) guests, and the documentation of incoming gifts, all of which are absent in nonritualized gift giving during little events."[23] Certainly, food gifts in Moonshadow Pond fall into all these categories, ranging from banqueting and food gifts accompanying ritual occasions, such as weddings, to the gifting of food items as a common courtesy when visiting on less grand occasions, to simple acts of reestablishing a social connection.

For instance, when I took the trip to Dabu County with Teacher Li and her husband, she returned to Meixian with a large box of greens, as well as a box of pink pomelos, a particular variety for which that area is noted, that her brother had procured for her from their ancestral village. When she and her husband drove me back to Moonshadow Pond, they insisted I take some of those pomelos to give to Songling and Baoli. Through my simple act of bringing them some of her pomelos, Teacher Li reconnected with Songling and Baoli.

On only a slightly more formal level, food gifts can be used to express regret or thanks, or to simply smooth over an interaction. For instance, in 2007, I was working on a village survey. The village head's wife had promised to help me with some details. Time elapsed and I was soon to leave the village, but I had not yet heard back from her. About one week before I was supposed to leave the village, she came over to our house with a live chicken. She said that this was a way to thank me and my husband for our contributions to the village (we had helped purchase a set of basketball hoops for the play area in front of the local elementary school). However, when she came to the house, she said she felt embarrassed that she had not yet provided me with the details I requested. She promised to do so before I left the village. For her to arrive at the house merely to apologize for being late on the survey would have seemed awkward. But by coming with the gift of the chicken (which Songling cooked for us that night), she ensured that the rest of the interaction was easygoing and essentially unremarkable.

Similarly, when I arrived in the village in 2012, I decided to donate to an academic award fund that I had established in the mid-1990s. The interest from the fund was not huge, but it could be used each year to reward students from the village for notable academic achievements, such as admission to college or even to graduate school. I wanted to inform the village head of my decision to make this contribution. One evening after dinner, I went to his house with Songling to share the news. I brought a durian fruit to his house, as these were available at that time of year and are considered a special and rather expensive treat. When casual visitors bring a food gift, a host will almost certainly say that the gesture is too *jiangjiu,* which means they are too particular and too concerned with appearance. The host may also add that the guest is being too "polite" (*keqi).* These are precisely the words the village head used on this occasion as he ushered us in to share tea and snacks. Nevertheless, my arriving with the durian fruit deflected the initial moments of my visit into polite talk, and eased what might have been initial awkwardness.

When visits, such as the yearly ones that occur between families and friends during the two-week celebration of the Lunar New Year Festival, are more formal and less spontaneous, then the gifts should not be ordinary items, such as greens, that are consumed daily. Packages of tea, citrus fruit, or factory-made cookies are common and acceptable food gifts for such occasions. A visitor can also bring packaged Hakka specialties made with glutinous rice flour and combined with natural flavors such as ginger or chrysanthemum. The quantity and quality of the food gifts may depend not only on one's resources but also on the nature of the relationship between the giver and the recipient, as well as on whether the gift is more "instrumental" (such as a gift to a local official) or "expressive" (one that is appropriate when visiting the family of a longtime friend).

Sometimes a high-quality gift (such as tea) need not be accompanied even by a visit but can simply be sent as a way of saying "thank you" for a previous act. Thus, when I returned to Moonshadow Pond in 2010, I arrived a day after the tragic death from cancer of Songling's sworn sister and close friend Xuelan. I did not go to the funeral, but since Xuelan had helped me in my previous fieldwork, I called on her family, accompanied by Songling and Baoli, a few days later. For this visit, Songling and Baoli brought along a box of apples and a bag of factory-made candies to give to Xuelan's family. Songling advised me that, after sitting for a while, I should present Xuelan's husband with a red envelope containing a symbolic amount of money (200 yuan). While visiting the grieving family, we talked about Xuelan, her accomplishments, and how well regarded she was within the community. An hour passed, and before we took leave I attempted to give the red envelope to Xuelan's widowed husband. After much protestation he accepted, although he repeated many times over that this was not necessary.

A few days later, Xuelan's daughter-in-law stopped by the shop that Songling's daughter Fengying owned in the county capital. She brought a bag filled with several packages of high-quality local tea meant for me. In commenting about this, Songling said that Xuelan's family was embarrassed (*bu hao yi si*) by the red envelope I gave them. When I called Xuelan's husband to thank him for the tea, he insisted that through my visit I had demonstrated my care and concern (literally, that I had a lot of "heart/mind," or *hen you xin*). I protested that my red envelope was just a small token of my regard (*yidian xinyi*).

Nonetheless, Xuelan's husband clearly felt that it was necessary for this token to be reciprocated with a more valuable gift, in this case, good-quality tea. The fact that I am a foreigner—and thus was visiting from so far away—certainly played into his estimation that my visit had to be repaid with the tea.

This story also shows the way food and money may substitute for each other within gift giving. When money functions as a gift, as mentioned in chapter 2, it is enclosed in a red envelope (*hongbao*). In the story above, I gave Xuelan's husband a red envelope rather than food, while Songling and Baoli brought food. In this case, Songling and Baoli had already gone to the funeral services and gifted money. As I had not gone to the funeral, the money I gifted on this visit was appropriate because it substituted for the incense-rites money (*xiang yi qian*), which I would have contributed had I attended the funeral rites for Xuelan.

Other considerations, such as the nature of the visit, or the identity of the recipient, can also factor into whether a gift exchange involves money or food. For a happy occasion, or for a holiday, and if visiting an elder or a person who has no employment, money enclosed in a red envelope would be a suitable gift. If visiting someone who is younger and employed, then bringing food, especially easily transportable food, such as fruit, cakes, and biscuits, would be more appropriate. Thus, when I went to visit Teacher Li at her flat in the county capital, I brought a box of apples (these are not grown in Meixian but are a popular gift during the Mid-Autumn Festival), as well as some moon cakes (the treat traditionally associated with the Mid-Autumn Festival). However, when I went to visit Teacher Li's relatives in Dabu, I gave her father a red envelope with a token amount of cash (100 yuan).

Both food and money, therefore, can function as either gifts in reciprocal exchanges or as payment for services rendered, depending on the situation and on the identities and relationships of the givers and receivers. Of course, with the commoditization of the economy, food as a means of payment applies only to limited situations. On the other hand, as we have seen, when it comes to the gift economy, food is still a vital element of both informal and more ritualized exchanges.

Banqueting is the most formalized and elaborate example of food in the gift economy. We therefore turn next to two examples of banqueting in Moonshadow Pond—the wedding banquet and the Zuofu banquet. We examine them here from the standpoint of food exchange. In chapters 5 and 6, we will examine banquets from the standpoint of both moral discourse and emotional bonding.

THE WEDDING BANQUET

The proverb "courtesy demands reciprocity" (*li shang wanglai*) is often quoted by villagers when talking about the etiquette of banqueting and hosting. The last characters, *wanglai*, are simply an inversion of *laiwang*, and literally denote "comings and goings."[24]

Banqueting is part of a continuum in the gift exchange of food that begins with assumed daily exchanges, such as the exchange of vegetables, and culminates in the feasting and banqueting associated with calendrical celebrations and life-cycle rituals. These include events as diverse as the Lunar New Year's unity meal, lineage-branch gatherings, weddings, birthdays for elders, one-month celebrations for infants, house movings, business openings, and even funerals. As Moonshadow Pond residents have prospered, or at least as the economy has expanded, villagers are able to celebrate more ocasions with banquests, and banquets are becoming bigger.

Wedding banquets provide a good example of this process. They were once reserved for only a small elite in the village, but they are now standard practice for all families, even as wedding banquets are also differentiated from each other by size and types of food. During the "old society," many marriages were not accompanied by any formal ritual at all, certainly not extravagant banquets. Many brides were sent to live with their future husbands' families as infants, an institution known as the "adopted daughter-in-law" (*tongyangxi*). This practice minimized friction between a bride and her mother-in-law, since she would not have to be integrated into her future husband's family as an adult. Upon reaching maturity, the adopted daughter-in-law and her adoptive "brother" would simply be left to spend the night with each another, and there was no formal wedding ceremony. The expanded social networks that are created by marriage ties in rural China were unavailable to families with adopted daughters-in-law, as these women had few ties with their natal families.

Needless to say, such marriages were not marked by large wedding banquets and the display of dowries and wedding gifts. During the collective era, adopted–daughter-in-law marriages were outlawed, as were forced marriages of any type. "Major marriage," or the marriage of an adult bride and groom, became the norm. However, the older generation often arranged marriages for their children. Courtship practices changed slowly over the course of several decades, however, and by the early years of the twenty-first century, almost all young couples in Moonshadow Pond were finding their own mates. Increasingly, as young people have been leaving the village to work in urban areas, their spouses have not been from the immediate vicinity, although the majority are still Hakka.[25]

Along with these transformations in courtship have come a greater emphasis on larger and more elaborate wedding banquets. As stated above, in the old society, wedding banquets, which were the responsibility of the groom's family, were held by only the small minority of families who contracted major marriages. Then, for the first few decades of the collective era, the size of weddings was curtailed for reasons of ideology and economics. Extravagant weddings were viewed as a remnant of the old society. Abbreviated rituals, followed by small banquets, were common in the 1950s. Aihua recounted her own wedding of 1956, for which the banquet consisted of a modest four tables (square tables of eight persons each). A few years later, with the massive food shortages of the Great Leap Forward, even simple wedding banquets were impossible. By the mid-1960s, small wedding banquets of a few tables re-emerged in Moonshadow Pond.[26] The early reform period saw a slow but steady increase in the size of wedding banquets. Aihua remembered her son's marriage in 1981, which was considered quite extravagant for the time. For the banquet, Aihua's family invited enough guests for twenty-five tables, including three or four tables composed of her son's friends. (Aihua and her husband sold everything in their store to pay for the wedding.)

In the mid-1990s, I attended more "modest" banquets of seventeen tables and more elaborate ones of almost forty tables. Wedding banquet "inflation" certainly was taking place because, each time I returned to Moonshadow

Pond, I always heard of a banquet that was bigger and more elaborate than any that had taken place the last time I had visited. For instance, a fifty-five–table wedding banquet was held for one villager's daughter in 2007. It was held not in the village but at one of the fanciest hotels in the county capital. In this particular case, the young woman married someone who was quite wealthy—a "big manager" (*da laoban*), as villagers usually refer to such people—and he actually invited his entire village to the banquet!

In addition to the number of tables at a banquet, the inclusion of more dishes and rare or more expensive items can differentiate banquets.[27] Villagers often told me that an elaborate wedding banquet is needed for *mianzi*; a word commonly translated as "face," *Mianzi* connotes status, and to have a big *mianzi* both indicates and creates ever-wider networks of social connections. Thus, a wedding banquet does more than display one's *mianzi,* it also improves and builds on it. While one can legally marry without a wedding banquet, villagers insisted that this was not sufficient from the standpoint of *mianzi*. In fact, I attended one banquet in Moonshadow Pond, for which the couple had registered their marriage a year earlier but had waited to host the banquet until they could get together enough money—a late banquet being preferable to none at all. And while a banquet is certainly a huge expense, costs are at least partially defrayed by the guests, who must bring a red envelope with cash to the banquet. Furthermore, the wedding banquet is a sufficient return in itself. The host need not send guests away with other gifts (as happened with the Zuofu banquet that we examine below).

Interestingly, aside from its role in banqueting itself, the role of food within marriage exchanges in Moonshadow Pond is less important than in the past. For instance, formerly, once the wedding date had been finalized, relationships between the bride's and groom's families were inititated through a number of exchanges that included both food and money. The groom's family delivered food items and the three sacrifical meats (chicken, pork, and fish) to the bride's family. They also sent money to the bride's side—expressed as a "thank you" for raising her. In reality, this payment was a way to partially defray the cost of a banquet hosted by the bride's family on the day before the wedding.

At present, aside from the banquet itself, the use of food in prenuptial exchanges is dwarfed by cash as gift. However, it is also important to point out that cash is key to this exchange precisely because the bride's family needs it to host a prenuptial banquet. And these banquets, like wedding banquets, are expanding in size and scale.[28]

FOOD, MONEY, AND GIFT EXCHANGE
IN THE ZUOFU BANQUET

The Zuofu holiday that we considered in chapter 2 from the standpoint of the labor of cooking is also an excellent lens through which to analyze the circulation of food and money in Moonshadow Pond. Unlike a wedding, which establishes a set of new relationships and integrates a new family member into the groom's family, the Zuofu holiday does not create a new set of relationships. It also does not entail the important transfers of money and property that occur in the dowry and bride price of marriage. Here food alone is central in *laiwang,* or ongoing relationships.

Zuofu emphasizes relationships and connections outside the core patrilineal family—such as matrilateral ties, affinal connections, and friendship. For instance, for Songling and Baoli's celebration, the guests included relations through Baoli's father's sister, his father's brother's daughters, Baoli's own daughter Fengying and her family, his daughter-in-law's aunt, and friends of his son. Similarly, in Wenping's Zuofu celebration, described in chapter 2, the guests included the parents of both his daughters-in-law, his wife's family, his mother's sister (Songling), as well as parents of his dry son[29] and one of his wife's cousins.

Indeed, the very fact that the Zuofu banquet is held in each of the township's villages on a different day over a two-week period is itself a testimony to the importance of social exchange for this holiday. The festivities are organized so that one is a host on one day and a guest on several other days. The arrival of guests for the event is a colorful and happy spectacle. Guests bring a variety of food gifts, including biscuits, specialty items such as moon cakes, and sometimes liquor. People may also bring red envelopes with money.

A number of considerations can affect what gifts the guests bring, and whether they bring food or money. If one is going to the home of very close relations or friends, then food is an appropriate gift. For instance, at Songling and Baoli's Zuofu event, their son's best friend came with two jars of expensive honey. As this is highly prized, it would be considered a more-than-sufficient gift. Another guest at the same banquet brought a live chicken. As Zuofu is held around the same time as the Mid-Autumn Festival, showing up with an expensive box of moon cakes would also be considered a more than adequate gift.

However, one villager pointed out to me that, if someone is invited to the home of a big manager or boss, who is not also a close relation, then food and money together are a more fitting gift. In either event, incoming gifts are often matched by parting gifts. High-quality gifts mean that the guest may also be sent away with something of high quality, such as expensive liquor. Certainly, both host and guest can exercise some discretion in the flow of food and money in these gifts. But no matter what, the guests at a Zuofu banquet are not supposed to leave empty handed. Most commonly, hosts send their guests away with items such as glutinous rice cakes, biscuits, and fruits.

On the day of Songling and Baoli's Zuofu banquet, the guests were ushered into the living room at the front of the house. Songling and Baoli poured endless cups of tea for them until it was time to eat. After the banquet, and more tea and talk, the guests began to take their leaves, and each guest departed with a bag of gifts. The contents of the departure gifts were similar to the items that the guests had brought, but some traditional Hakka-fermented rice flour buns were added to the mix. These treats are considered particularly apt for any happy occasion, since they are dyed the auspicious color red. Further, while the name *fajiao ban* literally means "fermented rice cake," the character *fa* in this name is also used in the words that mean "to prosper" (*fa cai*).

The custom of seeing guests off with a bag of treats is practiced at some other moderately sized banquets in Moonshadow Pond (but not at wedding banquets). For instance, in 2007, when Songling's daughter Fengying moved into her new flat in the county capital, she invited eight tables of guests to celebrate at a banquet hall. Songling readied herself for the event by ordering 170 fermented rice cakes prepared by a local woman. After the banquet was over, each guest went home with a bag of these cakes plus a package of factory-made biscuits.

The exchange in the Zuofu banquet, however, also has one more surprising element. In addition to its being a venue for the flow of food and money between hosts and guests, the banquet is marked by the arrival of beggars at the host's door (see fig. 17). I was shocked to see this because in Moonshadow Pond beggars were certainly not a part of the everyday landscape. I learned that, because each village held their Zuofu banquet on a different day, the beggars rotate from one village to another. As we sat down to eat at Songling and Baoli's banquet, beggars traveling in pairs, came to the doorstep, and then proceeded to the next house. I was told that, while hosts had put rice into each beggar's bowl in the past, they now put money into every bowl. Villagers assured me that this was because the conditions (*tiaojian*) of life had improved, and rice would no longer be acceptable to the beggars. Furthermore,

FIGURE 17. Beggars come to door during Zuofu banquet.

after each donation, the beggars say "good words" (*hao hua*) to the host. These words are also part of the exchange—money for good words—as "bad words" are considered extremely inauspicious.

And so, the gift of money now substitutes for the gift of food for the beggars. However, I remained confused about the role of the beggars. People said it had always been this way in Moonshadow Pond and in the surrounding township. Only when I put the local Zuofu banquet into a larger context, and considered the role of food exchanges within the cosmic world, was I able to understand this aspect of the event. We therefore turn next to the issue of the exchange of food and money with gods, ghosts, and ancestors. After this, we will come back to the Zuofu banquet and try to understand why beggars are incorporated only into this particular celebration.

FEEDING THE SPIRIT WORLD

Throughout China's long history, the exchange of food has structured not only relationships among humans but also between humans and the cosmic world. Studies of popular religion in rural China point to a tripartite division of the cosmological world into ancestors, gods, and ghosts. Ancestral spirits are those of the patriline, while the category of gods includes a large number of spirits selected on the basis of location. These spirits of the locality and community range from low-level gods, such as the Stove God, who tends to the business of one's immediate family; to space-placed gods, such as a god of a particular bridge or village; to higher level gods, who oversee larger domains like counties and entire cities.[30] Additionally, there are Buddhist and Taoist deities, who are popular across large regions, like the Buddhist Goddess of Mercy, Guanyin,[31] who is ubiquitous in southeastern China. Finally, there are the ghosts, who, unlike ancestors, are not cared for and "fed" by descendants. For this reason, ghosts are "hungry," and can disturb the living if not occasionally placated by offerings.

The offering of food, in this case in the form of sacrifice, is critical for humans' relationships to this world of spirits. Indeed, the nature of the food exchange goes a long way in defining a spirit's identity. Michael Puett has explained that ghosts, gods, and ancestors in ancient China were delineated according to who fed them, and what each was fed. His insight also pertains to Moonshadow Pond today. As Puett states,

> Ghosts are dead humans who are not fed by living descendants (and thus become hungry and highly dangerous. . . .); ancestors are fed by their living descendants (and thus are not dangerous and may even be helpful to the descendants); and spirits are fed by larger numbers of people than just simply their descendants (and thus become far more powerful than ghosts or ancestors). Moreover, each of these can become any of the others if the food offerings are changed. . . . It is living humans, through the act of feeding, who define the differences between spirits, ghosts and ancestors.[32]

In regard to feeding ancestors, Charles Stafford, as noted previously, has framed this as part of the "cycle of yang" or mutual nourishment; parents care for and feed children, who will in return care for and feed their parents when they are old. This obligation continues after death, with the worship and feeding of both immediate and distant ancestors.[33] Indeed, Stuart Thompson has pointed out that it is precisely the act of feeding that turns a mere corpse into an ancestor.[34]

In addition to demarcating the difference between ancestors and ghosts, food can also differentiate gods from one another. Certain gods accept only vegetarian offerings, while others will accept meat. As we shall see, the timing of a particular sacrifice—its order within a cycle of worship that occurs over the course of a year—may also be demarcated by the foods offered.[35]

Ancestors, deities, and ghosts are all etched into the landscape of Moonshadow Pond in a number of ways. First, the boundaries of the original settlement area of Moonshadow Pond (before the new house construction of the reform area) are marked by bridges over the river that flows through the village. These bridges, at the northern and southern ends of the village, are guarded by a number of locality gods, including the God of the Bridge, Earl of the Bridge (*Qiao Baigong*); the Duke King (*Gong Wang*), a village guardian god who can ease communication between the underworld of ghosts and the human world and is also a god of wealth;[36] and a community god (*Sheguan Laoye*), who is also a god of earth and grain.[37]

At the center of the village is the ancestral temple, dedicated to the village founder and his descendants in the patrilineage. This founding ancestor is said to have come to Moonshadow Pond at the end of the sixteenth century. There is also a second ancestral temple, dedicated to the founder of the largest lineage branch in the village and his descendants. Such an arrangement, with various locality or community gods at the periphery, to protect the village, and ancestors at the center, is found in many Hakka villages.[38]

In Moonshadow Pond's lineage-branch temple, there are also an image of *Guanyin*, the Buddhist Goddess of Mercy, who is very popular in southeastern China; markers for the God of Wealth (*Caishen*); and markers for two locality gods, the Dragon God (*Longshen*) and the God of the Earth, or Earl of the Earth (*Tudi Baigong*).[39] The open space or courtyard in each of the ancestral temples is also a place where sacrifices can be made to heaven (*tian*). At home, heaven can also be worshipped by placing offerings in a courtyard, or on a porch. In addition to locality gods at the village boundaries, and in the ancestral temples, a number of locality gods are on top of the hills that surround the village.[40] Markers for these spirits are placed near the graves, of distant as well as more immediate ancestors, which are located in these hills. Finally, there is also a local temple, with a number of popular Buddhist and non-Buddhist deities.[41]

The village, therefore, is a site that is rich in gods and ancestors, all of which must be fed. Remembering the scarcity of meat in the past, Big Gao, who had once served as village head, told me that the times one ate meat were easy to remember because they were tied to important days of sacrificial offering; these were the few times each year when the *san sheng* (or three sacrificial meats) were offered to ancestors or spirits. It makes sense that in a world where consumption of meat was extremely rare, and regarded as a special treat, it was connected to the times when offerings of meat were required. As Charles

Stafford has pointed out, "For the duration of their residence in any community, spirits can expect to be given periodic, and sometimes very elaborate, offerings of food. Such offerings are typically redistributed and 'consumed' in some form by the communities which provided them in the first place."[42]

Meat consumption in Moonshadow Pond, of course, is no longer solely reserved for key days of sacrificial offering. Nor does everyone presently residing in the village necessarily believe in a spirit world. In fact, some villagers told me they did not believe in gods or ghosts, or an ancestral life after death. There is no unitary set of beliefs in Moonshadow Pond. Many of my informants, particularly men, raised doubts about the existence of an afterlife. And while most villagers went through the formalities of a traditional funeral for family members, to minimally demonstrate that they were filial, they did not all necessarily think they were actually "feeding" the soul of the deceased. For instance, Red Chong, who had been a loyal Communist Party member during the collective era, told me that on death, he thought people just became a "pile of flesh and bones."

Still, the symbolism of feeding ancestors and gods is important. Some people still understand it as efficacious (often it was women who articulated belief in the reality of gods, ghosts, and ancestors). Other villagers often said that certain rites, such as giving sacrifices to one's ancestors during the Lunar New Year, are as much about commemoration as belief. Nonetheless, food figures critically in exchanges with the spirit world, whether they are understood as sacrifice and reciprocity, or as remembrance. Indeed, while food's role in exchanges with the spirit world is an old one in Chinese culture, it has been greatly elaborated during the reform era. (In this respect, it has followed a trajectory similar to that of banqueting, for which greater affluence enables more resources to be poured into ritual exchange.)

Below we examine the exchange of food between humans and the spirit world in Moonshadow Pond in more detail.

THE YEARLY CYCLE OF OFFERINGS

The Lunar New Year is not only a time of intensified food consumption within families and intensified food exchange among families, it is also the most important period of sacrifice to ancestors and local gods—in other words, it is a time of exchange between humans and the spirit world.

I participated in Lunar New Year's celebrations in 1996 and 2007. In 2007, we began New Year's Eve morning at Songling and Baoli's household by laying out offerings at home to *tian* (heaven). Once the food was spread out on a table, we lit incense sticks, recited our wishes for an auspicious future, and bowed three times. Offerings to *tian* included the three sacrificial meats, tea, wine, fruits, and *nianban* (more about this below). After worshipping *tian,* we packed up all the food items. Songling and Baoli's daughter-in-law Lianfeng carried them by shoulder pole to the village entrance. The area was already packed with other villagers, all of whom were also arranging their offerings on the ground in front of shrines to the village guardian gods. When we had finished displaying our offerings, we packed up again and brought them first to the main lineage temple and then to the temple for the second lineage branch, the largest one in the village. Finally, we made one more round and presented our offerings at a recently restored branch temple for the ancestors of a sub-branch of lineage branch 2.

At each stop, we spread out the food items as offerings. We then poured wine and tea into small tea cups, lighted incense, and bowed three times; burned spirit money and other paper offerings; and set off fireworks (this last step is to scare away the unruly hungry spirits and ghosts). On returning home, Songling and Yanhong laid out their offerings once again, this time in the kitchen for the Stove God. In this case, because the Stove God is a lower-order god (essentially just the guardian of a particular family), the food offerings were saved for later in the day; heaven, locality gods, and ancestors were fed first.[43] Nonetheless, the Stove God cannot be forgotten. The tradition of propitiating the Stove God during the Lunar New Year is an old one in China, with written descriptions of practices similar to current ones going back as far as the Sung dynasty (tenth through thirteenth centuries). Traditionally it was thought that the Stove God reported back to heaven on the behavior of the family, so it was necessary to feed him (bribe him) at least once a year.[44]

That evening, on New Year's Eve, we ate our reunion dinner (see chapter 3) and waited for midnight to welcome one more important god, the God of Wealth. Songling arranged her offerings for the God of Wealth on a table set out on the second-floor porch. She explained that, because the God of Wealth was only being asked in for tea, and not a meal, there was no need to offer him the three sacrificial meats. And indeed, the God of Wealth is never offered meat.

In addition to the food offerings they present on the eve of the Lunar New Year, many families and lineage branches try to visit ancestral graves, clean them, and provide offerings as soon as possible after the New Year's period.[45] This activity is called *guazhi,* which literally means "hang paper." It refers to the paper "spirit money" that is hung on the graves when the offerings are laid out. When members of a particular lineage branch or sub-branch visit the grave of their founder, they usually first sweep the area around it then place their offerings at the gravesite and worship, and finally gather together for a banquet.

In the old society, these feasts were supported by lineage land, or "ritual fields,"[46] and they accounted for as much as a third of all land in Guangdong before 1935.[47]

In many other areas of China, "tomb sweeping," or cleaning the ancestral graves, is performed later in the year during the Qingming Festival (in the third lunar month). In Meixian, people again visit their immediate ancestors' graves and make offerings during Qingming. But unlike their visits during the New Year's period, this worship is more individualized, and does not involve bringing together many members of the extended family. Also, Qingming is not celebrated with a feast in Meixian, as *guazhi* is.

In addition to the New Year's period, when village guardian and locality gods, as well as ancestors, figure prominently as recipients of food, there are many other calendrical rituals and life-cycle events, when food offerings to gods and ancestors are required. For instance, an individual can "contract" with a god for good fortune. Such a contract can be undertaken with Sheguan, the local guardian, or with a Buddhist deity.[48] In either case, the individual begins the cycle by praying to a god for good fortune (*qi fu*), followed by making a promise to the god (*xuyuan*), then by warming things up (*nuanfu*), and finally by redeeming his or her vow to the god (*wan fu*), which completes the cycle. For each phase of the cycle, different food offerings are indicated. To begin the cycle, and warm up the cycle, one offers only vegetarian items, such as buns, biscuits, candies, peanuts, and fruits. Burning spirit money and other paper representations of objects is also called for at all stages of the cycle. However, regardless of whether one contracts with a local guardian god, or a Buddhist deity, such as Guanyin, one must ultimately redeem one's vow with the three sacrificial meats. Part of the rationale behind this order of food offerings is that to complete the cycle one must give not only more, but something better, than what one started with. Meat has traditionally been regarded as "more," and thus is a necessity if one wants to fulfill one's contract with a god in the cycle. (For more details on the reasons for the high value of meat, see chapter 5.)

Such contractual offerings with gods are of less concern to men, who are more interested in rites focused on patrilineal ancestors. Contrastingly, middle-aged and older women, who are not part of their husbands' lineages, are more likely to take part in contracts with gods. Their motivation is to ask for good fortune for their immediate family members rather than to commemorate distant and unrelated ancestors. (This particular cycle of creating blessings springs from popular religious practice, and is a syncretic mix of many elements, Buddhist, Taoist, and the worship of placed based deities.)

A number of other considerations frame the choice of food items in exchanges with ancestors and gods. For instance, the rank of a god influences the food that is presented. When offered to one's own immediate ancestors, or to lineage ancestors, the three sacrificial meats typically consist of a cooked piece of pork, fish, and a whole cooked chicken. However, when making prestations to more remote ancestors, the group that gathers together is inevitably larger, since a wider circle of descendants is included. Thus, the event and the prestations are usually more elaborate. At one event I attended in 2012, the father of a distant lineage ancestor of Moonshadow Pond's own founder was honored at his grave. The celebration brought together lineage relatives who came from far and wide, as far away as Singapore. Naturally, for this celebration, it would not have been suitable to set out simple offerings. Hundreds of us met at the bottom of a hill, which we climbed until we reached the gravesite. Elaborate offerings had been prepared, including a whole goat, a live fish, a whole pig, and a rooster. (These offerings are more accurately deemed "sacrifices" because of their size.) The communal worship was followed by a large banquet at an associated lineage hall in the county capital.

On the other side of the equation of elaborateness, relatively minor gods can be satisifed with simpler offerings. For instance, for some gods, a whole chicken is unnecessary, and two hardboiled eggs will suffice.[49]

GHOSTS, BEGGARS, AND ZUOFU

So far we have spoken about feeding ancestors and gods, but what about ghosts? As ghosts are the uncared for and the unfed, they can make trouble for humans. Therefore, their hunger must also be periodically satiated. Traditionally, in Meixian and other parts of China, the fifteenth day of the seventh lunar month was known as the Ghost Festival.[50]

This festival is connected to the popular legend of Mulian. Mulian was a disciple of Buddha. According to the story, he traveled to the underworld in order to look into the fate of his deceased mother, who was condemned because of her bad deeds. When he found her, she was starving. As a filial son, who would do anything to help his mother, Mulian sought guidance from Buddha about how to help. He was advised to leave offerings to all the wandering ghosts and spirits every year on the fifteenth day of the seventh month (in the Lunar Calendar). In this way, his mother would be cared for. Hence, the Ghost Festival is a century's old tradition in China. In pre-Liberation Meixian, during the Ghost Festival, both Buddhist and Taoist monks would take part in rituals that focused on feeding lost souls, so as to keep them at bay.[51]

The needs of orphan souls (*dugu*) were tended to in other festivals besides the Ghost Festival in pre-Liberation Meixian. For instance, in a compilation on village religion in rural Hakka areas of northeastern Guangdong Province, one contributor reports on a religious festival that was held only once every five or ten years, over the course of several days. This was also called Zuofu (creating blessings) like the aforementioned banquet day in Moonshadow. For this particular Zuofu, monks carried out observances; late at night, on the last day, villagers ignited a large bonfire in which paper offerings were burned for lost souls.[52]

In a description of yet another pre-Liberation festival held in the same area, the observer recounts a ritual carried out by monks from the period after the end of New Year to Qingming; For this, a large altar to the Buddhist deity Guanyin was built. The religious festival concluded with a three-night ritual for saving orphan souls: "Rice and vegetables were offered and scriptures recited at the *dugu* altar, with food given to beggars as well."[53] This was a means of "summoning blessing and driving away harm" by taking care of previously uncared for souls, thereby preventing them from coming back to bother the living.[54]

Of significance, and certainly related to some of the parallel elements of the contemporary Zuofu Festival in Moonshadow Pond, villagers not only fed orphan souls but beggars as well. In addition, the festival ended with a large feast on the fourth day, on which people were again allowed to eat meat and fish. Everyone was invited to this feast, without regard to their status, and people talked about how to work together to do something that would benefit the village.[55]

In Moonshadow Pond, a number of customary practices still aim to keep ghosts and wandering souls at bay. For instance, during the *guazhi* ritual, spirit money stained with chicken blood is placed around the ancestral grave to scare away the unruly spirits.[56] Additionally, during the traditional Hakka funeral, still practiced in rural areas such as Moonshadow Pond, monks call back the soul of the deceased at several stages of the ritual. They then symbolically bathe and offer wine and food to the soul. Similarly, the monks call back different Buddhist deities and offer them food, tea, and wine. However, the ghosts are not fed but dispatched.

In all these cases, it is the ghosts' hunger that is threatening. But this is dealt with sometimes by feeding them and other times by dispatching them and scaring them away.[57] In contemporary Moonshadow Pond, the Ghost Festival itself is no longer an important ritual, in part, perhaps, because the general attack on "superstition" that occurred during the collective era led to the disappearance of a festival focused on feeding hungry ghosts and wandering spirits. Because the county gazetteer is an official publication, it attributes the lack of fanfare around the Ghost Festival to the fact that superstitious activities came to an end after Liberation. The gazetteer reports that, until Liberation, each town conducted a ceremony that was led by Buddhist monks and nuns, who erected an altar and held a memorial rite for the homeless souls and hungry ghosts.[58] I found similar articles in the local press explaining that, although many traditional rituals have reappeared in the reform era, the connotations of a festival devoted to ghosts and wandering souls are such that people do not dare to bring it back.[59]

That said, while there are no communal celebrations in Moonshadow Pond for the Ghost Festival, a few elderly people still leave individual offerings for wandering spirits on the fifteenth day of the seventh lunar month. Some villagers addressed the issue of the insignificance of the Ghost Festival in another way. They asserted to me that the ghosts had pretty much "disappeared" after Liberation, and were just not around as much as they had been in the old society!

However, the reason for the minimal importance of the Ghost Festival in Moonshadow Pond may have less to do with a decline in its importance after Liberation and more to do with the fact that many villages in Meixian have a long-established custom of postponing the Ghost Festival to a later date— the eighth month—when the harvest is complete. In a similar vein, Zuofu in Moonshadow Pond might also be viewed as a postponed, and currently less cosmically oriented, alternative to the Ghost Festival.

Fang Xuejia, a local scholar and specialist in Hakka history, has provided exactly this explanation for his home district of Bingcun, also in Meixian. According to Fang, Zuofu was synonymous with the Ghost Festival in traditional Meixian, but it was not always held on the seventh month, and could be as late as the ninth month. This was related not only to the fact that the seventh month was the most "intense period of agricultural work" but also to the fact that, by staggering the date of the festival for each village, the locality god of that area (Gongwang) could be brought to each village under his purview at the time of their celebration. In this way, Fang argues, "The people straightforwardly staggered the festival dates. This is how in the Hakka area, the Yulanpen Festival evolved into the Zuofu Festival, and this is why the Zuofu dates are not the same in each place." And, Fang adds, "Looked at in another way, this shows the Hakka people dare to put into practice a bold practical reformist spirit toward traditional holidays."[60]

BACK TO THE BEGGARS AT THE ZUOFU BANQUET

These considerations bring us back to elements of exchange during the Zuofu banquet in Moonshadow Pond, and can hopefully help us to understand what was previously unclear, the appearance of the beggars. As we pointed out, on the one hand, the banquet is a way for the host to bring together friends, affines (relatives by marriage), and matrilateral relatives (those related through the mother's side). Perhaps the most unique aspect of the Zuofu Festival is the emphasis on the circulating banquets that are held in a different village within the township each day, enabling everyone to be a host and a guest during the festival period. The celebrations also include gift exchange beyond the banquet itself, as the guests bring gifts when they arrive and receive gifts when they depart. Echoing my own informants from Moonshadow Pond, who spoke about Zuofu as an even bigger event than the Lunar New Year, Fang states,

> But there is one custom that has never been changed, but instead it is becoming increasingly more elaborate and intense, that is, on the date of the Zuofu, every family that is participating in the Zuofu inevitably pours out everything they have. . . . The guests are many, and the banquet is elaborate. Often it surpasses the spring festival. Putting this ever more elaborate trend to one side, you can also see the Hakka people's economy gradually expanding. . . . The Zuofu Festival in every Hakka area is the year's most intense day of social

activity. Because of this, if on this day the relatives and friends who come are not many, then it can be seen not as Zuofu but as "*bofu*." [the character *bo* means thin and meager].[61]

How does all this help us to understand the role of the beggars, who show up at the contemporary Zuofu banquets and are given cash, a substitute for the food that was placed in their bowls in earlier years?

First, we have learned that, in some parts of rural Meixian, the Zuofu festival of the midautumn period substituted for the traditional day to feed ghosts, the Ghost Festival on the fifteenth day of the seventh month. In other places, such as Moonshadow Pond, even though a few elderly individuals make offerings to wandering spirits during the traditional Ghost Festival, the holiday itself now passes unmarked as a communal time of worship.

Second, we should remember that in ethnographic descriptions of different Zuofu celebrations in earlier times and places, the feeding of ghosts often took place in tandem with the feeding of beggars. Indeed, Arthur Wolf, in his famous treatment of Chinese popular religion, makes similar connections between how beggars and uncared for unfed spirits are perceived. Speaking about his fieldwork in 1960s Taiwan, he stated, "When pressed to explain their conception of ghosts, most of my informants compared them to bullies or beggars. Why do you have to make offerings to ghosts? 'So that they will go away and leave you alone. They are like beggars and won't leave you alone if you don't give them something.'"[62]

Wolf continues as follows:

In the Chinese view a beggar's request for alms is not really begging. It is a threat. Beggars are believed capable of laying terrible curses on anyone who ignores their entreaties. The man who sends a beggar away empty-handed risks the possibility of illness or damage to property. Beggars are like bandits and ghosts in that they are feared, and bandits and ghosts are like beggars in that they are socially despised. The social identities of the three are so similar that bandits and beggars are sometimes treated like ghosts.[63]

Wolf also describes a Ghost Festival ritual in northern Taiwan, recorded in the late nineteenth century, in which food of every kind was hung from a large bamboo structure. The food included "chickens and ducks, both dead and alive, slices of pork and pigs' heads, fish of every kind, rice cakes, bananas, pineapples, melons, etc. This great feast was first offered up to all the wandering spirits who had answered the summons of the gongs, and then after the ghosts had had time to satisfy themselves, the entire collection was turned over to the destitute humans who had gathered for the occasion."[64]

Of course, the contemporary political, economic, and social contexts of Moonshadow Pond are not comparable to either late nineteenth-century Taiwan or pre-Liberation Meixian. But considering all of these past practices does help us to understand how certain themes have reappeared in an altered context. While people in Moonshadow Pond do not talk about ghosts and unruly spirits much, they do make some gestures to the idea of keeping ghosts at bay in funeral and graveside rituals. Further, there is certainly disagreement among Moonshadow Pond residents about whether spirits and ghosts exist at all. For instance, Songling criticized Miaoli for not being *xiuxin*—a word that can be translated as having a "cultivated heart," but actually conveys the quality of remembering one's ancestors properly. And Songling thought that some of Miaoli's bad luck was a result of this lack of filiality. However, Miaoli did not share this view and told me, "In old Mao's time, we tore these all down [referring to ancestral temples and tablets], and said these were feudal. Now we are [again] doing all these things [referring to offerings for ancestors], but I don't really believe that these are ghosts [*gui]* or spirits [*shen*]."

Still, the Zuofu banquet incorporates the giving of food (and now money) to beggars. They travel from village to village, as each village in a given township holds its banquet on a different day within a two-week period. Like ghosts and beggars in the traditional rural context, beggars must be served because of the potential for powerful inauspicious words or curses. The nature of their appearance at this event is also ritualized. There is no other banqueting activity in Moonshadow Pond where beggars appear. None of my informants specifically equated the Ghost Festival with Zuofu, and certainly no supplication of "ghosts" occurs during Zuofu. Even so, the role of beggars at the Zuofu banquet clearly parallels that of ghosts and beggars in the Ghost Festival and other traditional popular religious contexts.

THE NATURE OF THE SUBSTANCE AND THE NATURE OF THE EXCHANGE

As we have seen, food circulates in Moonshadow Pond as part of the commodity economy, as payment in kind, as small gifts that accompany the "comings and goings" from one place to another, and as ritualized gift exchange among people and between people and the spirit world.

Sometimes the nature of the food item itself is the most important factor in considering how it is exchanged. For instance, we have seen that commonly eaten everyday raw vegetables are exchanged among neighbors, or between mothers and married daughters. Such items would be inappropriate as either prestations for ancestors, or as gifts to bring on formal occasions, such as Lunar New Year's visiting. Similarly, grains (in this case rice) would never be gifted under any circumstance. As noted previously, cooked rice defines a domestic group. Uncooked rice, therefore, is not an item that would be gifted between families; indeed, its provisioning defines them. Rice may be self-provisioned, used as a rent payment, or bought in the market, but in any case it is never appropriate for gifting.

The line between accessing food as a commodity versus accessing food as part of gift exchange, gardening, or gathering, however, is not always clear and can change over time. For instance, some food items that were traditionally gathered have now become high-priced commodities. One example is swamp eels (*huangshan*). As mentioned in the last chapter, they were once abundant in the rice paddies, gathered and eaten as a free source of protein. Now with the greater use of nitrates as fertilizer, the eels are much less common and have become expensive items in the market. They can be found as an ingredient in special dishes at restaurants (stir fried with either *kumai cai* or bean curd).

A number of *yaocai* (medicinal grasses) have gone through a similar transformation from foraged to gourmet foods. For instance, an expensive combination of medicine grasses used to make soup is now a combination of the root of Chinese foxglove (*shengdi*) and a root called *tufuling* (Chinaroot greenbier rhizome, also called *yingfantou*). In the past, the foxglove root was ground up, mixed with water, and steamed to make buns during periods of food dearth and to give oneself a feeling of fullness. Similarly, the *tufuling* root was also made into a powder. It was mixed with boiling water and also used to give one a feeling of fullness. So here we have the curious transformation of foodstuffs from hunger foods to high-value commodities.[65] In the county capital, in fact, herbal medicine soups are marketed and packaged, so that overseas Chinese visiting their relatives in Meixian can bring the ingredients home.[66]

Such items are marketed with the traditional Hakka expression, "Rely on the mountains, eat the mountain's produce" (*kaoshan chishan*). But this phrase now has different implications. It once referred to the practice of gleaning as much as possible by foraging. Now it is used as a marketing phrase

FIGURE 18. Medicine grass soup ingredients for sale in county capital.

for products like the medicine grasses. Because it is a traditional Hakka adage, the phrase links these mountain products to Hakka identity. The essence of "the mountain" is now a commodity that can be purchased, and consuming medicine grasses becomes a way of reaffirming one's Hakka identity.

These *yaocai* are, furthermore, no longer used simply as medical treatments for specific ailments, though each one has specific medical properties, but are also sometimes consumed to buttress health in general. At the same time, as mentioned earlier, the high-value medicine grass market has not meant the end of older practices of gathering grasses for one's own medicinal use (see. fig. 18). I still saw villagers, particularly older women, gathering grasses for use at home.[67]

With the growth of restaurants and banquet halls, the illegal trade in protected animals, which should not be hunted at all, has also grown throughout Meixian. As one villager said to me, "The richer you are, the more natural you want your items, and this means people will also want things from the moutain tops." Animals, such as wild boar, wild rabbit, pigeons, doves, and even foxes, rare deer, and hawks may be captured and sold to restaurants for customers willing to pay a high price for them. The rarer the animal, the higher the price, and even its illegality can increase the prestige of the item. (As we shall see in the next chapter, however, this consumption of expensive, rare, and even illegal items does not go on without moral critique.)

As food moves and circulates throughout the village, therefore, any given food item may be at once, or a different times, an item gathered from the surrounding environment, a food cultivated for subsistence purposes, an everyday foodstuff exchanged with family, a ritualized gift, an offering to ancestors or gods, a payment in kind, or a commodity. Its consumption may be viewed as necessary, useful, prestige generating, or immoral. The meaning and value of that item changes as it circulates throughout the village, and as it is exchanged in different contexts among people, as well as between people and denizens of the cosmic world. A foodstuff's meaning can also change over historical time. As we have seen, some foodstuffs that were once ordinary have become rare and expensive, while others that were formerly special (such as bean curd) have become common and unremarkable features of the daily diet.

The varying situations in which food circulates illustrate the many forms of exchange operating in Moonshadow Pond. As Stephen Gudeman has reminded us, almost all economies have a mixing of categories within their economic systems. For instance, a trader who earns money through the market system may plow some of his resources back as donations to the community or use them to pay reciprocal obligations.[68] We should not assume that the increasing commodification of the Chinese economy has eliminated other forms of exchange, but rather that new forms are being added to the mix, even as market exchange assumes prominence.

Futhermore, the nature of food's role in reciprocal exchange itself is hardly of a uniform nature. Thus, to take the case of banqueting, in some contexts we can see it as a reciprocal exchange among equals, such as takes place during the Zuofu banqueting, where families take turns hosting on different days. But even here, the role of the beggars injects a hierarchical dimension. And we have also seen the competitive dimension, as banquets of many types increase in size—both in terms of the number of guests and the variety and rareness of the dishes served.[69]

In this sense, what the anthropologists Eiss and Pedersen call a "circulatory perspective" is most useful for thinking about the exchange of food in Moonshadow Pond. As they point out, any given item can undergo "continual metamorphoses of value in diverse social contexts."[70]

Thus, factory-made biscuits can become part of an important offering to the ancestors, a whole chicken can be used to contractually bind a god to give one good luck later in the year, or fresh vegetables from the village can be a mechanism for mothers and daughters to mutually nourish one another, even after the daughters have married "out" of the family. Contrastingly, foods that were once commonly available can become commodified—such as when a wild plant is sold as a costly medicine grass.

Still, whether engaging in gift exchange or in the market, Moonshadow Pond villagers ultimately subject the exchange of food to moral judgments. That food circulates in any number of ways and that its value transforms as it moves in different contexts are certainly true. What we need to examine more closely, however, is the ways in which the circulation of food is framed and understood within a moral discourse. Indeed, food is not only the focus of a moral discourse, but, through its circulation, consumption, and production, people can act as moral agents. An obvious example of this is that filiality requires one to feed one's elders and ancestors.

Moral discourse about food, as well as the use of food to enact moral obligations, is therefore highly elaborated in Moonshadow Pond. It is to these issues that we turn next.

FIVE

Morality

ONE AFTERNOON IN 2010, Songling and I visited her old friend Small Gao. Small Gao's husband began speaking about another family. The family had divided and all four sons were married and living independently. Three of the sons had remained in the village, and the fourth lived in Hong Kong. The Hong Kong son sent money to his mother every month. Typically, the mother might have rotated her meals between the other three sons. However, none of her three sons in the village would eat with her anymore.

As we spoke about the situation, Songling articulated the traditional view that the woman's sons, by refusing to feed her, were engaged in the most contemptible lack of filiality. Other stories of elders who were shunned, and had to fend for themselves for meals, often aroused similar responses from fellow villagers, especially other village elders. For instance, Meirong was a woman who suffered terribly during the Cultural Revolution because her family had a bad class status. (In fact, during the Cultural Revolution, her husband had been beaten to death by an angry mob.) She managed, however, to raise two sons, each of whom went on to marry and prosper. Nonetheless, by 2007, she was making her own meals and eating alone because she did not get along with her daughters-in-law.

One villager said to me, "Her story is a most bitter one." The villager went on to blame the woman's sons and daughters-in-law for her horrible fate in not being able to eat with her family. He particularly blamed the daughters-in-law for lacking *liangxin* (conscience, sense of obligation) and forcing their mother-in-law to eat alone.

The analysis of food exchange in the previous chapter noted that it is pro-pelled by many personal and social needs—nourishing oneself and one's fam-ily, earning a living, maintaining and expanding webs of social relations, and fulfilling obligations not only to family but to ancestors and gods. Food exchange also has a moral dimension. Most obviously, there is the "cycle of *yang*," a person's obligation to care for, and most importantly to feed, his or her family members. When that person ages, he or she will then be fed by the younger family members. Finally, families are obligated to "feed" those rela-tives who have died and are now their ancestors. But food's moral signifi-cance in the lives of Moonshadow Pond residents works in many other ways. This chapter will focus more directly on food in terms of its many moral connotations.

As we shall see, food is not only a powerful symbolic system, but is in particular a moral signifier. As chapter 1 notes, it was Mary Douglas who so famously articulated the idea that food was a "system of communication"[1] that encoded messages about social relationships, including degrees of hier-archy, inclusion, and exclusion.[2] For example, customs surrounding banquet-ing can either promote equality among the participants,[3] or reinforce hierar-chies among guests and between guests and hosts.[4] Rules prohibiting exchanges of food across caste or class lines can also buttress existing class or caste status.[5] It is not a coincidence that one of the first public arenas in which segregation was challenged in the American South was at lunch counters. Conversely, food can also express moral obligations that traverse caste and class boundaries, such as the food pantries or food stamp programs in the contemporary United States, or the free grain that landlords were obliged to provide to peasants during scarce years in precolonial India.[6]

Political rulers, too, can be judged in moral terms for how they fulfill their obligations to feed the people. This was especially the case in Imperial China, where "The moral requirement to 'nourish the people' underpinned an emperor's 'mandate of heaven' and gave rise to successive dynasties playing a highly proactive role in agriculture and in the development of ever-normal granaries."[7] As the historian Kathryn Edgerton-Tarpley points out, the requirement to nourish the people was one of the most important ways a ruler "could "demonstrate his moral legitimacy" to rule.[8] The old proverb "people consider food as heaven" (*Min yishi wei tian*) has also been glossed to signify that food overrides all other considerations for the people, and hunger will provoke discontent and revolt.

Food can therefore articulate a moral message about social relations and actions. And individuals can be judged morally with respect to their actions surrounding food. In the analysis that follows, we will define "moral" by using the framework of Stephen Parish, who conceptualizes the moral in everyday life, and in a given cultural context, as simply those things that are felt as "overriding obligations."[9] Says Parish, "'The moral' identifies the core commitments that define who we are and what we must do, overriding other considerations, at least in our rhetoric of the ideal."[10]

However, certain moral actions, such as helping people in need, are not obligatory. For this reason, we will use two additional frameworks for assessing the nature of the moral in an ethnographic context. First, the anthropologist Caroline Humphrey goes beyond defining the moral as mere obligation by stating rather succinctly that morality in a given cultural context is "the evaluation of conduct in relation to esteemed or despised human qualities."[11] Second, in discussing morality, both sphere and scale must also be considered. For instance, peoples' "ideas about moral obligations inherent in market-based exchange relationships may be different from those that they would apply to internal familial relations. And, obligations seen as applying to hierarchical or authority relations might not be the same as those applied to relationships amongst equals."[12]

In the case of rural China, moral judgments pertaining to food certainly apply to a number of different spheres: from the role of food in fulfilling moral obligations to family members, to ideas about profiteers or merchants who sell adulterated or poor-quality food to the public at large, to judgments about the morality of political leaders and eras, as viewed through the lens of food abundance or dearth. Furthermore, as the last chapter showed, the exchange of food goes beyond the market economy to encompass an economy based on social obligations. Such economies are often called "moral economies," a concept interrogated in more detail later in this chapter. In rural China, this moral economy thrives despite, or even because of, the expansion of China's market economy and globalization.

Indeed, the idea that the penetration of the market into local life will inevitably lead to a decline in mutuality, or moral ties, may not adequately describe the relationship between market economies and moral economies, especially with respect to food.[13] It is doubtful that food can ever be emptied of all values save those of the market. Its necessity for human existence and centrality in familial and other social relations mean food can never be completely detached from the social roles and obligations that underlie moral economies.

In considering the role of food as a moral signifier in Moonshadow Pond, this chapter begins by examining how the exchange of food (see chapter 4) is not only about provisioning and the strengthening of social networks but also about expressing, fulfilling, and creating moral obligations between people. In addition to there being a moral component in the sharing of food, food can also function discursively as moral commentary in Moonshadow Pond. Discourse about food expresses judgments about the rightness or wrongness of peoples' actions at the local and national levels. Finally, food choices themselves convey implicit and explicit moral judgments, for example, about the wider food system (as in decisions to purchase only local meat), or about food intake as a moral index (as in a decision to be vegetarian, which as we shall see is not common in Moonshadow Pond).

The chapter concludes by focusing on how the moral dimensions surrounding food's meanings and practices help to constitute a moral economy that retains a strong presence in daily life. Indeed, the moral economy of food in Moonshadow Pond may actually have been strengthened by the simultaneous growth of the market economy and the industrialized food system.

THE CENTRALITY OF MORAL DEBT IN RURAL CHINA

Before continuing, let us take a momentary sidestep away from the subject of food and briefly review some key points regarding the moral system in rural China prior to Liberation, including the impact of social transformations in both the collective and reform eras. We will focus in particular on the realm of family morality before examining food's role in this moral system.

Developing his theoretical formulations on the basis of fieldwork conducted in both Yunnan and Jiangsu provinces in the 1930s, the anthropologist Fei Xiaotong observed that peasants understood morality as best attained through superordinate control of subordinates and moral modeling.[14] This meant that those who were higher in the hierarchy corrected the mistakes of their subordinates. Furthermore, ethical rules were embedded in particular hierarchical relationships, such as those between parents and children and rulers and subjects. Moral modeling meant that those higher in the hierarchy were supposed to create morality through exemplary living, which would radiate outward to influence others. Morality, therefore, was situation specific and depended on the particular identities and relationships of the actors, rather than on abstract and universal standards.[15] Parents, for instance, had particular obligations to care for and teach their children. In return, these children were indebted to their parents forever. The nature of this obligation was different for sons and daughters. Grown sons remained with their parents after marriage. They were expected to support and care for their parents while they were alive, and to remember them through appropriate death ritual, as well as through subsequent worship and offerings, after their deaths. Daughters transferred their obligations from their own parents to those of their in-laws after marriage.

In this hierarchical moral universe, a key notion was that of reciprocity, or *bao,* which entails reciprocal obligations. According to Lien-sheng Yang, *bao* can imply many things: "'to report', 'to respond', 'to repay', 'to retaliate', and 'to retribute.'" But "the center of this area of meanings is 'response', or 'return', which has served as one basis for social relations in China."[16]

The concept of *bao* is a very old one in China (interestingly, food was a central metaphor to this concept from its beginning). Jean Levi points out that in ancient China high officials were called "meat eaters."[17] This was because the meat officials sacrificed to their ancestors was shared "downward" through various levels of officialdom, thereby creating an obligation of reciprocity on their parts. As Levi states, this "is a conversion of the leftover into an obligation of such a nature that it is virtually a categorical imperative. . . . For the ritual essence of the human being is to repay the gifts which Heaven distributed, from the top to the bottom, in the cascade of leftovers that, in its descent, determined the classes of beings. [In this conception,] the human being, constituted as Debt, is always in the position of being 'left behind' because he has something 'left to pay.'"[18] Sacrifice became the means through which reciprocity, or *bao,* could be enacted. Additionally, L. Yang pointed out that *bao* "strengthens the family system. For instance, the basic virtue of filial piety has ready justification in the concept of response."[19]

Many customary elements of family morality in rural China were tied to a combination of these two elements: moral modeling and reciprocal obligation within a hierarchical structure. For instance, the idea of *xiao,* or filiality, exemplifies this. Children are indebted to their parents for the gift of birth and for raising them. Therefore, they must repay them, not only through support in old age, but through support in the afterlife as well—through proper death ritual and ancestral worship. Moral modeling is also involved, since both parental investment and subsequent filial piety are embedded in actions that others should follow.

By the late nineteenth century, this hierarchical vision of moral debt was echoed not only in Confucian classics but also in "daily proverbs, ledgers of merit and demerit, and even the Qing law code," which "preached the accepted norm that to give birth to and rear a child meant pain and exhausting devotion, thus creating a lifelong debt that the son must strive to repay."[20] Moral debt, or the obligation to repay or respond, was also strengthened by Buddhist frameworks, which contributed the idea that moral retribution for one's acts might be meted out over one's own lifetime and even over subsequent generations.[21]

Lung-Ku Sun notes that in this framework indebtedness to parents begins at the moment of birth, and the debt to parents becomes the "prototype for all reciprocal transactions of society."[22] Ideas of moral debt were, therefore, applied to family relationships and more broadly because relationships outside the family were often understood through familial metaphors.

The concept of *liangxin* is central to these notions of moral debt. *Liangxin,* or literally a good or virtuous "heart/mind," is displayed by reciprocating other people's "good feelings." It is a quality of those individuals who remember their moral obligations and try to act on them. A person without *liangxin* is a person who either does not remember moral debt or at least acts as if he or she doesn't. In this sense, *liangxin* has implications different than the English word *conscience,* although that is often how it is translated. In English, we might speak of someone who commits a bad deed, but is subsequently disturbed by this, as a person with a "troubled conscience." But in Chinese, a person lacks *liangxin* if he or she violates moral obligations, even if these moral lapses mean spending sleepless nights battered by pangs of guilt. While memory is therefore critical to this process, as all reciprocity is dependent on it, *liangxin* entails more than memory because it also requires action.

It might seem that Mao-era morality would have upended the customary familial morality described above. As Richard Madsen has pointed out, revolutionary morality created an imperative to "serve the people."[23] All people, with the exception of "class enemies," were included in this injunction, and the morality was therefore meant to be universally applied and not dependent on particular hierarchical relationships, such as those between elders and their descendants. Additionally, putting your own kin's needs above those of the collective would have been a breach of a pure Mao-era moral code. But as

Richard Madsen has reminded us, this pure code was modified, had to be modified, even before the advent of the reform era.[24] It proved impossible for people to renounce all their family and kin obligations, not the least of which involved the need to care for one's elders. The state could not (still cannot) provide for all needs, and for this reason, it ultimately had to scale back on preaching a revolutionary morality that always puts the needs of the collective above those of the family unit.

With the integration of Chinese society into a capitalist economy during the reform era, notions of moral debt have remained central to family morality in rural China. However, when looked at in terms of traditional hierarchies of age, generation, and gender, rural Chinese families hardly resemble those of a century ago. No consensus has yet emerged in rural society on the exact nature of the obligations entailed in the particular family relationships that now take center stage. Nonetheless, as explained below, the idea of moral debt and obligation within the family has continued to be a critical element of family moral discourses and practices, even as family hierarchies and forms have changed.

INTERGENERATIONAL OBLIGATIONS

If one's debt to one's parents and ancestors is a prototype for moral debt, then it goes without saying that the family is a central domain of moral life. The traditional family system in China assumed a multigenerational household in which sons remained after marriage, sharing expenses and supporting their parents. In a perfect world, these households would extend to five generations, and authority would be allocated to the senior generation over the younger generation, to husbands over wives, and to older males over younger siblings. A woman had little initial power in this system, as she married into her husband's family and into a different village.[25] However, as the daughter-in-law became a member of the senior generation, she used her emotional bonds with her adult sons and her authority over her own daughters-in-law to exercise informal power. This informal power base is what the anthropologist Margery Wolf has called the "uterine family."[26]

The Mao era ushered in a number of profound changes in rural family life. Historian Neil Diamant points out that the roots of change go back to the early years after Liberation. The Marriage Law of 1950, the very first law passed by the Communist government, "put forth a decidedly modernist version of 'proper' family structure, based largely on the ideals of individual-ism, monogamy, and 'free choice in selecting marriage partners.'"[27] The Marriage Law also promulgated the view of marriage as a legal bond between two individuals, rather than as a contract between families. During the marriage law campaign, Diamant explains, older women were frequently targets of daughters-in-law during "speak bitterness" sessions.[28] Younger women seeking divorces also used the new law assertively and did not hesitate to appeal beyond the village authorities if they felt they were being obstructed.[29] The organization of collectives also had an impact on the family by undermining the authority of lineage leaders.[30]

The reform era was marked by further transformations in family life. A few of the trends detected in recent studies of contemporary rural families include a shift in power from the older to the younger generation, smaller households with less generational depth, and a growing equality and intimacy between husband and wife. In his study of rural families in North China, Yunxiang Yan noted a number of profound changes, including the rise of courtship and romance, changing youth employment patterns and more independent income, the spread of popular culture, birth limitation policies (resulting in a predominance of single-child families), and the spread of consumerism. All of these trends have helped solidify the predominance of conjugal families over complex ones, and given the junior generation more power over their elders.[31] Further, the labor migration to cities of tens of millions of rural residents, many of them young and unmarried, has enhanced their freedom to pick their own mates, as well as their sexual freedom.[32]

These changes have created more insecurity for the elderly. If households have less generational depth, what does this imply for the rural elderly, most of whom have no pensions and must rely on their grown children for support? If the conjugal bond is more important than ever, how can rural elders ensure the loyalty of their adult sons? Now that families are smaller, what happens if one's only child is a daughter? And if relations with daughters-in-law are more equitable, and the younger generation is more powerful, how can mothers-in-law count on their daughters-in-law to relieve them of burdensome household work as they age?

Many analysts concur that declining support for elders has been one result of greater conjugality in rural Chinese families. Pang, DeBrauw, and Rozelle's analysis of a nationally representative sample of rural elders shows that population policies limiting family size have reduced the number of children elders can rely on to support them. Coupled with rural emigration by young workers,[33] and decreasing numbers of elders living in extended families, this has led to the phenomenon of "working until you drop."[34] Most rural elders remain in the formal workforce until their seventies, and they may continue to work informally to help their adult children, even those in different households.[35] This help is provided partially in the hope that these adult children will reciprocate their elders when sickness or extreme physical disability leaves them physically unable to work.[36]

Such situations are, in a sense, a reversal of the reciprocity conceptualized in traditional hierarchical arrangements. Now the parents continue to work for the younger generation in the hope that these children will ultimately, and at a much later date than was the case with the traditional arrangement, feel a moral obligation to reciprocate. Their place in the family hierarchy is not sufficient in itself to ensure support in old age. As a result, elders may employ a number of strategies to bolster their security. These include the emerging trend of relying on married daughters to supplement support given to parents by sons, and meal rotation for the elder generation among the households of several married sons (more on this below).[37]

In these changing family situations, family members may articulate their actions in terms of ideas of morality and obligation. However, arguments break out over just what these obligations are. I found just such dynamics existing in Moonshadow Pond. For instance, some elderly and middle-aged women complain about being overworked by their own daughters-in-law, who, they claim, now expect them to do most of the housework. This is a reversal of the traditional image of the daughter-in-law, who labored under the yoke of a mother-in-law's unending demands. Indeed, some villagers pointed out to me that elderly people who cannot work are sometimes called *feipin* (literally "scraps, waste, or rejects") by many young people; they do not want to marry into households with in-laws who are too feeble to work, and are therefore perceived as an extra burden.[38]

Additionally, many grandparents now take care of their grandchildren while the children's parents go out to work during the day; in some cases, both sons and daughters-in-law have migrated to cities for employment, leaving the grandchildren with their grandparents, who raise them. The closer connections between married daughters and their parents, and the economic aid some married daughters now provide for their parents, also create new counterobligations. Not only are parents expected to help care for their sons' children, they may have to help take care of their daughters' children as well.[39]

Interestingly, despite the evidence that the elderly feel much more vulnerable in contemporary rural China, and also experience the need to "lock in" a sense of obligation to them in their adult children, to conclude that the younger generation no longer feels any moral duty toward their elders would be wrong. In fact, in interviews with a hundred young rural people, most of whom were labor migrants who had moved from rural areas to cities, the anthropologists Hansen and Pang found that most of them had deeply internalized a sense of obligation to family. According to Hansen and Pang, "Hardly any of them expected the state to take any responsibility for the old, and they took it for granted that they would have to support the elderly."[40] In addition to asserting that they felt a responsibility for their elders, many of these young migrants spoke of using their earnings to support the educations of younger siblings.[41]

In summary, despite decades of revolutionary, followed by capitalist transformation, the idea that there is a moral debt to parents, and even that siblings and affinal kin have some mutual obligations, still holds traction.[42]

FOOD IN THE FAMILY MORAL SYSTEM

After this brief detour into rural family morality, we can now consider the role of food in this system. In many respects, the flow of food has always been one of the most basic statements of obligation between family members in rural China. Indeed, in classical philosophical texts, the necessity of saving the best food for one's elders is identified as a key ingredient of filial piety. For instance, the *Liji* instructed daughters-in-law and sons to serve the husbands' parents generously while allocating only leftovers for themselves.[43] This was especially the case with meat and wine, which were to be kept aside for the elderly. Good rulers upheld these normative principles as well. Roel Sterckx observes that, "The *Guanzi* prescribes that a ruler ought to donate meat and wine on a monthly basis to people over eighty and daily to nonagenarians. . . . According to Mencius, ensuring that people over seventy can eat meat is part of good government."[44]

As we saw, the obligation to support family members (*yang*) implies mutual nourishment,[45] while family division is frequently indicated by the end of meal sharing. Indeed, this definition of the family as a unit that implies mutual nourishment is quite humorously conveyed in Meixian by the expression "*er nai,*" which literally means "second milk," and which refers to a situation where a woman has an affair with a married man and gives birth to his child. *Nai* can mean "breast," "breast milk," or simply "milk," and therefore evokes the act of feeding a baby.

This moral obligation to mutual nourishment, although a cultural ideal, has been challenged during times of famine as well as in times of relative food abundance, such as the contemporary era. As one might imagine, famine has often put this mutual obligation to the test, as the responsibility to mutually nourish flies in the face of the brute fact that there may not even be enough food to go around. During the relatively more prosperous times of the reform era, food has fortunately not been the focus of the stark moral choices presented by famine. Nonetheless, food sharing within families still functions as a material embodiment of moral debt, and conflicts over food also reveal tensions around obligations in contemporary families.

FAMINE AND FAMILIAL MORALITY

The absolute food deprivation of famine can severely challenge moral obligations within families. Hierarchies may either be reaffirmed or overthrown. From the end of the nineteenth century through the twentieth century, there were many regional famines in China. But two great famines, almost a hundred years apart, had momentous political, cultural, and economic consequences on a national scale. These were the famine in North China in the late 1870s, and the Great Leap Famine of 1958–62. These famines also illustrate the ways moral discourses and obligations in families were tested during times when they were under most severe stress.

The North China famine of 1876–79 was a catastrophic crisis of the late Qing period that resulted in an estimated 9.5 to 13 million deaths and imposed great suffering on many more people.[46] Historian Kathryn Edgerton-Tarpley has documented reports about the 1870s famine that chronicle sacrifices that parallel the lines of familial authority. As she notes, "County gazetteers are rife with detailed stories about sons who sacrificed their wives and children and sometimes even their own lives in order to feed elderly mothers. A gazetteer from southern Shanxi's Yishi County (1880), for example, introduces a filial son named Wu Jiuren who, during the 1877 famine, abandoned his wife but kept his mother alive by carrying her on his back while escaping to another area. People called him extremely filial."[47] Edgarton-Tarpley also narrates many other stories of filial sons who gave up food for their aged mothers. However, Confucian logic did not always lead to one answer. In one story recounted in the Jishan county gazetteer, a grandmother argued that she could rescue the family line by not eating, thereby saving the minimal food available for her grandson.[48]

Of course, such stories were as much intended to instruct people in orthodox Confucian morality as they were to record actual events. We cannot be certain that people followed such moral injunctions when faced with the actual horror of famine in their own lives and families. Edgarton-Tarpley tells us that available demographic evidence from famine stricken Liaoning Province suggests that, in fact, "Families faced with rising food prices shared their dwindling food supply relatively equally rather than allowing privileged family members to maintain their normal consumption rates while less privileged relatives starved."[49] Furthermore, females, ironically, may have had better survival rates than males during the famine because they were trafficked—sold from famine-stricken areas to regions where food was more available.[50]

Almost a century later, the famine of the Great Leap Forward also put issues of family morality into relief. Only this time, the state was not trying to shore up Confucian codes of familial hierarchy but to attack them. As chapter 2 mentions, the public mess halls established during the Great Leap Forward were, among other things, an attempt to collectivize cooking and childcare, thus freeing women from their domestic chores.[51] The destruction of the family kitchen, a symbol of family unity, was encouraged as families were pressed into giving up their family cookware for the backyard steel furnaces.[52] For instance, James Watson tells us, "In Guangdong Province, household stoves were dismantled, brick by brick, and the materials were used to build centralized mess halls."[53]

Interestingly, the symbolism of familial moral debt was used to characterize the communes and canteens. Writing about this massive (and ultimately disastrous) experiment, Watson states, "Week after week, month after month, the Chinese mass media urged China's farmers to 'make their way into the collective life of a large family.'"[54] And, he continues, "Another intriguing notion that emerged in late 1958 was the 'mess hall family,' meaning the collectivity of people who ate together—approximately 60 to 80 households on average."[55] The use of metaphors of family, with its obvious implications of obligation, to refer to the collective mess halls is testament to the power of linking ideas of moral debt, of family, and of the act of feeding in rural China.

Of course, the Great Leap policies led to horrific famine and the eventual loss of tens of millions of lives. Despite the symbolism of moral debt implied in the metaphor of the mess hall family, the actual practice of family reciprocity was often upended by the famine, not only because of the mess halls themselves, but also because the experience of starvation itself had a profoundly destructive effect on family relationships. For instance, in Ralph Thaxton's study of the Great Leap famine in one village, a villager recollected how loyalty to the party led his brigade's party secretary to allow his own mother to starve to death, thus creating an "unforgiveable moral predicament."[56] Trafficking of women, like earlier periods of famine, was also reported during the Great Leap famine,[57] and there was a general decline in family cohesion. Those who could labor got the meager rations that were available, and those who could not were defined as "without use." Therefore, elderly people and children were often "slowly starved to death."[58] Yang Jisheng's encyclopedic account of the Great Leap famine, based on province-by-province research, also recounts how extreme hunger prompted many instances of intrafamilial violence, including killing family members to get more food for oneself, as well as killing younger children or siblings for cannibalism.[59] As Yang reflects, "human beings at the extremes of hunger pay no regard to affection, morality, or dignity."[60]

By 1961, the debacle of the Great Leap was coming to an end. The collective mess halls and communal nurseries simply folded, and China's massive collectivization had to be modified to allow for some individual initiative and private gardens.

FOOD AND FAMILIAL MORALITY
DURING THE REFORM ERA

During the reform era, food continues to be symbolically loaded as a medium of familial moral obligation, although fortunately not in relation to hunger and famine as in the past. In my own field research in Moonshadow Pond, I found that the idiom of food was still used as the customary way to speak about family solidarity or family division. First, as we saw, families from Moonshadow Pond have dispersed geographically because of the demands of the labor market. Discerning which families are still single economic units and which are actually separate, therefore, is not always easy. However, as noted previously, the family you return to, *and share food with,* on New Year's

Eve, indicates the boundaries of the undivided family. One does not eat a New Year's meal with a family that has already divided economically.

Further, as we have seen in our discussion of food exchange, family division does not entail the end of all obligations and exchanges between adult children and their parents by any measure. We have already discussed the informal exchanges that take place between mothers and their married daughters in Moonshadow Pond. Brothers, who have divided and set up their separate households, also continue to have obligations to their aging parents; following the food trail is a good way of assessing the degree to which offspring feel the pull of these obligations. For instance, meal rotation (*lunliu*) is a common way for adult sons to divide responsibility for feeding aging parents. A parent may take his or her meals one month with one son, the next month with a different son, and so forth. Jing Jun, in reviewing several ethnographic studies of this practice, observes that it is considered routine in some villages and criticized in others.[61] As the stories at the beginning of this chapter illustrate, in Moonshadow Pond, both the practice and the discourse about meal rotation often reflect contradictory ideas about the nature of family obligations, ideas that mirror the conflicting demands on family members in the current economic and social context.

Such tensions surrounding food within families have been noted by other anthropologists of contemporary China. Since feeding and food sharing is such an important part of moral obligation within families, food's frequent prominence in disputes about such obligations is not surprising. Fei Wu's study of rural suicides highlights many cases in which conflicts surrounding food provoked the extraordinary reaction of suicide—a family member felt ignored or humiliated when they were left out of ordinary family commensality. These cases include elderly people who were fed rancid food; were not given a more nourishing and special part of a meal, such as an egg in one's soup; or were simply not included in the family meal.[62]

And yet, although abandoning one's elders to eat alone, is usually seen as a most flagrant violation of filial obligations, conflicting interpretations of such actions also reveal variations and contradictions in contemporary moral attitudes about these duties. Wu's study explained that villagers do not always attribute bad motives to a negligent daughter-in-law who does not properly care for her elders. For instance, they may remark that such a person is simply "confused."[63]

I found such variations in moral judgments in my own fieldwork. For example, while Songling harshly condemned Meirong's daughters-in-law for refusing to cook for her in the aforementioned story, this interpretation of the situation was not shared by all. One villager told me that the circumstances were not as they seemed. Rather, he asserted that it was quite "complicated," and that Meirong's daughters-in-law refused to cook for her because Meirong was really "arrogant" (*jiaoao*). Furthermore, she was still capable of making her own meals. "If she were truly disabled," this villager stated, "perhaps it might be a different story, but she is able to cook for herself now, so her sons and daughters-in-law should not have to endure her attitudes." In his assessment of the situation, this villager was not exactly throwing the need for filiality out the window. But he was willing to balance its requirements by considering the degree to which an elder was able to provide food and cook for herself, as well as her attitudes and behavior toward her sons and daughters-in-law.

The shifting relationship between the generations is also revealed by the delay in the reversal of responsibility for mutual nourishment. In many of China's rural communities, as the younger generation migrates to cities, or takes up nonfarm work, elders continue to provision their children and grandchildren not only by cooking for them but also by continuing to farm. They also take charge of key food rituals, such as the making of *nianban* (see chapters 2 and 3), when their adult children may no longer have the time. In this regard, they are continuing to provide food for their families into old age, rather than relying on their grown children.

For instance, we have already seen how Yinzhao persisted in farming for her adult children, and also organized the yearly activities of preparing New Year's treats (*nianban*). Additionally, with respect to the provision of food for adult children and daughters-in-law, some food-related tasks have always been allocated to the senior generation. For instance, as earlier chapters have noted, it is expected that a mother-in-law will make a special chicken dish for a daughter-in-law when she gives birth. This dish of braised chicken, ginger, and fermented rice wine is considered necessary to bolster the health of the new mother and ensure nourishing breast milk.

Thus, food exchanges are an important means by which elders in Moonshadow Pond can endeavor to make sure that the younger generation feels a continuing sense of obligation toward them. The flow of New Year's treats is just one example of this. In making *nianban* for other family members, an older woman enables them to fulfill *their* obligations to a wider circle of friends and community members, who visit them. This ensures their further indebtedness to her for helping to make this possible.

Preparing treats for their married *sons* and daughters-in-laws is one way in which mothers attempt to cement obligations, which previously were taken for granted. But with regard to married *daughters,* a slightly different phenomenon is occurring. In this case, by helping their married daughters, middle-aged and elderly women are trying to engender a new sense of obligation, which was not assumed in the past, when married daughters were expected to transfer their obligations to their in-laws. As Songling quite directly put it, "We don't have retirement or social security, and our children are our only security." Here, she was referring to all her married children, not just her son.

Further, the sharing of food among family members is not only about cooking for them, provisioning them with major staples like rice, or preparing special items like *nianban*. It is also enacted, as we saw in the last chapter, through an almost constant flow of very ordinary foodstuffs among family members, especially among women. The exchange of greens and other food items between mothers and married daughters, therefore, can be understood, not only as a way of continuing the emotional intimacy of the family, even after the daughters have long since married out, but of constantly reinvigorating a feeling of mutual obligation.

Of course, there are some who opt out of this time-consuming cycle of giving and cooking food for others, and the enmeshment of social obligations that ensues from it. For instance, A Xie was a young mother living in the county capital, whose elder sister had married into a family from Moonshadow Pond. Although both sisters were originally from Meixian, they had grown up in another province, where their father had been a professor. Not having grown up in a rural context, and not living in one now, A Xie had this to say about all the fuss that went into making *nianban* during the New Year's holiday: "People don't need these sweets, they are oily, heating, give you a dry throat and cough, they are time consuming to make and nobody can finish them. It's easier to just buy a small bag in town and give it to the children or guests when they come to visit."

A Xie, who had a rather tangential relationship to Moonshadow Pond, had never lived in any rural context. As someone who had grown up outside of Meixian, she was already less enmeshed in local relationships than others were. Hence, it makes sense that she approached *nianban* as neither an essential element of the New Year nor as a critical foodstuff that enmeshed her in a web of obligation to family or friends.

Political and Social Orders

In Moonshadow Pond, food is used rhetorically to make sense of both the past and present social world within and beyond the family. This includes articulating moral judgments about interpersonal behavior, as well as about past and present political regimes, and the social orders they ushered in.

Not surprisingly, as indicated previously, the relative prosperity of the present is often spoken about through food references and analogies. Food analogies and metaphors have also been used by political leaders to establish their moral credentials. As chapter 3 explains, during the Cultural Revolution national leaders urged peasants to begin their Lunar New Year's unity meal by eating a bitter dish, using the metaphors of bitter and sweet foods to evoke differences between the "bitter" society of the past and the "sweeter" present. Another metaphor—the "iron rice bowl"—is also frequently invoked in references to the collective period. The image conjured up by this metaphor is that there was a guaranteed subsistence, even if the standard of living was very simple. Of course, this metaphor clearly omits the period of the Great Leap Forward (1958–61), a time of mass starvation and food insecurity.

Nowadays, elders, and even middle-aged people who lived through the collective era, often refer to its hardships for a different purpose, to goad young children into doing the right thing by finishing their rice at mealtimes. In fact, the "goodness" of a child is not infrequently correlated with their pickiness about food. As mentioned earlier, children who eat all their rice are often praised, while children who do not eat their rice, and prefer biscuits and other factory-made snacks, are commonly reprimanded.

Food also figures as a moral critique in commentaries about the inequalities of the present era, especially in regard to the differences between rural and urban identities, or between ordinary people and officials. A myriad of expressions related to food is used by residents to locate themselves in the contemporary class structure as "peasants," and to contrast their situations with those of urban dwellers who work for a wage, especially those who work in white-collar desk jobs. Although only 6 percent of Moonshadow Pond households earn their income exclusively from farming, the traditional expression *qing kun fan,* or "rice cleared of tiredness and fatigue," is still used by village elders to refer to the rice that educated urban people eat. It means that, unlike peasants, educated people do not need to grow their own rice.

Proverbial figures of speech, such as "those who till the fields produce for those who sit at wide desks"[64] refer to the same social distinctions.

Food is increasingly viewed as an indicator of class differences and an index of corruption in reform-era China, and commentary about this often expresses implicit and explicit moral judgments. For instance, criticism of officials and their lavish habits is often articulated in terms of their extravagant banqueting behaviors. In chapter 1, we saw that our neighbor Red Chong characterized the growing number of restaurants and banquet halls as establishments that catered to cadres, or employees of office units. For many villagers, this conjures up images of places that cater to people who are not "spending their own money."

Villagers often told me that at banquet halls, officials were regularly plied with dishes I could not even imagine. People often focused on soups as examples. As we have seen, soup, and especially medicinal soup, is highly prized in Meixian. Soups that are made with foreign or exotic ingredients and are, therefore, more expensive are status symbols as well.

"We hear that they come to eat and will spend several thousand yuan for a bowl of soup for their table," one villager said to me. Such expensive soups, she said, might be abalone soup or a soup based on winter worm summer grass [dongcongxiacao] that they procure from Xinjiang or Tibet. The winter worm summer grass this villager referred to is actually caterpillar fungus, a form of fungus that becomes a parasite on caterpillar larvae. It kills the caterpillar and mummifies it. The fungus sprouts in spring—hence it is called both "winter worm" and "summer grass." Soup made from this is thought to cure a wide variety of ailments, but the fungus is extremely expensive because it is difficult to procure.[65] Hence, this villager would associate such an item exclusively with cadres eating at government expense.

Similarly, another villager, talking about the Zuofu banquet, told me that one cadre who grew up in the village held a large banquet of nine tables, including two tables that were reserved for members of his work unit. This villager complained that the work unit paid for these tables. Hence they were using government money for a private affair. While I could not verify this, it was a good example of how concerns about corruption are often articulated through examples of banqueting at the public's expense.

That complaints about cadre corruption are often connected to food does not, of course, mean that villagers themselves do not play their part in this system. Most people know someone who invited cadres to dine with them in order to procure a favor, such as help for a son or daughter who is looking for a job; minimally, it is routine to present cadres with gifts of fruit or other foodstuffs when visiting them in order to request attention or help. Such gifts are not really a direct exchange for the particular favor, but they grease the wheels of social interaction. Further, if someone holds a banquet for a wedding or other occasion, such as moving into a new house, observers will take note if any local cadres are among the guests. Attendance by many cadres is taken as an indication that the person is well connected.

Ironically, villagers often use the verb "to eat" to speak about how cadres "gobble up" the public's resources and money. At the same time, the metaphorical meaning can also be literal. Thus, a villager complained to me about payments that had to be made to the township government in order to secure a gravesite in the village. (In the past, no such payment was needed.) "The cadres just 'eat up' [chidiao] the money you give them," she exclaimed. The words "eat up" in this case can also be taken literally, to mean that they spend the money on banquets and expensive food, or idiomatically, to mean that the cadres use the money for their own purposes. In either case, the verb for eating is a very meaningful way of speaking about cadre corruption and waste. This relationship between food consumption and cadre corruption, however, is not new to the reform era. For instance, accounts from other areas of China about the difficult years of the Great Leap Forward often contrast stories of starvation amongst ordinary people with tales of cadre indulgence. Yang Jisheng describes the situation regarding county level cadres during the Great Leap Forward in Anhui this way:

> While peasants starved, cadres entertained at lavish feasts. Once, when the county party committee met, some committee members were so drunk that the meeting had to be adjourned. When the county's deputy head and party secretary of Xiaoxihe Commune, Miao Jian, went on inspection visits, he brought his own liquor, meat, and a chef. When the Zhetang production brigade leader was enjoying one of his lavish meals, a sick person asked for a swallow of fish broth, only to be slapped and sent off hungry. Lin Xingfu of the county party committee work group reported, "County party committee chairman Jiang Yizhou ate wheat flour and rice, with no limits on his consumption. He didn't eat at the communal kitchen, but had rice crusts fried in oil. [County party secretary] Zhou's family never ate coarse grain."[66]

Someone from the same province reported, "The Wudian on-the-spot meeting was very wasteful. There was no food at the communal kitchen, and thirteen people died at Zhoulou in two days, but at the meeting they still ate and drank—fried dough strips, fried glutinous rice cakes, boiled dumplings, steamed bread, twelve dishes in the morning and twenty-four at noon, and fancy liquor along with it."[67] Certainly, during the Great Leap Forward, access to the communal kitchen system also fostered cadre corruption with regard to food, as it gave cadres special access to food and enabled them not only to eat better than others but also to survive the famine itself.[68]

Later on, after the collective kitchens were dismantled, cadres still had access to collective resources. However, villagers in Moonshadow Pond, who had actually been cadres during the collective era, also pointed out that there was another side to the equation of food with cadre corruption during that period. Sometimes the accusation of hoarding food was baseless, but it was leveled at an adversary in order to bring him down. For instance, Big Gao was the head of the production brigade in Moonshadow Pond from 1978 to 1993. He had previously been forced to resign during the Four Cleanups Campaign of 1965. The accusations against him during the Four Cleanups Campaign focused on hoarding food—stealing fruit from the *longyan* (dragon eye) trees that he tended, killing oxen for meat, and taking extra pork and grain from brigade resources.[69] He was only exonerated during the reform era, when the accusations were officially withdrawn.

Villager complaints about present-day cadre corruption and food are hardly unique to Moonshadow Pond or Meixian. Indeed, in recent years, food as an indicator of cadre corruption has been recognized as a national problem and is widely reported in the Chinese as well as in the international press. An article in the English-language version of the *China Daily* indicated that one-third of all China's consumer spending on eating out was for official banquets.[70]

Of course, as previously described, even ordinary folk in Moonshadow Pond hold more frequent and larger banquets, with a greater array of dishes, than in the past. Nonetheless, this overall trend does not prevent banqueting from figuring prominently in the moral commentary of villagers and in their critiques of officials.

While a critical view of officials is often revealed in food images, by way of references to their sumptuous banqueting, the moral virtues of contemporary peasant life are also frequently expressed through food imagery. Villagers, as described in chapter 1, take pride in their ability to access fresh and nonadulterated produce. A moral judgment is implied in villagers' preferences for their own food—the assumption is that the village is a place where social relationships are more trustworthy and reliable, and schemes to adulterate food for profit are urban phenomena. Indeed, many people note that village pork is actually more expensive than that sold in the city; but buyers are willing to pay more because they can be sure the meat comes from freshly slaughtered local animals.

Ironically, as mentioned in chapter 1, the local government now insists that local pig farmers bring their pigs to the slaughterhouse in the county capital, instead of slaughtering them locally. This is part of an effort to ensure that all meat sold in the city can be trusted. Such meat is literally called "trustworthy meat" (*fangxin rou*), in contrast to *heixin* food, which literally means "evil food" but can be understood to mean "untrustworthy food." For this reason, official discourse on the "morality" of meat is not the same as that of the villagers. Whereas villagers trust their own pork vendors to sell them locally slaughtered pigs, the authorities view gaining oversight and control over the slaughtering process as a necessary means of rooting out untrustworthy meat.

Of course, this does not mean that people do not complain about the prices their fellow villagers set for local meat. Nonetheless, while local vendors are understood to want to earn money, their motivation is never imagined to extend so far as to cause injury to people, as occurred in national scandals around melamine in milk or dangerous protein compounds in meat. The face-to-face nature of such local transactions, in fact, would make such fraud impossible.

Food Discourse and the Rightness or Wrongness of Social Relationships

Aside from using food to speak about the morality of different political and economic orders and social groups, villagers refer to food when evaluating the rightness or wrongness of individual actions within social relationships.

Food scarcities in the past, therefore, might be used to explain, and even excuse, behavior that might normally be viewed as immoral, or as violating basic obligations. My informants in Meixian did not report (at least to me) the extreme behaviors, including a breakdown in family relationships[71] and even cannibalism,[72] chronicled in some other parts of China during the Great Leap Forward famine. However, they did talk about extreme hunger, and severe symptoms such as edema. Care packets from overseas relatives likely helped keep the ravages of the famine under control by providing direct nourishment to some Moonshadow Pond residents, thereby reducing the pressure on others for the limited amount of available food.

Villagers, nonetheless, still recite stories about the ways this famine changed social relationships and people's abilities to fulfill basic obligations. For instance, Jieguo is a villager, whose mother was widowed during the time of the Great Leap Forward. Her economic situation as a widow, combined with the very difficult food situation, made it impossible for her to feed her three sons. In response to these pressures, she gave two of her three sons to adoptive families in the Chaozhou area, a region of Guangdong Province that had a better food situation than Meixian's. One of the sons remained with his adoptive family, although he reconnected with his biological family as an adult. Jieguo, however, was taken back to Moonshadow Pond and was returned to his mother by two women from the village. In fact, he was secretly abducted. While neither of these actions—giving your son away or secretly abducting him to get him back—would have met with approval in normal circumstances, older villagers, recounting the story a half-century later, used the situation of food scarcity to explain and excuse both of these actions.

A number of phrases also use food analogies to invoke moral obligations between individuals. For instance, the phrase "when you drink water, remember the source" (*yin shui si yuan*) is a common way to reference the importance of remembering one's moral debt to people who have provided help. And the phrase, "when a person leaves, the tea turns cold," is used to criticize the ease with which people forget others and their obligations to them.

Stories about people who were refused food can also be used to illustrate the fate of those who violate social and moral expectations. In discussing a woman, who had a bad relationship with her husband and was having an affair with another man, a villager illustrated the community's disapproval of her by saying, "When she goes to buy pork, no one will sell it to her!" And in describing a cadre of the past, who was not well regarded, my neighbor said, "When he went to someone's house and asked for water, they replied, 'you can find it in the river.'" Such stores were more illustrative of the story-teller's disregard for the person than they were evidence of a common practice of refusing to share food with people who were not morally respected. Nonetheless, it was interesting to me that the example of food exchange was often used to illustrate a person's low moral standing in the community.

Even the verb "to eat" (*chi*) can be used as a metaphor for the violation of proper social relations and obligations. To say a person has "eaten" someone else's money is to say that he has swindled them. As indicated above, it can be used to refer to cadre waste of public resources, and it can also be used to refer literally to the act of wasting other peoples' money through feasting.

THE SUBSTANCE OF FOOD AND MORAL JUDGMENTS

Most of our discussion thus far has focused on the intersection of food and morality with respect to various social relationships, whether they are among family and acquaintances, between cadres and ordinary villagers, or even between the state and society at large. As we have seen, food and its exchange often function as an index of the rightness or wrongness of various social relationships.

But in Moonshadow Pond, is food choice itself an index of personal or individual morality? In all societies, consumption of certain specific foods is considered taboo. The particular foods that may fall under such a designation vary widely from context to context and according to social identity. (An orthodox Brahmin in southern India must refrain from all animal protein, while an untouchable may eat meat, including beef.) Like taboos on what not to eat, positive choices of specific foods can also be framed as moral. For instance, in the contemporary United States, the local food movement is not simply about purchasing food that is fresher and tastier but is also about taking a stance against industrial agriculture; it is also considered a way to help the local economy and global environment. For this reason, the act of purchasing something local can be framed as a moral act.

In Moonshadow Pond, individual food choice is also sometimes framed in moral terms. As pointed out earlier, Moonshadow Pond villagers mistrust the food found in the wider market—in terms of both taste and safety— compared to food they can either produce themselves or buy from local vendors. Growing one's own rice and vegetables, or purchasing meat from a local vendor, can therefore be understood as an implicit critique of the wider food system. This does not mean, however, that such actions are understood only in moral terms. As examined in chapters 1 and 2, residents of Moonshadow Pond who grow their own rice, plant their own vegetables, or purchase meat from a local vendor also explain their actions in terms of economics, taste, and health.

While food choices do act as an implicit moral critique of the wider food system, they are not usually viewed as an index of the consumer's *personal* morality. However, two possible exceptions to this pertain to the consumption of alcohol and the issue of vegetarianism, practices that often contain a moral component in a variety of different cultural contexts. In general, in Moonshadow Pond, consumption of meat and alcohol rarely defines the morality of the consumer in a negative way, nor does refraining from these substances cast one in a morally more positive light. To understand this, we need to take a closer look at the social and cultural contexts of both alcohol consumption and the rare instances of vegetarianism in Moonshadow Pond.

As explained earlier, drinking in Chinese society has traditionally been associated with banqueting (hence the colloquial reference to banquets as "eating liquor"). However, while drinking liquor is seen as part and parcel of banqueting, copious amounts of drinking are also linked to the image of excessive consumption attached to official banqueting. Interestingly, officials sometimes defend their extreme drinking behavior by arguing that drinking and toasting are an essential way of building the social relationships and networks that are critical to carrying out official business; and this business is at least in theory undertaken on behalf of their localities. Thus, officials find a moral justification for what others criticize. An official quoted in a *China Daily* article about one cadre, who died from excessive drinking at a banquet, stated "'We would lose face if we could not get our guests drunk. Refusing to drink is considered disrespectful.'"[31] The implication here is that refusing to drink by getting drunk with the guests is disrespectful and makes it harder for officials to get their necessary work done.

Nonetheless, while Moonshadow Pond residents include liquor consumption in their general moral condemnation of excessive cadre consumption, drinking is not subject to moral critique as part of banqueting in general because it is an integral aspect of sociality. Drinking at banquets in Moonshadow Pond is a primarily male activity (as in most of China), especially when the spirits are hard liquor. Women more frequently choose from a range of other options, such as soda, soy milk, or homemade glutinous rice wine (which is cooked and therefore has negligible alcoholic content). However, as people have prospered, the range of spirits available at banquets has expanded. I rarely witnessed red wine at banquets in the 1990s, but after 2010, it, along with beer and liquor, became a more common option. Women are not completely excluded from any of these choices. But even when women choose alcohol, their toasting behavior is rarely as ostentatious as that of men (and it never continues to the point of drunkenness).

Therefore, while certain social conventions frame drinking, and excessive or wasteful consumption is linked to cadre corruption, the consumption of spirits is not itself subject to moral critique, nor is refraining from all liquor consumption a way to boost one's moral standing. One needs to keep in mind that both spirits and tea have long been important substances in sacrifices to ancestors and gods. Furthermore, not to offer any alcohol at a banquet would certainly be considered shoddy treatment of one's guests. (In the next chapter, liquor as a substance that promotes conviviality and emotional closeness is dealt with in greater detail.)

Similarly, vegetarianism plays only a minimal role in establishing a moral persona in Moonshadow Pond. Few vegetarians live there, and meat, as described previously, is an integral and valued part of the diet. We also saw in chapter 4 that the three sacrificial meats are important in worship, and are even offered to some Buddhist deities, like Guanyin. There are, therefore, only a few spaces for vegetarianism in Moonshadow Pond. For instance, Buddhist lay, female religious practitioners in Meixian are referred to colloquially as "vegetarian mothers" (*zhaima*). But even here, when it comes to the actual food practices of vegetarian mothers, and even of nuns themselves, to whom one might assume the rules would be applied more strictly, the contemporary village practice is quite different from that of more formal Buddhist institutions in urban areas. For instance, in Moonshadow Pond, two nuns are associated with the village temple, which contains a mixture of Buddhist and non-Buddhist popular local deities. These two women belong to two different generations, but neither is a vegetarian.

The first nun, Auntie Zhao, was an elderly woman when I first met her in 2007. Before Liberation, because she was a sickly child, she was sent to live in the temple. At that time, it was believed that, if a girl with precarious health were sent to live in a temple, she would be protected by the goddess Guanyin and cured. (Ironically, these girls were the only ones in Moonshadow Pond who were educated in the old society, because they had to learn how to read scripture.) After Liberation, the temples were disbanded until the reform era. Monks and nuns went to live among the general population and married. Auntie Zhao married and had children. But in the reform era she went back to the temple to live. She is now over eighty and still has relations with her children and grandchildren, who visit frequently. When I queried Auntie Zhao about vegetarianism, she replied, "People have different tastes, but what matters is what is in your heart." Her meaning, in other words, was that one's morality depends more on inner character than on the particular substances one eats. The other nun in Moonshadow Pond was a young woman who was not from the area. She lived in the temple and also acted as a caretaker. She had not married, but she also did not follow a vegetarian diet.

Interestingly, the origins of vegetarianism in China are closely connected to the introduction of Buddhism. Although Buddhist monks in Southeast Asia can eat meat, Chinese Buddhism adapted a vegetarian diet for both monks and nuns. The adaptation of this practice took place over the first few centuries of Buddhism's spread in China, and, by the tenth century, vegetarianism was the presumed practice in all Buddhist monasteries.[74] An elaborate vegetarian cuisine developed, and Buddhist-inspired vegetarian restaurants can be found today around Buddhist temples in urban areas. This strict vegetarianism also includes prohibitions on fish, eggs, alcohol, garlic, and onions.[75]

Village popular religion, however, has always been syncretic and has been geared more toward the practicalities of rural life. Indeed, the only devoted vegetarian whom I knew in Moonshadow Pond was a young woman named Bright Ling. She was a college-educated, unmarried teacher, who participated in the activities of a Buddhist center in the county capital. This center appealed to educated urban residents, and they gathered together to take classes in Buddhism, recite sutras, and sing songs together as a congregation.[76] Buddhist associations such as this one, which are based on voluntary membership, began to expand greatly in the late nineteenth century. Ironically, this kind of congregationalism was formed on the basis of the Christian model and was a response to it. They had "their own scriptures, philosophical systems, liturgies . . . congregational modes of participation, and hierarchical national organizations."[77] These redemptive societies often focused on "morality, discipline, and self-cultivation—many of these groups campaigned against opium and alcohol and advocated the more traditional vegetarian diet."[78] Their emphasis was on "immediate forms of salvation outside the ancestral line."[79]

Unlike village-based religion, which emphasized lineage and place (ancestors and gods based on locality), these societies did not place importance on the interaction between the dead and the living. It makes sense in this context that Bright Ling, who was not married and therefore was not bound by obligations to in-laws and children, might be drawn to this approach. In her own words, she saw her involvement as a form of "philosophy," and she characterized the villagers' religious practices as "blind superstition."

For Bright Ling, vegetarianism was a way to amass virtue. Unlike other villagers in Moonshadow Pond, she was not only a vegetarian herself but also considered the offering of the three sacrificial meats to ancestors and gods impermissible. Bright Ling was also following a wave of post-1980, reform-era expansion in Buddhist congregations on the mainland.[80] The search for some kind of moral system in the wake of rapid urbanization has made Buddhist congregationalism attractive to many urban residents during the reform era. In a number of urban areas, vegetarian restaurants detached from Buddhist institutions have even begun to crop up, although they often distribute Buddhist-inspired literature and morality books. A consequence of this is that both Buddhism and vegetarianism have recently become popular among urban residents and recent migrants from rural areas, who are searching for a moral framework in rapidly changing circumstances.[81]

Villagers in Moonshadow Pond, however, need look no further than traditional family morality to justify their nonvegetarianism as moral. Indeed, vegetarianism in China has always conflicted with other moral demands, most importantly, the moral requirement of filiality, which obligates one to nourish one's elders and ancestors.[82] Meat, as we have seen, is associated with a good diet, and the three sacrificial meats are also essential as offerings to ancestors and many gods. The importance of meat in Moonshadow Pond is not simply a reaction to the deprivations of the collective era. Indeed, the association of meat with the good life goes back to ancient China, where the expression "meat eaters" (roushizhe) was associated with the ruling class. The expression that referred to vegetarianism, on the other hand, literally means "plain eating" (sushi).[83] As mentioned earlier, even as far back as the classical philosophers, reserving meat for the elderly was identified as a key ingredient in filial piety. The association of meat with moral obligations, filial piety, and even good government, therefore, has deep roots in China.

In Meixian, even popular legends confirm the connections between meat and filial piety. For instance, in the neighboring Hakka county of Dabu, beef balls in soup are a popular snack. The story surrounding their origin concerns a filial daughter-in-law whose mother-in-law was old and could not chew meat. The daughter-in-law chopped the beef and added a bit of salt to make beef balls, which she cooked into soup to make them edible. It is said that, in inventing beef balls, this filial daughter-in-law created a perfect dish for old people and children.[84]

This example perfectly embodies the ideal cycle of yang, or mutual nourishment, as a definition of family—for the snack can fulfill obligations to both the very young and the very old. That this treat is said to have been invented by a loyal daughter-in-law is even more telling. As we have seen, the daughter-in-law is precisely the individual traditionally given the task of taking care of both the very young and the old; her "failure" to live up to these traditional expectations can be a source of tension in contemporary rural families.

Bright Ling's very social marginality made it possible for her to practice vegetarianism, but, at the same time, her example helps to explain why this would be a difficult moral choice for most other villagers in Moonshadow Pond, where food still plays such an important role in structuring everyday family relationships and moral obligations. In villagers' eyes, providing good nutrition for family members, especially one's elders, entails providing them with meat. (Our focus here, of course, is on the moral aspects of the choice to be a vegetarian. But vegetarianism is also a difficult choice in Moonshadow Pond from the standpoint of sociality, because of the importance of serving meat in banquet settings, a subject we will explore in more detail in the next chapter.)

FOOD AND MORAL ECONOMY

In this chapter, we have examined the moral significance of food in Moonshadow Pond: its centrality in fulfilling moral obligations, and its use as a trope in discourse about morality. Finally, we explored ideas about whether certain foods might somehow embody higher moral values than others.

How do these issues connect to debates about "moral economy" versus "political economy"? In his famous essay on eighteenth-century food rioters in England, E. P. Thompson pointed out that several centuries passed before the logic of the political economy of the free market was able to break down an earlier logic characterized by what Thompson called the "moral economy of provision."[85] The moral economy that Thompson wrote about was marked by substantive obligations and reciprocities within an admittedly paternalistic and hierarchical set of relations. Nonetheless, it was sharply differentiated from an emerging "political economy," as articulated by thinkers such as Adam Smith, which was "disinvested of intrusive moral imperatives,"[86] and within which the laws of supply and demand were supposed to operate unimpeded by moral obligations. In theory, this free-market political economy would work intrinsically to create an outcome for the greater good.[87]

In his discussion of moral economy, Thompson focused on food riots, a not insignificant point. For food is certainly a most fundamental need, and it makes sense that, even when other items have worked their way into the commodity economy, it is in and through food that we might see the most resistance to the logic of pure political economy, as opposed to that of moral economy. For instance, the sharing of food within the immediate family is almost always done on the basis of the logic of a moral economy, even in the most capitalist of societies. It would be hard to find a society, in which the logic of provision based on moral obligation did not apply within the family—at least, at a minimum, to children! Even in the most highly rationalized and commoditized food systems, the exchange of food is never based solely on market principles; food still enacts some meanings that are embedded in particular times and places, minimally expressing the fulfillment of obligations to specific family members at certain points of the life cycle or the calendar year.

As we have seen in the specific case of contemporary Moonshadow Pond, a good deal of the food consumed within the family is not even acquired from the market but is self-provisioned. We have also come to understand that the sharing of food within families, and its exchange within wider circles of kin and community, enacts and communicates both social and moral obligations. As this chapter has also made clear, beyond its role in fulfilling obligations in everyday life, food as a symbol has great discursive power in judgments about the morality of individuals and regimes.

However, considering the issue of food as part of a moral economy in contemporary rural China involves a twist. While the moral economy and capitalist political economy may be seen as alternative domains here, one should not forget that the current system of smallholder agriculture (the responsibility system implemented after 1978) was itself a response to the failure of the collective, which was an earlier attempt at a moral economy. Although this collective system failed spectacularly in the late 1950s, and was reorganized into a less draconian and more workable model during the late 1960s and 70s, the current system has reintroduced the market and has gradually reduced (to zero at this point) the state's role in extracting food from villagers.

According to Chris Hann,[88] the transition from the collective era to the current market economy in China has, ironically, ushered in a new moral economy. Hann argues that it was actually the collective regime that obstructed villagers' attempts to fulfill basic moral obligations to kin, lineage mates, and ancestors. And he points out that it is the reform-era market economy that has enabled villagers in many areas to revive traditional rituals of reciprocity.[89]

Hann's observations are certainly relevant to the historical experiences of rural Chinese. As Ralph Thaxton has written, the Great Leap Forward and Maoism in its most extreme collectivist form were seen by peasants as "a threat to long-standing household entitlements."[90] And Stephen Feuchtwang quotes a villager in north China, who relevantly states, "'No matter the dynasty, we ordinary people are always the victims and have no one to rely on except our own relatives and close friends. . . . I lost my mind once and devoted myself completely to the collectives, but after the three difficult years [of the famine], no more!'" Commenting on this, Feuchtwang observes that this villager "had abandoned the moral discourse of self-sacrifice to the greater good led by the party in favour of an older moral discourse of mutual, interpersonal reciprocity."[91]

Like the villager quoted above, older Moonshadow Pond residents have lived through the famine of the Great Leap. They have also experienced the drastically different situation of the reform era—more ample food supplies but also the uncertainties of an unregulated market. Indeed, both of these historical contexts—collective and market—can help explain the impulse to maintain traditional modes of reciprocity and alternative moral economies. For such moral economies are an alternative to both state collectivist and purely market-based regimes.

Furthermore, while villagers' ideas about these past and present political and economic regimes certainly contain contradictions, food remains an important lens through which they assess how and whether basic obligations have been met—by the state, as well as by family members, kin, and community members.

In Moonshadow Pond, food therefore powerfully communicates and fulfills moral obligations, and is also a potent symbol that is used to judge morality in others. Further, villagers' stated preferences for their own food are articulated, not simply through an economic rationale, but also through an attention to concerns such as health, safety, reliability, and taste of food-stuffs. Such choices are also an implicit moral critique of the wider food system. While food is thus undoubtedly a commodity in contemporary rural China, its meanings are too rich to be contained only by its value as a commodity. As this chapter demonstrates, the moral significance of food resonates on many levels.

SIX

Conviviality

TWO SMALL BANQUETS WERE PARTICULARLY memorable for me. They were hardly the most sumptuous meals I ever attended in Meixian. Perhaps they proved unforgettable because of their qualities of fellowship. As we have already seen, excessive feasting—especially on the part of officials— can certainly provoke critique on moral grounds. But we should not overlook the role of communal eating in creating sociability, fellowship, and emotional ties. This chapter will focus on precisely these aspects of food consumption, beginning with an account of the two banquets I remember so well.

RENAO, "RED HOT SOCIALITY"

The first banquet occurred in spring 2007. During the weeks that follow the Lunar New Year, members of the lineage branches and sub-branches of Moonshadow Pond's founding ancestor visit the graves of their founders (the *guazhi* described in chapter 4). After laying out food offerings to their ancestors, burning spirit money, and setting off fireworks to scare away wandering spirits, branch members hold a banquet.

This particular banquet was in honor of Jinchenggong, who was a first-generation descendant of the founder of Moonshadow Pond's largest lineage branch. The descendants of Jinchenggong were therefore members of a lineage sub-branch, and they had all been members of the same production team during the collective era. (Production team membership was determined on the basis of physical propinquity in the village; as descendants of a sub-branch of a lineage, their old village homes were all clustered together.)

FIGURE 19. Creating *renao* before a lineage-branch banquet.

Jinchenggong's original house had once served as a memorial hall for their sub-branch, but it had fallen into great disrepair during the collective era. Furthermore, as it was located high on a hill, and because most residents of Moonshadow Pond built their new homes conveniently closer to the highway, its condition only deteriorated further during the reform era, when no one regularly keeping an eye on it. Before long the courtyard of the old house was being used by an old man to raise chickens.

However, as lineage branch members began to prosper, they started to think about refurbishing the branch hall. They raised money to fix the hall and the stairs ascending the hilltop where it was located. So on this day in 2007, not only were branch members honoring Jinchenggong, they were also celebrating the renovation of the hall. The renovation was still just minimal, and the building needed much work, but the central courtyard was now usable for holding a small banquet. As it was during the Lunar New Year's holiday, many young people who worked in the cities were home, and children were off from school. While a local couple prepared the food in the courtyard, lineage-branch members sat outside and banged on gongs, cymbals, and drums, making a general racket (see fig. 19). Children joined in, and my husband and I also took part. The atmosphere was free spirited and informal.

After exploding fireworks to ward off wandering ghosts, we sat down to a relatively simple (by rural Meixian standards) banquet. There were no rare and exotic dishes. Instead, the menu consisted of a number of standard Hakka country dishes: braised pork (*hongmen rou*), fried noodles, soup with beef and daikon radish, dog meat, stir-fried peapods and pig liver, fish ball soup, fried lettuce (*sheng cai*), and steamed chicken with ginger and red chilies (*jiangyou ji*). Drinks were a choice of cola or a strong local liquor.

Lineage-branch members raised money for the feast in advance, and contributions were posted on the wall. But the price per table was also low compared to the escalating costs that accompanied banquets for more formal occasions. Indeed, the cost was just one hundred yuan for a table of eight. To give a sense of how inexpensive this was, an elaborate wedding banquet at that time could come to several hundred yuan per table; and, as noted in the last chapter, villagers told tales of cadres who spent hundreds of yuan on just one rare dish.

What was important in this lineage-branch banquet was that the atmosphere was festive, very *renao*. *Renao* connotes a bustling and busy event. As Adam Chau points out, the word *renao* can be translated literally as "red hot sociality."[1] He states, "*Re* means hot, heat, heady, emotional, passionate, fervent, or feverish,"[2] and "*Nao* means to stir up and connotes a wide range of excitement: rambunctious, agitated, hustle, bustle, playful, busy, noisy, conflicted, exuberant, colorful, to express dissatisfaction, to vent, to plague, to turn upside down, to be naughty, to create a scene."[3]

Renao, therefore, is a desired element of all ritual and public events, as well as a coveted aspect of family life in rural China. Even for sad occasions, such as funerals, some phases of the ritual demand an atmosphere of *renao*. For instance, in Moonshadow Pond, gamblers come out the night before the funeral, gamble throughout the night in the main ancestral hall, and enjoy congee together at midnight. This *renao* counteracts the loneliness of death.[4] Speaking about *renao*, the anthropologist Hans Steinmüller describes it as "social heat," and he notes that it is a kind of "social effervescence" that is positive, as long "as it remains within certain boundaries."[5]

The boundaries between excessiveness and appropriateness are not always clear cut. Certainly, *renao* can also be part of the conspicuous consumption that villagers critique in cadres (see chapter 5). By the same token, *renao* is also an important part of ordinary sociality. As Steinmüller observes, "The production of 'social heat,' as, for instance, in banquets and family celebrations . . . is constitutive of living in a socially meaningful way."[6] Thus, elderly people will often speak about the importance of having descendants, not only because they need people to take care of them in this life and the afterlife, or only because of the importance of carrying on the lineage, although these are both critical, but also because having children in the house creates *renao*.

For these reasons, at this banquet in honor of Jinchenggong, the quality of *renao* surrounded the entire occasion and made for a most memorable event. This was so, even though it was certainly neither a sumptuous nor an expensive banquet.

NANDE: RARENESS

The second banquet that was memorable for me occurred in spring 2010. It exhibited another important quality for banquets, in addition to *renao*: rareness, or *nande*. *Nande* literally means "difficult to attain," and it pertains to a very special event that can seldom be realized.

In this particular case, I had returned to Moonshadow Pond for a few weeks in the spring of 2010. I was accompanied by Ruolan, my friend from Hong Kong, who was related to Songling and Baoli. Ruolan was returning to Moonshadow Pond with both her husband and her brother, who lived in Guangzhou. As they seldom had any opportunity to visit, we all gathered at a restaurant in town that is popular with many local people from the surrounding countryside. All together, we were about twenty people, including Songling and Baoli, their two daughters and sons-in-law, their son Yanhong, and their grandchildren—all of us were seated at two round tables.

As Ruolan arrived with her husband and brother, the atmosphere became joyous. There were smiles all over, and people began to exclaim at how rare this opportunity was.[7] For this occasion, we were allocated a separate room—not an unusual arrangement for restaurants like this, which cater to both large and small parties. The guests—Ruolan, her husband, her brother, and I—sat at one table with Yanhong and his father, Baoli. Yanhong also initiated the toasting, not because he was the oldest, he was not, but because he was the host that night. However, as this was a family event, with children running around the tables, and continual exclamations on the rareness of this special occasion, the toasting and drinking were celebratory but not prolonged to the point of inebriation

In this case, the food was certainly memorable as well! We enjoyed fourteen dishes, including many Hakka specialties, such as steamed dumplings made from daikon radish and pork (*luobo yuan*), deep-fried chashu mushrooms balls, braised pork, duck, fish heads, shrimp and celery, and rice noodles. However, it was the quality of the social, rather than the culinary rareness, that everyone continually noted. The banquet was the necessary medium through which the pleasures of this out-of-the-ordinary coming together could be enjoyed.

Both of these occasions, the gathering with Ruolan and her family and the lineage-branch celebration, show the pleasure in sociality—its rambunctious aspects, as well as the fact that such occasions should be savored while they happen because they are rare. Certainly banquets can also be about social obligation and connections, status display, official excess, and even corruption. But to think of social occasions for banqueting as entangled only with such matters misses the role of food in communal pleasure and as an instrument of emotion and caring.

Even in an ordinary interaction, food in Moonshadow Pond is the most common means through which people enjoy each other's company. For instance, if you are visiting someone, the easiest way for that person to delay your departure is to say simply, "Stay here and eat, don't leave yet!" People will indeed go to great lengths in using food to delay a departure. A typical example occurred when I stopped by Fengying's store while running some errands in town.

"You came just in time for my eggplant fritters!" Fengying came out excitedly with some on a plate. "Take some," she urged. Although I had errands to run, I could not turn her down, as she had already brought the treats out. After tasting them, I told her I had to go to the bank and run some more errands.

"Well, take some now, and then come back after your errands are completed and drink some tea," Fengying urged.

I dutifully undertook my chores and did return to Fengying's store. Tea was poured, and we talked and chatted. Finally, it was time to return home.

"Oh, do you want a sweet potato before you go?" Fengying asked, delaying my departure one more time.

Casual visitors are often urged to stay back for a meal, although politeness requires that, unless the circumstances are unusual, this gesture be refused, certainly at the first offer. Indeed, good manners dictate that one should avoid dropping by someone's house before lunch or dinnertime; lingering too close to mealtimes should also be avoided. Otherwise, hosts will feel compelled to invite their visitors to share a meal.[8] This may be awkward for both sides. Hosts may think they are not prepared, and feel embarrassed by the food on offer, and guests will not want to look like they were intentionally trying to take advantage.

As the examples above illustrate, food can be used to stretch out even the most ordinary communal occasions; it is not reserved only for banquets and celebrations that are both rare and hot and noisy. Below we will further examine the connections between food and forms of sociality in Moonshadow Pond. But first we need to take a step back and consider somewhat more abstractly this relationship between eating and sociality.

CONVIVIALITY AND COMMENSALITY

In social science writing, and even in popular discourse, the word *society* most often refers to social organization: "institutions and relationships within which a relatively large group of people live [*sic*]."[9] In this sense, according to Joanna Overing and Alan Passes, the term *society* often conveys something structural that not only shapes possibilities but also sets limits to human action; or, in the worst-case scenario, it is a kind of unyielding edifice,[10] as in Durkheim's notion of a "social fact."[11] However, Overing and Passes remind us that, until the eighteenth century, the word *society* did not always convey these meanings. Rather, it once referred to "sociability, companionship, fellowship, or a mode of living"[12] Because society now implies social structure, Overing and Passes suggest, the terms *sociality* or *conviviality* are currently used to refer to ideas previously connoted by the word *society*.[13]

Cross-culturally, commensality has always played a critical role in promoting just such conviviality and sociality. Discussing the general attributes of commensality, Warren Belasco comments that "Sharing food has almost magical properties in its ability to turn self-seeking individuals into a collaborative group."[14] This is so in part because sharing food establishes a "common substance among those who commune together."[15]

As Maurice Bloch observes, families, themselves, "may be understood as being continually unified not only by biology but also by being commensal units."[16] And as we have seen in Moonshadow Pond, families are defined very much in this way—as people who share a stove and eat together, even if their commensality must sometimes be delayed until a holiday when physical reunion is possible. Thus, it makes sense that, even when sharing food with a guest, and regardless of whether it is a planned banquet or a spontaneous event, hosts use the metaphor of "family" to frame the situation. For instance, in trying to make me feel at home, and urging me not to be shy about eating, hosts often said to me that I was just like family (*gen ziji jia yiyang*).[17]

The sociality inherent in food consumption in Moonshadow Pond can emphasize either hierarchical or more egalitarian social relationships, depending on the context. For example, eating from one big pot (*chi da guo fan*) can occur when a large group shares food in an informal situation.[18] During the spring of 2007, my husband and I took a day trip with the Moonshadow Pond Council of Elders (*laorenhui*), to make offerings at the grave and memorial hall of a distant ancestor of Moonshadow Pond's own founder. This memorial hall was a few hours away from Moonshadow Pond, and there were about eighty of us on the trip. When we arrived at our destination, several of the women prepared a huge pot of rice; they then added fried pork, mushrooms, dried squid, and scallions to the pot, and mixed these ingredients with the rice to flavor it (see fig. 20). When the morning's ceremonies were over, they filled our bowls with this savory rice dish, and then to complete the meal, refilled our bowls with a simple soup made from salted, preserved vegetables and pork bones.

Such a meal emphasizes the equality of all participants. In that sense it is similar to the celebration of Jinchenggong's descendants (even though that banquet was certainly more elaborate than a simple shared pot of savory rice). Such gatherings cannot be described as "balanced gift exchange,"[19] for which the dynamics of status competition prompt each side to try to outdo the other. Rather, they are closer to what David Graeber calls the "timeless commitment" of more "open-ended communistic reciprocity."[20] Indeed, such shared meals did not really have a "host," as the participants essentially organized the meal for themselves.

However, in most other banqueting or special meal contexts, even in a fairly informal family gathering such as the reunion with Ruolan's relatives, there is usually a distinct divide between host and guest. The host is, of course, clearly responsible for the quality of the food on offer, and urges guests to eat. Any number of other conventions may indicate the relationship of the host to the guests, as well as the relative status of different guests. Much literature on Chinese banqueting emphasizes its role in expressing and reconfirming social hierarchy. As Roel Sterckx comments, "A meticulously stage-managed Chinese banquet today still echoes some of the precepts and rules

FIGURE 20. Making "one big pot."

of etiquette set out in ritual codes traceable to early imperial China."[21] And in describing banquets in contemporary rural North China, Andrew Kipnis elaborates at length on rules of seating that express not only express status difference between hosts and guests but also the relative closeness and importance of various guests in terms of their relationship to the host.[22]

Nonetheless, in Meixian, even though there is a hierarchical division between host and guest, linguistic protocols may also politely downplay this hierarchy. In Moonshadow Pond (and Meixian in general), the host of a dinner will often demur that "there is no food here" (*meiyou cai*). In literal terms, this expression means, "there are no *cai*" (dishes). As noted earlier, *cai* refers to the dishes, or trimmings of a meal, and *fan* refers to rice, the staple. The host will say this, however, even when the dishes are quite plentiful. It is way of apologizing for the ostensibly poor quality and small quantity of the food on offer, a polite expression that Charles Stafford calls, a "characteristic show of modesty."[23]

At the same time, while hosts may overtly express embarassment at the poor quality and small quantity of their food, they will also try simultaneously to find means to convey that the actual quality of their ingredients is high—drawing attention to the chemical-free vegetables from their ancestral villages, for instance, or to the rare and healthy medicine grasses in the soup. For instance, when I visited my colleague at a local university, he had not anticipated that the private dining room for faculty guests would be closed because of a school vacation. So we ended up at his home, where his wife asserted that she had nothing to serve me. Nonetheless, she managed to come up with a number of special items from her native village, and also make a soup with a rare ingredient: a dried medicinal powder made from a fungus with mist like spores (*lingzhi baozi fen*).[24] Thus, while reiterating that there were no dishes, my host's wife was able to ensure that I would not lose sight of the fact that I had eaten something rare. In this way, hosts can "have their cake and eat it too"; they can reiterate that their food is inadequate, while also indicating that they are not such bad hosts after all, having offered their guests something very special.

In all cases, whether a meal involves one big pot or is much more elaborate, and whether the symbolism emphasizes equality or hierarchy, feasting in Moonshadow Pond creates a platform for conviviality, enhancing social relationships and creating conditions for the desired red hot sociality.

REUNION

We described one reunion meal at the beginning of this chapter, and we saw how reunion meals celebrate the concept of *nande,* or the rareness of an opportunity to bring a group of people together. Indeed, reunion without commensality is hard to imagine in the Chinese context. Charles Stafford observes, "Commensality *is* reunion."[25] The emotion of family reunion is impossible to imagine without food. In a study of Chinese students returning home from study abroad, Anna Kajunus observes, the "proper avenue for the expression of familial emotion was the sharing of food."[26]

Chapter 3 described the importance of the reunion meal on Lunar New Year's Eve from the standpoint of memory revival and connections to tradition. The Lunar New Year is filled with other reunion meals as well, and integrally related to their memory function is their role in sustaining emotional connection. One of the most important reunion meals during this period is a married daughter's return to her natal family on the second day of the New Year.[27] Even daughters who frequently interact with their natal families (such as Songling's daughters Fengying and Meiying) will honor this tradition. And, of course, there are those who return from more distant cities, in which case the return to the natal family is indeed a "rare" occasion.

In 2007, I participated in one such celebration at the house of Song Hongwei, a young unmarried man from Moonshadow Pond, who was himself returning home for the New Year's holiday from his job in Shanghai. His mother was the third of seven daughters (all clearly born before China's birth-limitation policy was in effect). Since there were no sons in the family, she remained in her natal family after marriage, and her husband married "in." This is a less-than-high–status arrangement in patrilineally oriented rural China, but, nonetheless, it is necessary to continue the family line in cases in which there are no sons. Because his mother remained with her natal family after marriage, she was responsible for hosting the return visit meal for her other married sisters and their families. In addition, her own children, Hongwei and his younger sister, were also returning from work in distant cities.

After I arrived at the gathering, I chatted before the meal with the other guests (the returning sisters and their families). We sat in the living room drinking tea, eating sweet and savory New Year's snacks, as well as seeds and nuts. Hongwei and his father also sat with us and served tea. Meanwhile, Hongwei's mother, grandmother, and an unmarried sister and aunt finished preparations for the meal of twelve dishes. When we all sat down, the men drank and toasted with hard liquor, while the women drank soda or hot glutinous rice wine.

Unlike the Zuofu celebrations described earlier, where friends, affines, and matrilateral relations are key, this occasion was essentially a family affair, truly focused on intimacy rather than being a demonstration of contacts and connections with the outside world. The family reunion of married daughters with their natal family is not, therefore, accompanied by the gift giving noted in the Zuofu banquets. Although the dishes were much more numerous than on an ordinary day, they were not exotic or expensive. The basis for most was the ingredients that were cultivated, raised, or produced by Hongwei's mother and father. These included the glutinous rice wine, vegetables, duck, chicken, and even the pomelos and New Year's treats that we consumed after the meal.

When married daughters and their families return to their natal homes for the Lunar New Year, the theme of family reunion can also be emphasized by sharing a meal of hotpot. With hotpot, a simmering pot of boiling water is placed in the middle of the table, and the diners choose various fresh food items arrayed around it. They then dip these items into the shared pot to cook. Such sharing of food boiled within one pot is associated with the intimacy of the family in many cultures. For instance, Claude Lévi-Strauss calls boiled food an "'endo-cuisine,' prepared for domestic use, destined to a small closed group"; contrastingly, he calls roasted food an "'exo-cuisine,' that which one offers to guests." As an example, he cites France, where "boiled chicken was for the family meal, while roasted meat was for the banquet."[28] Lévi-Strauss also points out that, whereas "boiling conserves entirely the meat and its juices . . . roasting is accompanied by destruction and loss," and while boiling connotes "economy," roasting is associated with "prodigality."[29]

For instance, during the same Lunar New Year discussed above, Songling's family enjoyed a hotpot, when her daughters Fengying and Meiying returned. In some ways, hotpot is the perfect endo-cuisine, as it involves consuming food from a shared pot. However the concept of "endo-cuisine," as discussed by Lévi-Strauss, implies not only intimacy but also frugality. In the Chinese context, by comparison, hotpot is generally associated with festive occasions, and the ingredients are always more various than at a normal meal. (On that night, for instance, we consumed shrimps, squid, seafood rolls, bean thread noodles, bean curd, fish pieces, beef, pork balls, mushrooms, and greens, just to name a few; this was hardly a typical day's fare.) The hotpot meal can also last for a long time, as the host continuously brings new items to the table to cook until the guests are quite full.

Indeed, reunion meals, whether hotpot or other fare, are differentiated by the quantity and quality of the food and their duration. The end of the gathering can be put off further as family members may play mahjong with each other and later cut up fruit or bring out other snacks to share. For example, as mentioned earlier, the Mid-Autumn Festival is now a national holiday and like the Lunar New Year it is an important time for family reunions. When I traveled with Teacher Li and her husband to her natal home over the holiday in 2012, we shared a hotpot dinner. There were ten of us, including Teacher Li's three siblings and their spouses, Teacher Li's son, and her elder brother's two sons. As is usual at such reunions, the time was stretched out by predinner tea and snacks, followed by a long dinner of hotpot and hours of talking and playing mahjong. When the mahjong playing finally petered out, one of Teacher Li's sisters brought out a large durian fruit, which was cut up and shared by all. By this point, it was already past midnight, and we finally all went to sleep.

Games, particularly mahjong, play an important role in stretching out a meal, and lengthening the time spent socializing. Gambling in rural China can certainly rise to the level of a problem—and when it does it is considered antisocial and wasteful behavior. But playing mahjong is also an important form of sociality and a common activity at formal banquets, as well as at family reunion gatherings. As Hans Steinmüller explains in regard to gambling in rural Hubei Province,

> [There are] two words that are most commonly used for "gambling": *wan* and *du*. The first is more entertainment and play, whereas the second clearly denotes the involvement of money and betting. . . . This *wan* side of gambling is also extremely important for the celebration of kinship, of friendship, even of relatedness in general. To "play" (*wan*) together is the best way to cement a relationship. *Wan* can involve gambling, but also many other social activities, such as playing games of any kind, eating, making an excursion, chatting, joking, and so on. The social exchanges in these activities ideally should be lively, hot, and noisy.[30]

Just as with "social heat" itself, gambling (and drinking!), as long as they remain within certain limits, can add to the sociality that the sharing of food enabled in the first place.

Indeed, as Steinmüller points out, mahjong equipment and food are often considered equally important elements of good hosting.[31] As mentioned earlier, in Moonshadow Pond, the rooms to which hosts invite guests at local restaurants contain not only tea tables for people to gather around and enjoy tea and snacks before and after each meal but also mahjong tables and tiles. Mahjong can continue long after the end of a meal in these cases; it is also part and parcel of the aftermath of larger banquets that accompany weddings, house moving, birthdays, and other celebratory events.

The category of *wan* that accompanies festive meals and banquets, however, is not restricted to gambling games. *Wan xinniang*, or "playing jokes on the bride" is a tradition that occurs during Hakka wedding banquets as the bride and groom go from table to table to toast the guests. It also occurs before and after the banquet as bride and groom serve tea to the guests. According to Hakka custom, one's wedding day is one's youngest day (*zui xiao de yi tian*). Everyone, even one's equals, must be addressed by the bride and groom as if they were at least a generation older. A friend who is older, for instance, might be addressed as "father's older brother," while a friend who is younger might be addressed as "mother's younger sister" or "father's younger brother."

On the wedding morning, the groom escorts the bride from her family home to his family home. Guests soon begin to arrive at the groom's house, and the bride and groom must serve them tea. As they do so, they may receive gifts of jewelry or money (in red envelopes) from various family members. This is called "four-hands tea" (*si shou cha*). However, while the atmosphere is initially rather respectful because the first persons to be served tea are usually family elders, four-hands tea takes a much more playful turn after the wedding banquet—which takes place at midday in Moonshadow Pond. At that time, many of the guests being served are the bride and groom's contemporaries, and these guests can joke and make fun of the bride and groom. Because the wedding is at the groom's house, only a few of the bride's friends and relations are present (although there is a banquet at her house a few days before the wedding). For this reason most of the friends who engage in this banter are male friends of the groom, although not exclusively so.

A typical exchange during the four-hands tea occurred during the wedding of Fengying's brother-in-law, which was captured on videotape:[32]

GROOM: What should I call you?

FRIEND 1: I don't know either.

GROOM: How about uncle, right?

FRIEND 1: It's up to you!

BRIDE: Uncle, please take the tea.

FRIEND 2: It's not simultaneous enough, you [both] have to say this again.

BRIDE AND GROOM: One, two, three, Uncle! Please drink some tea.

FRIEND 1: *laughs and then drinks the tea.*

GROOM: *turns to the third friend.* Boss, please take the tea.

FRIEND 3: *does not take the tea from the bride and groom.* You should both stand still and you need to stand closer to each other. (*Looks at the groom.*) Now you have to put your arms around the bride. (*Tells them to lock their feet together.*) You have to put your arms around the bride tighter! (*Turns to the bride.*) You need to put your arm around the groom. You two should be romantic today; it's your marriage day! (*Speaks to both of them.*) You two should stand with good posture. Otherwise I won't drink the tea! (*And then, finally.*) Your feet are not in the right position, and I only see three hands, not four hands, serving the tea.

BRIDE AND GROOM: *again,* Uncle, please drink the tea.

FRIEND 3: Still not ok. Do it again.

GROOM: What am I supposed to say so that you will drink the tea? I know I am not doing a good job, you should forgive me!

(Another friend comes over, friend 4.)

FRIEND 4: Put your hands behind your waists.

GROOM: *does according to his demand,* Is it OK now? Now, you should drink the four-hand-tea! Please forgive [my rudeness], please drink it.

FRIEND 3: No, it's not an issue about forgiving, don't use the word *forgive.*

BRIDE AND GROOM: *finally put the tea in front of friend 3, who then lifts up the teacup, and drinks the tea.*

Similar kinds of banter and games can take place as the bride and groom go from table to table during the actual wedding banquet to toast the guests. As they move to each table, the groom is able to introduce the bride to his relatives, friends, and associates. But the joking that accompanies this toasting varies depending on the identities of the guests. If the guests at the table are their elders or relatives, then the toast may be simple. The bride and groom may propose a toast to the guests and the guests may wish them a happy marriage, or reply with an old (and patriarchal!) proverb such as "May you have a distinguished son early" (*zaosheng guizi*). But if the guests at a particular table are the newlyweds' peers, then more joking is allowed. For instance, since the bride and groom must toast the guests at each table, they may actually not be drinking real liquor; hence one common joke is to tease them about whether their liquor is real or fake. Friends will also challenge the bride and groom to engage in stunts, such as simultaneously eating a pea or small piece of meat that is dangling on a string.

That these games revolve around two important beverages—tea and alcohol—that enhance sociality in rural China is not surprising. Below, we look in more detail at the role of various foods and drinks in terms of their roles in enhancing sociality.

SUBSTANCE AND SOCIABILITY

As Maurice Bloch observes, "Particular groups of people may view some foods as better social conductors than others: in France, for example, the eating of soup together implies a greater degree of togetherness than eating popcorn."[33] Bloch calls such food substances "social conductors,"[34] but he also goes on to observe that different foods sustain different kinds of relationships. As he continues in his observation about soup versus popcorn in France, "The sharing of soup here is . . . a sign of strong familial *organic* solidarity among people who are joined by their dissimilarity, whereas the sharing of popcorn is, to a certain extent, a sign of an egalitarian *mechanical* solidarity of a different sort. In this case, therefore, we find two co-occurring but different registers within which social conductivity is evaluated."[35]

As we have seen in Moonshadow Pond, and much of rural southeastern China, rice is a key social conductor when it comes to the family—"sharing the rice pot" is a quintessential ingredient of family solidarity. Meat, tea, and alcohol, although in different ways, *are* important social conductors when it comes to relations outside the family.

Tea

Of the two beverages mentioned above—tea and alcohol—tea is the more versatile because it works as a social conductor within a greater variety of situations than liquor and wine do. But in every case, the format for drinking tea inevitably involves sociality. No matter whether the occasion is informal or formal, ordinary or celebratory, tea marks a great variety of social encounters. In a given day, I could be served tea when visiting a friend's store, visiting a colleague's office at the local university, or just sitting in the front room of Songling and Baoli's house while neighbors dropped in. Tea also follows most daily meals, and is served before and after meals when special guests come to visit, at which times it is also accompanied by small treats. As mentioned in chapter 1, the essential element of a home's public space is a place to serve tea, usually a set of chairs and a sofa arranged around a low table, on which the host steeps the tea in a teapot before pouring it into small cups for guests.

Drinking tea in Moonshadow Pond can therefore never be a solitary act—as in taking a cup of tea up to one's study. Tea drinking means that someone is responsible for steeping and serving the tea for others. Even at the wedding banquet described above, four-hands tea simply doubled this ordinary equation—with both bride and groom serving tea to the guests. On this occasion, the number of guests did not allow the couple to actually prepare the tea, but they still made the rounds of their guests to serve tea from a tray filled with tiny cups.

Like many foods, of course, tea can also be about status—the perceived status of the guest may determine the grade of tea that the host decides to serve, and a host can also, correspondingly, increase his or her own status by serving a higher grade of tea. But beyond such status competitions, tea is also a key substance in promoting sociability. Tea breaks down the initial awkwardness of a visit, and can extend the visit's duration as the host steeps tea and continues to pour small cups for guests. Tea also provides a venue for winding down after an ordinary dinner or sumptuous banquet. But, again, it is always taken communally. In short, it is a key medium of sociality in a diverse array of social encounters.

Spirits

As a medium of sociality, tea's contexts of uses are very broad, whereas alcohol's are more specialized. Like tea, its consumption is immensely social. In distinction to tea, alcohol accompanies meals, usually banquets or holiday feasts, whereas tea is consumed outside of mealtimes.[36] Indeed, in Hakka society, a banquet without alcohol would be seen as insufficient, and, as noted earlier, alcohol marks a banquet as distinct from an ordinary meal. Furthermore, when drinking at a banquet, one must properly toast another person before imbibing one's own drink, and the person or persons who are toasted must accept the toast and drink up (although this convention is beginning to change as will be explained below).

In toasting, there is also a set order. Usually, the host of the banquet will begin by toasting an honored guest or guests. Then, if there are many tables involved, the host will proceed from table to table and toast each one (as a whole) to get things started. To not toast all one's guests would be seen as a sign of disrespect.[37] As explained above, if it is a wedding, the bride and groom must also go from table to table and toast all guests in similar fashion. In toasting, saying "good words" (*hao hua*) is important. They can be general as in "To your health" or "Happy New Year," or more specific, as in the wedding toasts discussed earlier. As a banquet proceeds, however, this set order of toasting begins to break down, and people at each table can and do begin toasting each other. Those who want to drink up must continually find partners to toast because drinking cannot proceed individually.

The need to find a toasting partner, and the set format of toasting, does not mean that drinking at banquets cannot become rambunctious, or that drinking is merely restrained and formal. As a social conductor the world over, alcohol certainly has few rivals in its ability to break down social boundaries, and in Chinese banqueting it certainly plays such a role, enabling more freewheeling expressions of feelings or emotions (*ganqing*) than would occur without it. As Andrew Kipnis observed in a rural northern China context, drinking at banquets is used "to break down excessively formal postures. . . . Toasting materialized respect, while drinking deconstructed the boundaries that distinguished guests from hosts, thus allowing *ganqing* to flow. The local saying, 'exchange feeling by toasting,' (*jingjiu jiao qing*) sums up this side of drinking."[38] Thus drinking creates informality, which can soften future relationships.[39]

Alcohol consumption at banquets is also heavily gendered. Women do not have to refrain completely from drinking and toasting, but they do not engage in competitive bouts of toasting and drinking as men do. As mentioned previously, women can use many alcohol substitutes, such as carbonated drinks, sweet-cooked glutinous rice wine, or other sweet drinks, including soybean milk.

Focusing on alcohol consumption as part of banqueting in Chinese *urban* contexts among professional men and women, Katherine Mason describes the role of toasting and drinking as a way to break down social barriers, and details the difficulties that professional women have in negotiating the territory of alcohol. As Mason states, "My male informants would frequently taunt a colleague whom [*sic*] they thought to be not drinking enough by shouting, 'Aren't you a man?' (*ni bu shi nanren ma?*) This was an effective means of coercing him to drink more."[40] As a form of male bonding, male drinking, therefore, presents conundrums for professional women, who do not wish to drink to the point of inebriation. They may, therefore, subvert the process by filling their toasting glasses with tea or soda or by abstaining from drinking altogether. Mason also notes that some women respond by simply trying to equal men in prodigious alcohol consumption.[41] Lately, however, as women in urban China have begun to assume more government posts, some have tried to redefine this excessive drinking as immoral because it interferes with family life and is unhealthy.[42]

In a rural context such as Moonshadow Pond, however, alcohol consumption is not about creating new relationships and professional connections. Rather, it cements already-existing relationships, more often those of kin and friends rather than of coworkers and colleagues. While consuming alcohol is still heavily gendered, women do not face a conflict (in deciding whether to drink) between creating bonds with their colleagues or declining to drink. Instead, local gender norms frame most drinking behavior in Moonshadow Pond. Toasting behavior, especially competitive and exuberant toasting, is still a primarily male activity, and women commonly consume alcohol substitutes.

Like gambling, there is a moving boundary between what constitutes the playful side of alcohol consumption and what crosses over into antisocial behavior. This line is not clear cut and it often depends on context. However, just as at a certain point the *wan* or play of mahjong crosses over into the *du* of gambling, so too can drinking and toasting move beyond an acceptable point. When and how this occurs depend on the audience and the context as much as the drinker's state of inebriation.

For instance, in 1996, my parents came to visit me in Moonshadow Pond. As they were the only foreigners besides me to have ever visited the village, it was a very special event. We hosted a banquet for about sixty people, to thank villagers who had helped me in my fieldwork. At that time, villagers' access to foreign liquor and wine was not great, so my parents purchased some high-quality scotch and rye in Hong Kong and brought it with them to the village. To further the feeling of uniqueness on that day, we invited an American anthropologist of China (Myron Cohen) and his wife, who happened to be visiting Meixian at the same time.

The event was very festive, and toasts were traded back and forth—to our health, to American and Chinese friendship, and even to R. H. Macy (that one from my father!). By the end of the banquet, the older men in particular were obviously thoroughly inebriated. They said they were especially "happy" (*gaoxing*) with the scotch and rye because at that time these items were still considered very rare. In this context, their drinking and toasting all added to the "happy" aspect of the occasion, and many people talked about their "happiness" for days afterward.

However, in yet another case, the boundary between happiness and unacceptable inebriation was a bit more blurred. In 2012, after the Zuofu banquet, our neighbor Weiguo, who had arranged for the neighborhood caterers, stopped by Songling and Baoli's house. He started grumbling about his younger brother, and rehashed a dispute between them from earlier in the day. (The younger brother had complained that the caterers had set up their stoves and cooking equipment in his garage without permission.) By the time Weiguo came over to the house, he was clearly drunk from the banqueting of the day, and he would not stop griping about his brother. Although the others listened and indulged him for a while, Baoli finally tried to quiet him and send him home. Afterward, people dismissed most of what he said as being a result of his drunkenness.

During the course of a banquet, there is also a limit on how many times a guest needs to accept a toast and invitation to drink up. "In the old days," one middle-aged man told me, "if someone toasted you who was a generation above you, you had to drink." But now, he said, "You can decide not to drink and it would not always be considered disrespectful." Interestingly, when he told me this, he was referring specifically to Weiguo, who was often exuberant at banquets, and who would toast endlessly. His behavior could easily create a quandary for someone of a younger generation, who wanted to refuse his toasts but also did not wish to appear disrespectful.

Even so, while people might recognize Weiguo as more than a high-spirited drinker at banquets, his drinking would not be regarded as an indication of either a drinking problem or immorality. Men who are perceived as drunkards or gamblers or both are viewed as unmarriageable, and alcohol abusers are referred to as "drunken ghosts" (*zuigui*). But these are people whose drinking does not take place within an ordered and communal banquet format, whereas Weiguo's drinking occurred within the social context of banqueting and toasting, venues where heavy drinking is not only acceptable but is sometimes viewed as necessary for sociability, especially for men. Heavy drinking at banquets is condemned morally when it involves public officials, but that condemnation is more about the waste of the public's resources than about the drinking itself.

Interestingly, the difficulties of finding the right balance between sociability and excessive drunkenness go back to ancient times in China. Even in the Confucian *Analects,* men are given the rather demanding (if not impossible) task of learning how to drink "without limit" and yet not to the point of "becoming disorderly."[43]

Meat

Earlier chapters noted that increased consumption of meat is one of the ways Moonshadow Pond villagers have marked their increased prosperity over the years. Chapter 4 described how the elements of a banquet, in particular the rareness and cost of different dishes, are important ways to distinguish oneself and to maintain or improve on one's status. Meat is also integral to a host's presentation of self as a generous person and is therefore a substance that also enhances sociability.

To be a good host, one has to serve things that are more valuable than ordinary fare, and despite great changes in living standards, meat still embodies value. In part, this is because ordinary meals are still structured by the *fan/cai* distinction, with meat as it occurs in such meals, being only a complement to a grain staple. This is not the case for either banquets or meals served for guests, where the various dishes are complemented by liquor rather than rice. As the author Wang Zengneng has observed regarding Hakka banqueting, "For contented guests there must be plentiful alcohol, and meat cannot be insufficient."[44] His remarks were echoed by local informants. As noted in chapter 4, during the old society, most people had meat only three times a year, and these were the three times that the three sacrificial meats were offered to the gods and ancestors—the Lunar New Year, Zuofu celebrations, and the Qingming Festival. In fact, according to Baoli, what distinguished "landlords" in many villagers' minds was, not their landholdings, but the fact that they consumed meat more often—about three times a month instead of three times a year!

It should not be surprising, therefore, that meat in a contemporary banquet is not simply an index of status. As a material expression of a host's generosity it is an essential conductor for sociality, crucial for ensuring that an occasion is both *renao* and *nande*.

"MAGICAL" FOOD

Everyone who has experienced banqueting, or even the simple sharing of food in a Chinese context, can remember some incident, in which he or she felt completely unable to eat more but was still enthusiastically urged to continue eating. On innumerable occasions, an exuberant host has urged me on, placing more food into my bowl, exclaiming how fresh or rare a particular dish was, and warning me not to miss the opportunity to try it.

One night in Hong Kong, in September 2012, when I was about to travel to Meixian, I met Ruolan for goat curry. She took particular delight in sharing this with me, precisely because I would not find it in Meixian. "They don't have anything like this in Meixian!" Ruolan exclaimed, while dumping a second goat chop on my plate, next plying me with fish curry over noodles. These followed a cold dessert made with sweet red beans, and finally green tea ice cream. It was delicious, but I was full and felt that I could eat nothing more. Ruolan countered my protestations, telling me that I would not get these dishes in Meixian (the host's insistence on the rarity of an opportunity to eat a particular food makes it even harder for a guest to refuse). When

I again protested that I was really satiated, Ruolan acknowledged this might be so. But, she added, "I feel so happy when you eat!"

Charles Stafford recounts a parallel incident that occurred during his fieldwork in North China, when he visited a family in the countryside. "As the conversation went on, I was pushed to eat and drink more but kept saying I was full. The grandmother said, 'We feel so happy when you eat!' (*ni chi an men jiu le*).[45] And, writing about Hakka culinary culture in particular, Wang Zengneng states, "The more the guests eat, the happier the host is. If the guests don't even taste one bit, then the host will lose psychological equilibrium."[46]

But what about the happiness of the guest? How happy can he or she be if forced to eat? For a long time, because I was more often the guest than the host, and often the recipient of repeated urgings to eat more, I pondered this. Was I the mere instrument of my hosts' satisfactions? Thinking of these incidents in such terms, one might certainly conclude that the function of the guest is simply to make the host happy. However, if one thinks of food as a medium of sociality and as a social conductor, then one can begin to see that eating together is exactly what overcomes the boundary between host and guest; the point is not the misery of the overstuffed guest and the cheerful gloating of the host but rather that the joy of the host will be felt in parallel by the guest.

How is this so? First, remember that the host often tells the guest that they should feel as if they were in the same family (*gen ziji jia yiyang*) and should not feel reticent. The assumption, of course, is that shyness, and not wanting to look greedy, might prevent the guest from eating as much as she wants. Some urging is necessary to overcome these inhibitions to enjoying the meal together. Also, remember that the most precious gatherings are those that are rare or difficult to achieve. In banqueting, the play of toasting also helps overcome inhibitions and barriers among guests. And we have also seen a selection of different food substances functioning as social conductors, from rice, which brings the family together, to tea, alcohol, and meat, which link people outside of the family.

As food and drink in Moonshadow Pond are the conduits for human connections, they are also culturally shaped vehicles for shared states of human feelings, or what Melissa Caldwell, using Milan Kundera's framework, refers to as "co-feeling."[47] Eating together expresses, but also creates, connections, and it does so in part by evocation. That is, through sharing food and drink, one not only expresses what is but also evokes hope of a more ideal state through analogy.

In understanding this, I have found the work of anthropologist Stanley Tambiah very useful. Tambiah proposes two alternate "orderings of reality": one based on "participation" and the other on "causality." As he explains, "The discourse of participation can be framed in terms of sympathetic immediacy, performative speech acts, and ritual action. If participation emphasizes sensory and affective communication and the language of emotions, causality stresses the rationality of instrumental action and the language of cognition."[48]

For a moment, let's backtrack and see where we have come so far. In previous chapters, we have seen how food in Moonshadow Pond is a central focus around which labor is organized and divided. It is also understood as medicinal and health bolstering. It ties into a variety of systems of exchange and conveys a multitude of interrelated meanings, since it embodies historical memory and moral meanings. But in this chapter, we have focused on the affective side of food, its role in sociality and fellowship, and in breaking down boundaries between people and creating co-feeling. These experiences certainly partake of the participatory ordering of reality that Tambiah refers to.

Of course, any one food event can partake of both participatory and causative frameworks. To take banqueting as the most elaborate example, we have seen that banquets are hosted for all kinds of reasons, from celebrating life-cycle rituals such as birthdays and marriages, to marking yearly holidays, to thanking mourners after a burial. Each of these banquets can also provide a template to index one's social status and to create a new set of obligations and debts on the part of those who attend. Certainly, such motives cannot be understood outside of a cause-and-effect framework. But, by the same token, the banquet is able to achieve these cause-and-effect goals in part because of its affective dimension—people experiencing co-feeling, greater intimacy, and a general sense of fellowship. As Tambiah explains, in actual social life, actors "make shifts into and out of . . . [these] different orderings of reality."[49] Therefore, by using his framework, one can see that food partakes of both "technico-causal and expressive-performative features."[50]

As a substance used to reaffirm and create social ties, however, food is particularly evocative. Looking at banqueting as a form of ritual can help us further understand this phenomenon. Banqueting in Moonshadow Pond embodies many elements of ritual, as it is ordered and uses multiple media: for instance, fireworks blasting before the start of the banquet, a specific ordering of dishes, symbolic connotations to some of the elements of the dishes, and a concern with the dishes' aesthetic appeal.[51] Toasting behavior is also highly structured, as word and physical actions are joined in one expressive act.

At the same time, while food in banqueting becomes a template for the expression of emotions, it is also a way around communicating these emotions directly. Rather, emotions are invested in, and signified through, the shared meal. Here Tambiah's analysis of ritual is quite apt. One can understand ritual, Tambiah points out, not as a " 'free expression of emotions' but a disciplined rehearsal of 'right attitudes.' "[52] As in the case of ritual, the emotions expressed during banqueting are not always direct and sincere but are sometimes formulaic. We might think here of the context of toasting, or of the hosts' protestations that they "don't have any dishes," or even of the host's insistence that the guests eat more. Such gestures may be invested with emotion, or may be simply polite.

Roy Rappaport's analysis of the meaning of signs in ritual is quite apt here. First, as he points out, unlike ordinary speech, ritual does not merely indicate a past condition, it signifies something that is in the process of coming to be: "In the casual usage of everyday, we usually, and rather carelessly, take signs, indexical or otherwise, to report, describe, represent, denote, designate, reflect or otherwise signify states of affairs existing independent of, and usually previous to, our references to them. In the case of the ritual acts and utterances with which we are concerned, the sign brings the state of affairs into being and—here is the sleight-of-ritual—having brought it into being cannot help but indicate it."[53] So, too, we can think of sharing food at a banquet, as well as on less extravagant occasions, as both a sign of a social relationship and a way of bringing a closer social relationship into being.

Rappaport also observes that ritual words are both illocutionary and perlocutionary. They are illocutionary in that they often perform something just by virtue of being said ("I pronounce you husband and wife"). But their persuasiveness and the way they can move people ("perlocutionary force") can also affect the ritual.[54] Similarly, the sharing of food can, in and of itself, reaffirm and strengthen old social ties, or create new ones. But, of course, the elements of the meal, the number and quality of the dishes, may also contribute to the end result—and in this sense can be thought of as the "perlocutionary force" of the meal. What is key here is not whether the emotion is sincerely felt, or simply expressed in a polite and even formulaic way. In either case, through commensality, food becomes the medium for expressing and creating co-feeling, that is genuinely felt, politely simulated, or evoked and hoped for.

To understand this further, I have taken one other element of Tambiah's analysis of ritual, and of his notion of the alternative modes of participation and causality, by using his examination of "magical" acts in ritual. To be clear, the word *magic* is a loaded one, and is invested with negative connotations. In Western religious history, magic was branded as playing dangerously with the manipulation of the supernatural. And in Western intellectual history, magic has often been viewed as ineffective science.[55] But Tambiah points out that understanding magical acts in ritual necessitates a comprehension of the difference between exactly these two orderings of thought—the persuasive/participatory versus the causative.

In ritual, magical acts are often based on "analogical thought and action."[56] As Tambiah states, "In ritual operations by word and object manipulations, the analogical action conforms to the 'persuasive' rather than the 'scientific' model," in which the attempt is to transfer through persuasion or evocation the "properties of the desired and desirable vertical relation to the other which is in an undesirable condition, or in attempting to convert a potential not-yet-achieved state into an actualized one."[57] One example of such analogical speech acts would be a paternalistic employer who tries to compare his relationship to his employees to that of a father to his children. Of course, as Tambiah points out, this is really a case of propaganda, as the employer is highly unlikely to care about his employees as if they were his children. And the employer cannot cause his employees to see him as a father figure simply through use of this analogy. Rather, all he can do is to evoke the parallel and hope his employees buy into it.

Now to use this framework in a somewhat different situation, that of commensality and the sharing of food in rural Meixian, we can see how a host's telling guests they should not feel uncomfortable because they are like members of his or her own family operates on this same level—through analogy and evocation. But in this case, the evocation is not merely verbal but is something that comes about through the shared experience of eating together: "We are like family, because we are sharing food, as families share food." In such a circumstance, whether guests and host really end up feeling like they are "all in the same family," and whether the polite and appropriate words that accompany eating and toasting are heartfelt or not, is somewhat beside the point. Sharing food and drink is richly evocative of a shared state of feeling that should ideally come about, and sometimes really does transpire, in the course of sharing a meal, especially a memorable and flavorful one.

Similarly, the emotive aspect of sharing food together—through banqueting, feasting, or more ordinary meals—can also provide us with another angle with which to think of food and gift exchange. As mentioned in chapter 4, food can be used to delay a guest's departure: "Please stay and try my eggplant fritters!" But when departure must take place, food gifts can also extend co-feeling, and even co-presence, when actual physical co-presence is no longer possible. Here we are referring not just to the "spirit of the gift" in the sense of the obligation to repay a gift received, which is the focus of so much literature on reciprocity.[58] We are seeing the affective dimension again, that is, food becomes an instrument of right attitudes and appropriate feelings, either genuinely felt or at least politely and properly expressed.

As an example, a departure of a long- or short-term guest is not marked in Meixian by hugging or much of any physical demonstration. The verbal and physical expressions of emotion when visitors depart are muted when contrasted to the exuberance articulated when they are urged to stay longer for tea and snacks, or when compared to the verbal energy spent coaxing banquet guests to eat more. While an actual departure may not be marked by much overt emotional expression, hosts put a great deal of effort into procuring foodstuffs before a guest's departure, in hopes of sending their guests off with more pomelos, tea, or whatever local specialty they want them to carry home.

I have left Songling and Baoli's house many times, and each time, the moment of my leave taking is rather muted. On the other hand, the preparation for leaving certainly is not. As described in chapter 4, in the days before I leave, Songling's family members and neighbors, as well as others, bring tea, Hakka specialties, or other items they hope I can carry with me. If I protest that I can't carry everything, I can expect an immediate reply that, definitely, there is room somewhere in my suitcase. As noted earlier, sometimes the food gifts are for someone else, and I am the critical link. But this is not merely about instrumental exchange, it is also a way to carry over an affective link.

Understanding food as a materialization of emotional connection makes sense in both the specific Chinese context, as well as in terms of anthropological analyses of emotion in a variety of cultural contexts. Such analyses focus on emotion not only as an expression of an individual's inner psychic state but also as something that is socially generated. For instance, in Kipnis's study of sentiment in rural North China, he describes the role of *ganqing* as shared emotion. In this role, emotion helps define group boundaries—"the boundaries (ever shifting) of the groups of people whose 'magnetic fields of human feeling' (*renqing de cilichang*) constitute individual hearts/minds."[59] As he points out, *ganqing* in a Chinese context, "is not primarily an individual matter. . . . It is a type of feeling that must be conceived of more socially than psychologically (i.e. that is held to exist between and among people as much as within individual heads)."[60]

As food flows between or is shared among people, it embodies their affective ties and establishes the very fields of feeling that Kipnis refers to.[61] This flow of food and its role in constituting emotion can also be understood as part of what Sara Ahmed has termed an "affective economy."[62] As Ahmed explains, feelings do not reside in subjects or objects themselves, but are produced through circulation among them as "emotions circulate between bodies and signs."[63] What Ahmed means by this is that emotions often grow as they move from one symbol to another, and as they move backward in time to both conscious and repressed memories. Ahmed's own examples are political and examine how emotions circulated from symbols like the American flag to the actual bodies of immigrants from Muslim countries, generating growing distrust and even hatred of asylum seekers in the post–9/11 world.

However, this notion of floating or circulating emotion can also make sense in this much more benign case of food as both a medium and symbol of emotion in Meixian. As food gifts circulate, webs of human feeling are both reinvigorated and produced. This was made palpably clear to me in December 2012, when my husband and I were leaving Meixian after a short visit. We carried with us on the bus to Hong Kong one of Songling's freshly slaughtered chickens and some of her homemade glutinous rice wine to give to Ruolan. That we did not forget to take these gifts was particularly important since it was my second attempt. My first attempt had been during a visit I had made on my own earlier that year. When Yanhong drove me to the bus station in the county capital that time, and as I was about to get onto the bus, he remembered that we had left the bag with the chicken and rice wine at home, and it was too late to go back for them.

Luckily, there was a second chance to bring the food gifts to Ruolan a few months later. When we arrived at the bus station in Hong Kong, Ruolan and her family were there to greet us. We went off happily and rather noisily to the nearest dim sum restaurant, and had our own reunion with one another, precipitated by the food gifts from Songling to Ruolan that we had carried from the village.

Although physical reunion and the sharing of food together may be *nande,* rare or hard to achieve, the food gifts sent by Songling to Ruolan could at least evoke memories of prior times together. They could thereby create a bridge between past times together and anticipated future reunions by renewing feelings in the wake of spatial separation. The gifts also generated additional webs of mutual emotion, as our delivery of the food gifts precipitated our getting together with Ruolan and her family to enjoy dim sum.

The concluding chapter looks further at the role of food in linking disparate parts of a fragmented world together, and considers its implications for understanding contemporary China.

Conclusion

STITCHING THE WORLD TOGETHER

IT WAS AROUND FIVE in the late afternoon. Songling and I were returning from visiting a friend in another part of the village. On the way back, we saw Songling's sister-in-law and a friend pulling carts loaded with bags of chicken droppings. They had purchased these for just ten yuan per bag from another villager who raised chickens, and they planned to use them for fertilizer. As we walked home, we also passed several local women hauling water and fertilizer, on their way to their vegetable gardens as is common in the late afternoons, when women go out to tend to their gardens. It was a scene in continuity with the past. But it was impossible to watch without wondering what the future would hold.

The foodways discussed in this book can be understood as being simultaneously part of a national culture and an historical tradition, in addition to being something expressly local. Residents of Moonshadow Pond routinely refer to their practices as "Hakka" ones. And, of course, these foodways are also shaped by local ecologies and economies. Yet, at the same time, many of these specifically Hakka food practices reflect widely shared Chinese traditions around food. These include concepts about the relationship of food to health and to the body, as well as ideas about the role of food in social relationships and among family members, ancestors, and the cosmos. Further, transformations and upheavals in the national context have all influenced these food practices as well, from the creation and breakup of collectives, through the opening of China to a market economy, to the urbanization and mass migrations of the reform era.

Altogether, these contexts might be understood as the conditions that shape the food habitus of Moonshadow Pond. The concept of "habitus," developed by Pierre Bourdieu, describes a set of internalized dispositions and accepted practices. But while the idea of habitus often presumes a set of largely unchanging social conditions,[1] rural Meixian, and indeed most of rural China, can hardly be described as a steady state. Nonetheless, despite more than a century of rapid transformation in China, and changes in food practices brought on by greater affluence, a common food culture still exists in Moonshadow Pond. We can indeed talk about Moonshadow Pond food-ways as a set of shared practices and beliefs. And these foodways still connect people to their pasts and to each other.

But what will happen to this food culture in the face of continued migra-tion, the declining involvement of young people in agriculture, and the rapid industrialization of China's food system, not to mention the growing threats that come from soil and water pollution and the adulteration of food? As the middle generation that still farms the land becomes the older generation, will anyone be left to carry on the particular food practices and traditions described in this book? The future, of course, can never be discerned accu-rately. But at least for now, one can argue that the food practices depicted here play a critical role in ameliorating the impact of these very same disloca-tions, connecting people through a sense of shared tradition, even as their circumstances continue to change rapidly. Indeed, by using food as a lens, we not only gain insight into how people respond to such rapid change but may also view these very transformations somewhat differently.

For instance, China is without question undergoing a momentous rural-to-urban transition, in which a large proportion of the agrarian population is migrating to the cities. But at the same time, those rural dwellers remain-ing in their villages will go to great efforts, including communal protests, in order to protect their land when they feel that their access to it and its quality are threatened by development efforts and pollution. After all, when there is an economic downturn, migrants return to these rural homes, which at least for now are places of food security. As long as the land can be pro-tected, one can eat, even if one cannot prosper. And, even in good times, it is to their village homes that urban migrants return for family celebrations. In the face of doubts about the wider commercialized food system, people con-tinue to invest food from their rural homes with values of both taste and safety.

Critics of the industrialized food system have argued that a move to more sustainable forms of agriculture would have an enormous impact on mitigat-ing global warming. A study undertaken by several international organiza-tions, including the Food and Agriculture Organization, the United Nations

Development Program, and even the World Bank, concluded that small-scale farming, which relies on biodiversity and often uses more ecological methods than industrial farming, not only is capable of producing enough food to meet the needs of a growing world population,[2] but is essential "in the face of worsening, climate, energy and water crises."[3] As China faces great challenges from climate change, therefore, what would be the impact of the disappearance of smallholder agriculture? Contrastingly, might there not be a reassessment of its value in the face of the climate crisis? And, if so, should this not provoke measures to make small-scale agriculture in rural areas a more feasible way to make a living? Although this might sound like pie in the sky in the face of the reality of a rapidly urbanizing China, it is clear that even China's economy will not grow forever, and urban areas will not be able to absorb all the surplus labor.

The agricultural practices and food choices of Moonshadow Pond residents also serve as reminders that rural dwellers are not simply passive in the face of unstoppable economic and social forces but are also actively responding to them. For instance, Moonshadow Pond foodways illustrate how new meanings can be invested in old practices. As we have seen, many of Moonshadow Pond's middle-aged and elderly residents continue to grow their own vegetables, and even to cultivate rice, not only for economic reasons, but also because the final product is trustworthy. Thus, in the current context, the decision to self-provision as much of one's own food as possible is in part influenced by doubts about the safety of the wider food system. In the past, whether to engage in subsistence agriculture was not really a decision at all, but was simply the unavoidable toil necessary for survival. In this case, therefore, an old practice has been invested with new meanings that would not have been relevant before.

So, too, the ways in which food in Moonshadow Pond is implicated in a deeply embedded and multilayered meaning system can add a new dimension to recent discussions about both the legacies of the state socialist past and the impact of contemporary globalization on peoples' moral, cosmological, and psychological orientations.

For instance, China's history over the twentieth and twenty-first centuries has often appeared as a headlong embrace of "modernity" with very little "religious fundamentalist reaction-formation."[4] Mayfair Yang points out that, unlike in the Middle East and South Asia, where direct colonial rule created feelings of loss and nostalgia for a past golden age, in China, the old order was brought down by the Chinese themselves (first with the overthrow of the Qing dynasty in 1911, and then with the Communist overthrow of the Nationalist government in 1949). Thus in China, at least since the Boxer Rebellion in 1901, there have been no more movements that aimed to resurrect China's role in the world by looking backward. Yang argues that, in the twentieth century, "China experienced perhaps the world's most radical and systematic secularization process and the decimation of traditional religious and ritual cultures."[5]

However, if we use food as our lens, and consider the ways in which in Moonshadow Pond it is implicated in calendrical rituals, connections with the past, relationships with ancestors and contemporaries, moral economies, and ideas about health and disease, then this picture of a decimated traditional culture and headlong embrace of Western ways is harder to maintain.

Similar to Yang's points about secularization in the religious and cultural sphere, much recent anthropological work on China has focused on a parallel transformation in the psychological sphere. For instance, the contributors to a collection of essays on reform-era morality in China call attention to a number of trends that indicate the rise of a new individualism. In *Deep China,* Arthur Kleinman and his coauthors mention studies revealing that migrant workers, while bound in some ways to contribute funds to their rural families, also express the desire to have the "freedom and choices for making a life of their own."[6] And they also observe that there is a "widespread public perception of moral crisis because of conflicts between individualistic values and collective values of both the officially endorsed socialist morality and the Confucian tradition."[7] Yunxiang Yan elaborates on this theme, remarking on the "rise of a new ethics discourse that favors the individual," and states that "The contemporary individual is more interested in his or her personal happiness and the well-being of a narrowly defined private family."[8]

A number of different terms to describe these more individualistic Chinese selves have emerged, ranging from the idea of the "desiring subject"[9] to the "enterprising self."[10] Of course, no one can deny that urban migration, changes in women's roles, and an emerging consumer economy have had an impact on peoples' psychological and moral orientations. But when food is used to frame our analysis, creating a narrative of a straight path from a traditional, less individualistic orientation to a contemporary focus on the self is harder.

For example, as we have seen, during past food crises, like the famines of the late nineteenth century and Great Leap Forward, filial devotion and a general sense of duty to family were often suspended in the face of dramatic threats to individual survival. And contrastingly, the ability to act on a notion of moral debt to family members may actually be stronger in these relatively more prosperous times. Indeed, food remains a potent means of fulfilling obligations to elders, children, and ancestors, and of cementing and reinvigorating social and emotional connections to friends and relatives. Furthermore, far from living in an individualistic bubble, Moonshadow Pond residents, as well as their children who have migrated to larger cities, confirm and express their connections to one another through continuous food exchanges. Food gifts also play a critical role in bringing together not only family but also friends separated by geographic dispersion.

In parallel fashion, food both bridges spatial divides and works to connect past and present. In these ways, food may diminish some of the sense of disruption felt by people living through rapid change. As offerings and sacrifice, of course, food connects people to their ancestral past. And as chapters 2 and 3 illustrated, food can also invoke past practices through reenactment. But food practices are equally powerful in prompting people to reflect on what has changed ("all we used to eat were sweet potatoes"). And finally, the labors of agriculture and cooking anticipate the future, whether through daily, seasonal, or longer term cycles. Food, therefore, is a continuous bridge through both time and space.

In an interesting piece on temple networks in historic and contemporary China, Michael Puett points out that, in Chinese popular religious practice, temple offerings illustrate one way that a world perceived as discontinuous and fragmented is brought together. He uses the example of the very popular deity Mazu. Mazu was believed to be the ghost of a girl, who drowned in the tenth century and was subsequently thought to drag humans to their deaths at sea. As a result, fishermen began to sacrifice to her, and over time she gained additional supporters. An ever-expanding temple network to Mazu spread throughout southeastern China as more and more people gave offerings to her. In this way, a ghost was converted through offerings to a god, and the temple networks to Mazu also began to connect people in an ever-expanding web.[11]

As Puett states, regarding traditional Chinese cosmology, the "world is fragmented and fractured, and filled with capricious ghosts. Within such a cosmology, the goal is to work endlessly to create continuity—to make connections, to form networks, and to domesticate the world such that these networks grow, flourish, and expand."[12]

Puett's example is drawn from temple networks. But it can also serve as a paradigm for the way food, at least in rural China, becomes a medium through which connections are forged and strengthened; thus is the world "domesticated." Food in gift giving, in banqueting, as the product of labor for others, and, of course, as offerings to the gods, ghosts, and ancestors remains a critical medium of connection. Looked at in this way, we see a world in which obligations and links to others are constantly being reiterated through the medium of food.

If contemporary rural Chinese live in a social world marked by rising individualism, they simultaneously live in a world where ties between people are continuously reaffirmed through the labors of producing, preparing, and exchanging food, as well as through the sharing of meals. If it is a social world where food scandals and pollution driven by a headlong drive for profit create apprehensions about some foods, it is also a world of deep appreciation of the value of "sweet" homegrown vegetables and local meats. Although the young residents of Moonshadow Pond have scattered to urban locales, the memories of past reunion meals, and local fresh food, inspire eager anticipation when they return home for the Lunar New Year and the Mid-Autumn Festival.

Whether food can continue as a great connector in the face of all the aforementioned challenges is an open question. But the very centrality of its role suggests that its social, symbolic, and indeed existential importance may prove a great motivator in confronting the dangers of pollution, the overwhelming drive for profit, and the fragmentation and potential loss of social solidarity and connections in a rapidly urbanizing society.

Of course, tackling these challenges is a tall order, and only time will tell what the future portends. Moonshadow Pond's residents, themselves, have plenty of theories about this. For instance, A Hui, who raises pigs and fish for a living, told me that he thought the village would not disappear at all. As city life becomes more complicated, he asserted, some people will move back to Moonshadow Pond. There will be fewer farmers, he predicted, but they will be able to make farming into a real business, as urban customer's desires for unadulterated local food from nearby villages will grow. As a resident of Vermont, who has witnessed the steady expansion of the local foods movement, I naturally find this an attractive, comforting, and optimistic prediction, even as I wonder how realistic it is in the face of the food needs of over a billion people.

As of this writing, no place on earth has actually implemented a sustainable food system on a national scale. At the same time, such systems must begin with smaller models, and are more likely to succeed when they have deep cultural roots. For now, the residents of Moonshadow Pond continue to cherish their own "sweet" food, grown, raised, and prepared mainly through their own efforts. This food continues, at least for the time being, as the language through which relationships are made, broken, and assessed.

APPENDIX A

Changes in Agricultural Production from 1949 through the Reform Era in Meixian

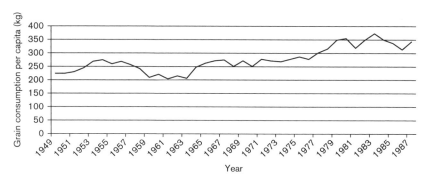

FIGURE A.I.   Grain consumption per capita in Meixian. (Data from *Meixian Zhi,* 247–48.)

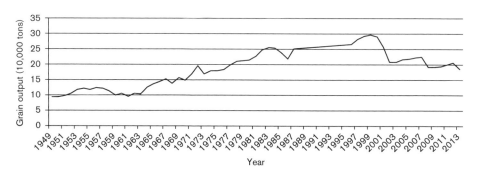

FIGURE A.2.   Grain output in Meixian. (Data from *Meixian Zhi,* 233–34, 258–59; University of Michigan China Data Center, "China Data Online.")

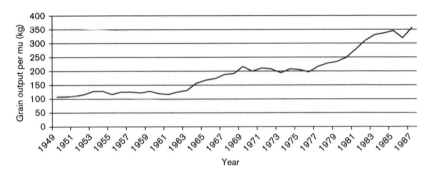

FIGURE A.3. Grain output per mu in Meixian. (Data from *Meixian Zhi,* 258–59; Meizhou City People's Government, "Meixian Qu, 2008"; Statistical Bureau of Meixian District, *Meizhou Statistical Report;* Luo, Chen, and Zhang, "Current Situation and Advantages.")

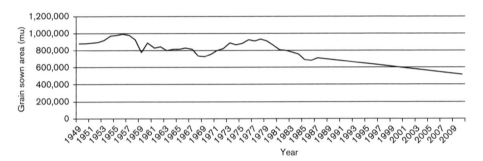

FIGURE A.4. Grain sown area in Meixian. (Data from *Meixian Zhi,* 258–59; Meizhou City People's Government, "Meixian Qu, 2008"; Statistical Bureau of Meixian District, *Meizhou Statistical Report;* Luo, Chen, and Zhang, "Current Situation and Advantages.")

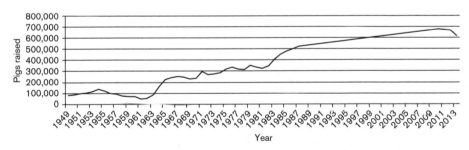

FIGURE A.5. Pork production in Meixian. (Data from *Meixian Zhi,* 234; Meizhou City People's Government, "Meixian Qu, 2008"; Statistical Bureau of Meixian District, *Meizhou Statistical Report;* Luo, Chen, and Zhang, "Current Situation and Advantages.")

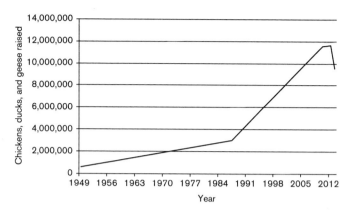

FIGURE A.6. Poultry production in Meixian. (Data from *Meixian Zhi,* 266, 267; Meizhou City People's Government, "Meixian Qu, 2008"; Statistical Bureau of Meixian District, *Meizhou Statistical Report;* Luo, Chen, and Zhang, "Current Situation and Advantages.")

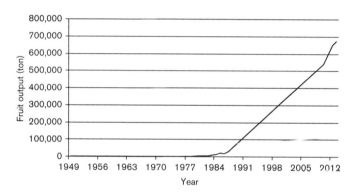

FIGURE A.7. Fruit output in Meixian. (Data from *Meixian Zhi,* 272–74; Statistical Bureau of Meixian District, *Meizhou Statistical Report;* Luo, Chen, and Zhang, "Current Situation and Advantages.")

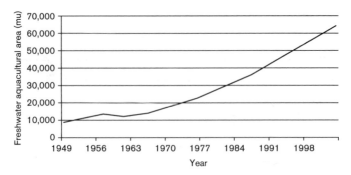

FIGURE A.8. Freshwater aquacultural area in Meixian. (Data from *Meixian Zhi*, 287; Statistical Bureau of Meixian District, *Meizhou Statistical Report*; Luo, Chen, and Zhang, "Current Situation and Advantages.")

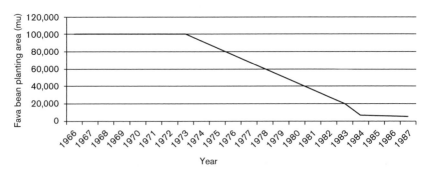

FIGURE A.9. Fava bean planting area in Meixian. (Data from *Meixian Zhi*, 268; Statistical Bureau of Meixian District, *Meizhou Statistical Report*; Luo, Chen, and Zhang, "Current Situation and Advantages.")

APPENDIX B

Preparing a Holiday Meal

MID-AUTUMN FESTIVAL AT SONGLING
AND BAOLI'S HOUSE

HOUR 1: 6:15 P.M.

- Songling and Baoli's son Yanhong (YH) chops ginger, starts flame, adds ginger to hot oil, followed by duck meat with bone, then glutinous rice wine, salt, white pepper, and soy sauce. YH puts ingredients into braising dish for an hour.
- YH takes wok out backdoor, cleans it out with hot water and brush.
- YH slices carrots into matchsticks, adds them to chive flowers, slices rehydrated dried squid.
- Songling removes straw mushrooms (*caogu*) from boiling water.
- Meanwhile, pig's stomach is boiling in another pot.
- YH washes pork spareribs one more time, adds egg, cornstarch, and salt directly to the ribs.
- YH washes off thick cutting board and knife and restarts the flame on the wok.
- Songling peels pineapple in backyard behind the kitchen.
- YH puts oil in wok and deep fries ready-made frozen shrimp croquettes.
- YH cuts the pineapple. He cuts the rest of the carrot into chunks, which he adds to the pineapple.
- Baoli and Songling take out a big round table top and set it atop a smaller table placed in the open courtyard of their house. This way it can seat up to twelve people.
- The shrimp cakes are done. YH next deep fries the pork spareribs. The clams have been taken out of the broth in which they have been cooked, and the chicken is placed in boiling water to make soup (with ginseng).
- YH puts another whole chicken in a dish and places it in a pot to steam.
- YH takes deep-fried ribs out of the wok, saves the oil and puts it through a strainer.

- YH again washes out the wok with boiling water in the backyard behind the kitchen, and throws the water out in the yard.
- YH's two sisters arrive with their husbands and two of their daughters, a middle school and a high school student. YH's son Jiabing, a middle school student, is also present.
- YH slices pork, then smashes garlic and chops it.
- Songling sits on a low plastic stool outside the kitchen, in the backyard, and chops greens on a thick cutting board.
- YH's older sister Meiying enters the cooking space and starts chopping greens and garlic.
- YH's younger sister Fengying enters with *nangua bing* (fried pumpkin cakes) and asks me to taste one.
- YH adds salt to boiling water, followed by some Chinese kale.
- Songling goes into the backyard and chops some chive flowers (*jiucai hua*).
- YH takes the Chinese kale out of the boiling water and strains it in a colander. Meiying carefully takes it out of the colander and puts it on two plates.
- YH chops more ginger, smashes garlic, chops green and red chilies. and mixes them all together.
- Meiyiing brings some bean thread noodles into the kitchen. Then she takes the steamed chicken off the stove and puts the soup back on.
- No more than four burners are ever going at once: an electric burner in the courtyard, and two more gas burners and an electric burner in the kitchen.
- YH puts the garlic, chilies, and ginger into the wok. He adds the clams, basil leaves, and fermented sweet wine rice (hongzao), which is an early byproduct of glutinous rice wine production. Then he adds a bit of fish sauce, oyster sauce, and soy sauce. Fengying adds water.
- Meanwhile, YH chops up the steamed chicken and puts it out on a serving plate.

HOUR 2: 7:15 P.M.

- Everyone is ushered in to start the meal while YH finishes the cooking. He still has to complete several dishes. He fries some chopped pork, adds straw mushrooms and a bit of the chicken stock to it, and pours it over the Chinese kale.
- We have started eating. It is a family meal, so there is just a little bit of toasting. YH brings out a few more dishes, including sweet and sour pork ribs; stir-fried squid with chive flowers and carrots; stir-fried bean thread noodles with mushrooms, pork, and scallions; stir-fried greens; and finally chicken in soup with ginseng.

- Yanhong joins us to eat at 7:45 p.m., and we finish at 8:20, after which we retire to the living room upstairs.
- On the upstairs porch balcony, Songling has arranged offerings to *tian* (heaven) on a table. We light incense sticks and pay our respects. Then we retire to the living room, drink tea, eat moon cakes and other snacks, and talk until late into the night.

NOTES

PREFACE AND ACKNOWLEDGMENTS

1. John S Rohsenow, ed., "*Bao ren bu zhi e ren ji*," in *ABC Dictionary of Chinese Proverbs* (Honolulu: University of Hawaii Press, 2002), 4.

CHAPTER ONE. THE VALUE OF FOOD IN RURAL CHINA

1. The three grasses are *chou ye* (ramie or China grasses), *ai* (mugwort), and *jishiteng* (Chinese febervine herb).

2. "Clear bright" (*qing*) versus "green" (*qing*).

3. According to the Hakka historian Fang Xuejia, "The traditional custom is that beginning the first meal after giving birth, women have ginger wine chicken for at least one month. . . . This nutritious chicken has sweet and fragrant tastes, and can remove moisture, clear veins and five internal organs, promote blood circulation, and protect kidneys. When a woman gives birth her family shares this ginger wine with other families. This is called *songjiangjiu*." See Fang Xuejia, *Kejia Minsu* (Guangzhou: Huanan Ligongdaxue Chubanshe, 2005), 12.

4. K. C. Chang, introduction to *Food in Chinese Culture: Anthropological and Historical Perspectives,* ed. K. C. Chang (New Haven, CT: Yale University Press, 1977), 11.

5. Two excellent examples are Eugene Anderson, *The Food of China.* (New Haven, CT: Yale University Press, 1988); and Chang, *Food.*

6. See James L. Watson, "From the Common Pot: Feasting with Equals in Chinese Society," *Anthropos* 82 (1987): 389–401.

7. Yunxiang Yan, "Food Safety and Social Risk in Contemporary China," *Journal of Asian Studies* 71, no. 3 (2012): 705–29; James L. Watson, ed., *Golden Arches East: McDonald's in East Asia* (Stanford, CA: Stanford University Press, 1997); Jun Jing, ed., *Feeding China's Little Emperors: Food, Children and Social Change* (Stanford, CA: Stanford University Press, 2000).

8. For instance, the contributors to a new book on reform-era morality in China call attention to a number of trends that indicate the rise of a new individualism. In *Deep China*, Arthur Kleinman and his coauthors cite studies revealing that migrant workers, while bound in some ways to contribute funds to their rural families, also express the desire to have the "freedom and choices for making a life of their own" (Arthur Kleinman et al., introduction to *Deep China: The Moral Life of the Person in a New China, What Anthropology and Psychiatry Tell Us about China Today*, ed. Arthur Kleinman et al. [Berkeley: University of California Press 2011], 4). They also observe that there is a "widespread public perception of moral crisis because of conflicts between individualistic values and collective values of both the officially endorsed socialist morality and the Confucian tradition" (10). Yunxiang Yan elaborates on this theme, remarking on the "rise of a new ethics discourse that favors the individual"; he states that "The contemporary individual is more interested in his or her personal happiness and the well-being of a narrowly defined private family" (Yunxiang Yan, "The Changing Moral Landscape," in *Deep China: The Moral Life of the Person*, ed. Arthur Kleinman et al. [Berkeley: University of California Press, 2011], 45).

9. For a discussion of the rise in petrochemicals in agriculture in China, see Vaclav Smil, *China's Past, China's Future: Energy, Food, Environment* (New York: Routledge Curzon, 2005). An interesting analysis of economic relationships between peasants and agribusiness in China can be found in Qian Forrest Zhang and John A. Donaldson, "The Rise of Agrarian Capitalism with Chinese Characteristics: Agricultural Modernization, Agribusiness and Collective Land Rights," *China Journal* 60 (2008): 25–47. The growth of fast food in China has been the focus of many studies, including Jun Jing, ed., *Feeding China's Little Emperors: Food, Children and Social Change* (Stanford, CA: Stanford University Press, 2000); Watson, *Golden Arches East*. Still, while the total power of agricultural machinery has increased over threefold between 1980 and 2002 (Robert Benewick and Stephanie Hemelryk Donald, *The State of China Atlas* [Berkeley: University of California Press, 2005], 41), China's agriculture is still low on the mechanization scale compared to the United States (Erik Millstone and Tim Lang, *The Atlas of Food: Who Eats What, Where, and Why* [Berkeley: University of California Press, 2008], 35).

10. Lu et al., "Impacts of Soil and Water Polution on Food Safety and Health Risks in China," *Environment International* 77 (2015): 5–15. See also, Y. Yan, "Food Safety."

11. John Lossing Buck, *Land Utilization in China*. (Chicago: University of Chicago Press, 1937), 17.

12. Ibid., 11.

13. Ibid., 204.

14. Ibid., 19.

15. Ibid., 125.

16. Ibid., 127.

17. Ibid., 369.

18. For recent estimates of the death toll during the Great Leap Forward and for studies of the period, see Frank Dikötter, *Mao's Great Famine: The History of China's Most Devastating Catastrophe* (New York: Walker and Company, 2010); Xun Zhou,

ed., *The Great Famine in China, 1958–1962: A Documentary History* (New Haven, CT: Yale University Press, 2012); Jisheng Yang, *Tombstone: The Great Chinese Famine, 1958–1962*, ed. Edward Freidman, Guo Jian, and Stacy Mosher, trans. Stacy Mosher and Guo Jian (New York: Farrar, Straus and Giroux, 2008).

19. Vaclav Smil, *China's Past, China's Future: Energy, Food, Environment* (New York: Routledge Curzon, 2005), 77.

20. Ibid., 82.

21. Ibid.

22. *China Statistical Yearbook, 2015* (Beijing: China Statistics Press, 2015), tables 6.10, 6.15.

23. Millstone and Lang, *Atlas of Food*, 36–37.

24. Ibid., 83.

25. Ibid., 34–35.

26. Benewick and Donald, *State of China Atlas*, 51.

27. Sidney Mintz, *Sweetness and Power* (New York: Viking, 1985). David Sutton also addresses this issue in his study of food and memory in Greece. He points out, in reference to the standardization of food, "Commodity fetishism is the process by which objects are compared based on a price derived from their market value rather than on the history of labor relations that went into producing them . . . a purposeful forgetting of the past that went into the making of the present" (*Remembrance of Repasts: An Anthropology of Food and Memory* [New York: Berg, 2001], 64). Sutton's discussion also references Carole M. Counihan's work on rural Sardinia, *Around the Tuscan Table*, in which she recounts the ways in which the standardization of food and the decline of self-provisioning mean that the exchange of products individually made or grown declines, along with not only the social relations created by the exchange but also the association of these food products with particular times and places (Sutton, *Remembrance of Repasts*, 60).

28. Xin Liu, *In One's Own Shadow: An Ethnographic Account of the Condition of Post-reform China* (Berkeley: University of California Press, 2000), 82.

29. Liu, *In One's Own Shadow*, 82.

30. Roel Sterckx, introduction to *Of Tripod and Palate: Food, Politics, and Religion in Traditional China*, ed. Roel Sterckx (New York: Palgrave Macmillan, 2005), 3.

31. A good example of the ways in which the assumptions of "modernity" in the West have obscured anthropological analysis is provided by Deborah Reed-Danahay in her examination of a "curious practice" in rural Auvergne, where a newly married couple is presented with a chamber pot of champagne and chocolate (signifying urine and feces). As Reed-Danahay points out, although versions of this practice are widespread in rural France, researchers have never mentioned it—perhaps because of a form of "'reverse Orientalism' that constructs France as a 'nonexotic' place" ("Champagne and Chocolate: 'Taste' and Inversion in a French Wedding Ritual," *American Anthropologist* 98, no. 4 (1996): 750). Another example, though not food related, is the importance of connections in the United States for home repair and construction. Once embarked on a project, contractors will usually suggest their

own friends or associates for work they cannot do themselves. Reciprocal exchanges do not evaporate just because people are embedded in a highly commodified economy. The issue is always the intersection and articulation of these different domains.

32. The entire area is now referred to as Meizhou, and it is composed of seven counties as well as the county capital. The counties are Meixian, Wuhua, Dabu, Xingning, Pingyuan, Jiaoling, and Fengshun.

33. Ellen Oxfeld, *Drink Water, but Remember the Source: Moral Discourse in a Chinese Village* (Berkeley: University of California Press, 2010), 12–13.

34. On the trips in 2006, 2007, and winter 2012, I was accompanied by my husband, Frank Nicosia.

35. The local gazetteer gives some sense of the rapid decrease in per capita grain consumption (in kilograms) in Meixian from the first year of Liberation (1949) through the Great Leap Forward, as well as of the gradual increases thereafter until the late 1980s: 1949 (225), 1953 (268), 1959 (209), 1961 (204), 1964 (248), 1967 (276), 1968 (249.5), 1971 (278), 1975 (287), 1977 (300), 1979 (350), 1983 (373), and 1987 (344). See *Meixian Zhi* [*Mei County Gazetteer*], ed. Meixian Difangzhi Bianzuan Weiyuanhui [Meixian Gazetteer Compiling Committee] (Guangzhou: Guangdong Renmin Chubanshe, 1994), 247.

Similar statistics provide a view of the changes in meat production for that period as well. While the population of Meixian did not quite double during that time, the production of meat increased over six times (*Meixian Zhi*, 203). The numbers that follow show the extreme dip in production, measured in the number of pigs raised during the famine years, and the steady increase after that through the collective era and into the early reform period: 1949 (81,530), 1959 (71,500), 1961 (48,197), 1964 (165,576), 1967 (250,435), 1975 (320,273), 1983 (407,383), 1987 (522,507). See *Meixian Zhi*, 278.

The gazetteer also shows a similar rise in the area set aside for raising fish, from 8,558 mu in 1949 to over 35,000 mu in 1987 (*Meixian Zhi*, 287). One acre is equivalent to 6.07 mu.

36. Oxfeld, *Drink Water*, 184.

37. By 2012, Songling and Baoling's son, Yanhong, and youngest daughter, Fengying, had recently purchased cars as well. Although car owners in the village were certainly in the minority, and motorcycles were still the most common form of private transportation, I was amazed in my 2012 visit at how fast car ownership was spreading through this part of the countryside.

38. These numbers come from household surveys I conducted in the summer of 1997, and again in the spring of 2007.

39. I conducted household surveys in both 1997 and 2007. While the official census counts migrants who live in the city as part of the rural household (as long as they have not changed their registration), I calculated both numbers. So the population of Moonshadow Pond, if migrants were included, was 918 in 2007. However, when migrants were not included, and only household members in the village were counted, then the number in 2007 was 872.

40. These numbers also come from my 1997 and 2007 household surveys.

41. This situation is different from the one reported in rural Sichuan by Anna Lora-Wainwright. Lora-Wainwright found that goods bound for market were

treated with the very chemicals farmers deplore when they are used on products intended for their own families ("Of Farming Chemicals and Cancer Deaths: The Politics of Health in Contemporary Rural China," *Social Anthropology* 17 no. 1 [2009]: 56–73). Perhaps one key difference between these two cases is that many of the agricultural products, such as pork, that are produced in Moonshadow Pond are sold within the county or even within the village itself. Thus, people can easily gain knowledge about the conditions under which these items were produced.

42. Anna Lora-Wainwright noted the same issue in a village in Sichuan that she studied. She notes that nitrogen-fertilized paddy fields create a cancer risk if they are too close to wells. Nonetheless, while locals in the village she studied expressed negative attitudes about farm chemicals, "these substances were not condemned outright" ("Farming Chemicals and Cancer," 65). She notes that chemicals were popular for two reasons. They "produce[d] literally spotless food" for the market, and they made "the workload lighter" for the elders, who were usually the farmers, since younger villagers had migrated to urban areas to work (65).

43. This survey was focused on assessing daily food intake in April 2007. I chose April because it was not a festival time, like the Lunar New Year, when people ate more abundantly. I asked thirty-five families to record their dietary intakes over four days. I also asked them to note if they used farm chemicals on their rice and if they used their own fertilizer or farm chemicals (*nongyao*) on their gardens. No one said they used chemical fertilizers on their gardens, but the answers on the use of farm chemicals on rice were interesting. Twelve families reported using farm chemicals on rice, while eight reported not using any chemicals. Another seven said they used farm chemicals but tried to use small amounts. This is interesting because I gave people the option of answering only that they used or did not use farm chemicals, yet many felt compelled to insert more-nuanced answers, saying that while they used farm chemicals, they tried to minimize their use. Two organic ingredients traditionally used for fertilizing are composite manure and oil cakes made from the residue left after making peanut or soybean oil. This use of oil cakes for fertilization is an old method in South China and was noted by John Lossing Buck in *Land Utilization*, which was based on research in the 1930s. Additionally, people burn rice stalks and plow them back into the soil as a fertilizer. Cakes made from the residue of pressing oil from the seeds/fruit of the tea tree (camellia), mixed with grass and dried, are used as a kind of natural pesticide to kill snails in the rice paddies, which prey on rice seedlings.

44. In a survey I conducted of thirty-five families in April 2007, I found that some form of cooked rice was consumed by all families for almost all meals; rice porridge or congee (mainly for breakfast) was still consumed at least once a day by all but five of these families. Clear soups, made from a combination of one's own and purchased ingredients were, like rice, a seemingly non-negotiable part of meals, consumed every day by all the families in the survey.

45. Katherine A. Mason, "To Your Health! Toasting, Intoxication and Gendered Critique among Banqueting Women," *China Journal* 69 (2013): 108–33.

46. Only one of the families surveyed bought all of its vegetables at the market, while twenty-three families provided all of their vegetables themselves.

47. *Meixian Zhi,* 268.

48. In twenty-seven of the thirty-five families surveyed in April 2007 (see notes 37 and 38), meat was eaten every day. There were an additional five families that ate meat in three out of the four days, and only two families that ate no meat at all. This is significant because, as stated earlier, the survey was not undertaken during a festival time, when meat consumption would be expected to be higher than usual.

49. Of the thirty-five families surveyed, only one was entirely self-provisioning in the domains of meat, poultry, and fish.

50. Of thirty-five families surveyed, twenty-seven reported eating fruit, twenty-four consuming eggs, and ten consuming milk over a four-day period.

51. A few examples of these include common scouring rush herb or horsetail grass (*suomu cao,* also called *bojiecao,* or *muzeicao*), which is boiled in water and used to treat eyes that are red or scratchy; *fenjidu* (stephania longa), which is also boiled in water and can sooth a sore throat; and Chinese chesnut (*banliren*). The boiled chestnut can be made into a tea that helps bring down blood pressure

52. One example is a soup that comes from several wild grasses, including *maidong* (radix ophiopogonis) and *dengxin cao* (soft rush). These are both gathered in the wild. To these are added *hongzao* (red dates) and pork bones to make a soup. This soup protects bones (*bao gutou*), counteracts heat and moistens lungs (*qingre, runfe*), and cools blood (*liangxue*).

53. Tan Chee-Beng and Ding Yuling offer an insightful analysis of the promotion of fine tea drinking as an "invented tradition" in South China during the reform era. See "The Promotion of Tea in South China: Re-inventing Tradition in an Old Industry," *Food and Foodways* 18 (2010): 121–44.

54. For those familiar with the Cantonese food culture, what is known in North American as *dim sum* is a meal for which tea is perfectly appropriate as an accompaniment—that is, the tradition of *yincha,* literally "drinking tea." These meals take place from late morning through early afternoon. *Yincha* is not a Hakka tradition, but its structure does not contradict the Hakka separation of tea drinking from ordinary meals, for which there is a grain staple, such as rice. If tea is accompanied by food among the Hakka, that food should be treats that are deep fried or steamed. Plain boiled rice—the staple of ordinary meals—is not served with *yincha.*

55. These qualities are cold (*lengxing*), cool (*liangxing*), hot (*rexing*), warm (*wenxing*), dry (*zaoxing*), and neutral (*zhongxing*). Some examples of the medicinal grasses used in Meixian in soups are *tiejia cao* (dictyocline griffithii), to reduce inflammation; *shancha shugen* (camellia sinensis roots), to heal bones and increase life; *niunai shugen* (ficus hispida, a tropical fig root), to eliminate blockages and strengthen kidneys; *shiganlan* (pholidota chinensis Lindl), to lubricate lungs, stop cough, and relieve heat; and *wuzhi maotao* (wild peach root), to strengthen and protect the liver. There are many more examples.

56. Vivienne Lo, "Pleasure, Prohibition, and Pain: Food and Medicine in Traditional China," in *Of Tripod and Palate: Food, Politics and Religion in Traditional China,* ed. Roel Sterckx (New York: Palgrave Macmillan, 2005), 64.

57. Sidney Mintz, *Tasting Food, Tasting Freedom* (Boston: Beacon Press, 1997), 96.

58. Mary Douglas, "Food as a System of Communication," in *In the Active Voice* (London: Routledge and Kegan Paul, 1982), 82–104.

59. Mary Douglas, "Deciphering a Meal," in *Implicit Meanings: Essays in Anthropology* (London: Routledge and Kegan Paul, 1975), 249.

60. Douglas, "Deciphering a Meal."

61. Ibid., 269.

62. Ibid., 251.

63. Ibid., 255.

64. Douglas, "Food as a System," 96–97.

65. Douglas, "Deciphering a Meal," 251.

66. Douglas, "Food as a System," 102.

67. Ibid., 98.

68. Working in a similar tradition, the anthropologist Louis Dumont analyzed how a different conceptual distinction—the opposition between purity and impurity—underlies another social order—the caste system in India, which is based on a hierarchical ranking of castes according to their relative "purity." In this system, one can accept food only from someone of equal or higher caste rank than oneself. Additionally, food consumption is itself linked with one's relative purity, as high-caste individuals eat a "purer" diet. Brahmins in most parts of India, for instance, will not consume meat (*Homo Hierarchicus: The Caste System and Its Implications* (Chicago: University of Chicago Press, 1980). Dumont and Douglas, of course, both drew inspiration from the work of Claude Lévi Strauss, who considered fundamental categorical distinctions as the basis of societal order and organization.

69. Mintz, *Sweetness and Power*, 200.

70. Ibid., 201.

71. Ibid., 202.

72. For instance, Pierre Bourdieu's study of taste in mid-twentieth-century France emphasizes the way in which "signs" embody and then reinforce class positions. For Bourdieu, "taste" is a set of embodied dispostions. Further, "taste" and "class" are mutually reinforcing, as both are related to material conditions (*Distinction: A Social Critique of the Judgement of Taste,* trans. Richard Nice [London: Routledge and Kegan Paul, 1984], 175). An example in the French context that Bourdieu uses is that of working-class families, who have a taste for heavier food (more for your money), while many rising upper–middle-class, white-collar professionals prefer "light" food, which is not so much about "filling the stomach" as aesthetic presentation (177). These tastes not only signify and express one's class, but also reinforce one's place in society, as those who are in power valorize their own tastes as "good" taste. Ultimately, for Bourdieu, cultural categories and concepts not only signify class distinctions, they are themselves generated by particular historical conditions, including the economic and class contexts of peoples' lives. At the same time, the categories themselves help reinforce particular socioeconomic and political orders.

73. Jean Baudrillard, "The Ideological Genesis of Needs," in *The Consumer Society Reader*, ed. Juliet B. Schor and Douglas B. Holt (New York: New Press, 2000), 60.

74. Ibid., 60.

75. Ibid., 59.

76. Baudrillard's aim was ultimately to reveal the logic of commodities in capitalist society, in which in his view all objects function primarily as signs. Thus, in a full-fledged capitalist system, there is little room for symbolic exchange and even the logic of utility because, in his view, all goods under capitalism are turned into signs of differentiation. Indeed, for Baudrillard, the exchange value of different commodities under capitalism is simply the relative value, on a common scale, of all these different "signs" ("Ideological Genesis of Needs," 77).

77. David Graeber, *Toward an Anthropological Theory of Value: The False Coin of Our Own Dreams* (New York: Palgrave, 2001), 94.

78. Ibid., 45.

79. Ibid., 65.

80. Graeber uses the example of the Baining, a society in Papua, New Guinea. The Baining, although they do not have elaborate banqueting or gift-giving ceremonies, are constantly exchanging food on an informal basis. Each person has enough to eat without exchange, and often people will exchange the same amount of the same item (such as taro). However, this exchange reproduces their social ties, or "society." For the Baining, "Producing food through the labor of gardening is seen as the origin of value. This value is only 'realized,' however, when one gives some of that food to someone else" (*Theory of Value*, 70).

81. Jonathan Parry and Maurice Bloch, introduction to *Money and the Morality of Exchange*, ed. Jonathan Parry and Maurice Bloch (Cambridge: Cambridge University Press, 1989), 24.

82. Ibid., 25.

83. Janet Carstens, "Cooking Money: Gender and the Symbolic Transformation of Means of Exchange in a Malay Fishing Community," in *Money and the Morality of Exchange*, ed. Jonathan Parry and Maurice Bloch (Cambridge: Cambridge University Press, 1989), 117–41.

84. David Sutton, "Comment on 'Consumption' by David Graeber," *Current Anthropology* 52, no. 4 (2011): 507.

85. See Joanna Overing and Alan Passes, eds., *The Anthropology of Love and Anger: The Aesthetics of Conviviality in Native Amazonia* (New York: Routledge, 2000). I discuss the category of "conviviality" further in chapter 6.

CHAPTER TWO. LABOR

1. *Yi li liang shi, san dian han.*

2. There were only nine college graduates in the village in 1997; this number had risen to forty-five by 2007.

3. Each month during the collective era, villagers were allocated small amounts of peanut oil, about 1–2 jin per month, a jin being about half a kilogram or 1.34 pounds. Peanuts were one of a group of food items called "miscellaneous staples" (*zaliang*). These included the following: *sumi*, millet; *fanshu gan*, dried sweet potato; *fanshu mo*, bits of sweet potato; *doujiao gan*, dried tofu paste; *yu gan*, dried taro; *yu mi*, corn; and *hu dou*, fava bean. Not surprisingly, the production of these staples declined rather rapidly during the reform era, when meat, fruits, fish, and poultry became a more important feature of the Meixian diet. According to the Gazetteer, sweet potato production in the county declined from 47,000 tons in 1955 to 26,100 tons in 1987 (*Meixian Zhi,* 265). The production of other miscellaneous staples, including corn (*Meixian Zhi,* 265) and fava beans (268), also declined.

4. The *Mei County Gazetteer* does mention some localities planting a third crop in addition to their two rice crops as far back as the 1930s, before Liberation. And, it states, this third crop was sometimes wheat (*Meixian Zhi,* 262). If one looks at the production figures for wheat in Meixian, one can see that it virtually disappeared in the reform era and peaked during the Great Leap Forward. In 1949, over 80,000 mu (one acre is equivalent to 6.07 mu) were devoted to wheat production in Meixian, and production peaked at 140,000 mu in 1958 (264). But this figure had declined to an almost negligible amount by 1987, with only 729 mu in the entire county devoted to wheat production (265).

5. Like the tractors, the milling machine is no longer the property of the collective but is operated privately, with people paying a fee for its use.

6. Hok Bun Ku. *Moral Politics in a Chinese Village* (Lanham, MD: Rowman and Littlefield, 2003), 71; Jonathan Unger, *The Transformation of Rural China* (Armonk, NY: M. E. Sharpe, 2002), 87.

7. Jonathan Unger, *Transformation of Rural China,* 87.

8. Fishpond area increased from 8,558 mu in 1949 to over 35,000 mu in 1987 (*Meixian Zhi,* 287).

9. Fruit production rose from 2,020.35 tons in 1949 to 31,300 tons in 1987 (*Meixian Zhi,* 270).

10. The gazetteer records 81,530 pigs in 1949 and 522,507 in 1987 (*Meixian Zhi,* 278).

11. For instance, in Moonshadow Pond, which was part of a two-village administrative district, total fruit production rose from 114 tons in 1997 to 181 tons in 2011. Fishpond area expanded from 121 mu in 1997 to 536 mu in 2011, and fish production grew from 48 tons in 1991 to 117 tons in 2011. Additionally, by 2011, there were 420 pigs and over 38,000 chickens being raised. Interestingly, rice paddy area in total has not decreased, and, in fact, has slightly increased despite all of this. In 1996, 1,204 mu in the area were devoted to paddy fields; this area was enlarged slightly to 1,436 mu in 2011. Dry fields expanded from 103 mu to 260 mu, and the vegetable area remained fairly constant—1,140 mu in 1996 and 1,154 mu in 2011 (Chengbei Xiang [Chengbei township], *Ge Guanliqu Zhuyao Jiben Qingkuang* [Basic information on each administrative district]. Unpublished Information Sheet (Chengbei Township, 1997, 2007, 2012).

12. Now called *cunmin xiaozu,* or villagers' small units.

13. In my last book on morality in Moonshadow Pond, I observed, "The energy and involvement of women in economic activities is still referred to by Hakka in communities throughout the world as a unique aspect of their identity.... As Hakka men began to migrate throughout southeast China and abroad, it became even more important for women to hold down the agricultural economy at home" (Oxfeld, *Drink Water,* 10).

14. She could earn about 30 yuan a day in 2007.

15. Oxfeld, *Drink Water,* 102.

16. Hsiao-tung Fei and Chih-I Chang, *Earthbound China: A Study of Rural Economy in Yunnan* (Chicago: University of Chicago Press, 1945) 300.

17. A few of the notable participants in discussions of peasant identity include Teodor Shanin, ed., *Peasants and Peasant Societies* (Oxford: Blackwell, 1987); Robert Redfield, *The Little Community, and Peasant Society and Culture* (Chicago: University of Chicago Press, 1960); and Eric Wolf, *Peasants* (Englewood Cliffs, NJ: Prentice-Hall, 1966).

18. Oxfeld, *Drink Water,* 178.

19. Ibid., 178.

20. Ibid., 180.

21. Jonathan Unger, *Transformation of Rural China,* 46.

22. Pun Ngai, *Made in China: Women Factory Workers in a Global Workplace* (Durham, NC: Duke University Press, 2005), 116.

23. Hairong Yan, "Spectralization of the Rural: Reinterpretng the Labor Mobility of Rural Young Women in Post-Mao China" *American Ethnologist* 30, no. 4 (2003): 586.

24. H. Yan, Spectralization of the Rural," 586.

25. According to some of my older informants, one mu of land produces about 1,000 jin of rice. But this same amount of land produced only about 800 jin during the collective era and only about 440 jin during the old society. After factoring in the cost of the trays now used to plant the seedlings, the seeds, the fertilizer, and the pesticides, the cost to produce 1,000 jin of rice would be about 300 yuan. But the same amount would cost about 1,000 yuan to buy in the market.

26. Elizabeth Fitting, *The Struggle for Maize: Campesinos, Workers, and Transgenic Corn in the Mexican Countryside* (Durham, NC: Duke University Press, 2011), 100.

27. Stuart Thompson, "Death, Food, and Fertility," in *Death Ritual in Late Imperial and Modern China,* ed. James L. Watson and Evelyn S. Rawski (Berkeley: University of California Press, 1988), 93. The David K. Jordan quotation is from *Gods, Ghosts and Ancestors: The Folk Religion of a Taiwanese Village* (Berkeley: University of California Press, 1977), 118.

28. In 2007, 57% of all families were made up of three generations.

29. Ellen Oxfeld, *Drink Water,* 80.

30. Ibid., 96.

31. Some examples are *faban,* steamed rice flour, dyed red; *tianban,* glutinous rice flour and brown sugar steamed overnight; *jianban,* a deep-fried combo of sticky rice flour, sugar, and sesame seeds; *jiaoban,* which is sticky rice cake with the vegetable *jiaocai,* a kind of leek; *niu er gong,* made from deep-fried wheat dough filled with sesame seeds, peanuts, and sweet bean paste; *jian chan zi,* which are savory deep-fried wheat treats; and *jianyu pian,* which are fried shredded taro cakes.

32. Mid-Autumn, Duanwu, and Qingming, all traditional festivals, became paid national holidays in 2007.

33. David Sutton, *Remembrance of Repasts: An Anthropology of Food and Memory* (New York: Berg, 2001), 64.

CHAPTER THREE. MEMORY

1. Mintz, *Sweetness and Power,* 205.

2. Sutton, *Remembrance of Repasts,* 18.

3. Anthony Giddens, *The Consequences of Modernity* (Stanford, CA: Stanford University Press, 1990), 17.

4. Giddens, *Consequences of Modernity,* 9.

5. Ibid., 20.

6. Ibid.

7. Sutton, *Remembrance of Repasts,* 8.

8. Ibid., 8.

9. Krishnendu Roy, *The Migrants Table: Meals and Memoires in Bengali-American Households* (Philadelphia: Temple University Press, 2005).

10. Sutton, *Remembrance of Repasts,* 31.

11. Jon D. Holtzman, "Food and Memory," *Annual Review of Anthropology* 35 (2006): 364.

12. Holtzman, *Uncertain Tastes,* 41.

13. Ibid.

14. Ralph A. Thaxton, *Catastrophe and Contention in Rural China: Mao's Great Leap Forward Famine and the Origins of Righteous Resistance in Da Fo Village* (Cambridge: Cambridge University Press, 2008), 302–4.

15. Sutton, *Remembrance of Repasts,* 17.

16. See Holtzman, *Uncertain Tastes,* on the issue of ambivalence in memories of food.

17. Ralph Thaxton (2008, 293) points out that in Da Fo Village, the subject of his study of the Great Leap Forward famine, villagers dislodged "local party agents of the Great Leap" sometimes even "twenty or thirty years after the famine."

18. It is indicated by different character combinations that both sound like *kumai.* (In addition to being written as 苦脉, it is also sometimes indicated by 苦荬, but in both cases the character for "bitter" remains in both.) The English name for this leafy green vegetable is "sowthistle-leaf Ixeris," and its Latin name is *Ixeris*

sonchifolia Hance. It comes in several varieties—some straight edged and others uneven edged.

19. *Meixian Zhi,* 269.

20. *Xian cai,* sometimes translated as "Chinese spinach."

21. Although there is not sufficient space or time in this chapter to go into all the examples of commodification of foraged foodstuffs that were previously widely available, several other cases of this existed in Meixian. A particularly famous example is *yaocai,* medicinal materials made from various trees that were once widely available for anyone who chose to forage in the mountains. Now they sell in the market for a high price and are used as the basis for soups. They are consumed not so much for use as a cure but to maintain health and to defend against illness through the strengthening of different internal organs, enhancing of bodily function, and balancing of hot and cold in the body.

22. Wang Zengneng, *Kejia Yinshi Wenhua* (Fuzhou: Fujian Jiaoyu Chubanshe, 1995), 11.

23. Frederick J. Simmonds, *Food in China: A Cultural and Historical Inquiry* (Boca Raton, FL: CRC Press, 1991), 102; Jonathan Spence, "Ch'ing," in *Food in Chinese Culture: Anthropological and Historical Perspectives,* ed. K.C. Chang (New Haven, CT: Yale University Press, 1977), 262.

24. Spence, "Ch'ing," 263.

25. Lillian M. Li, *Fighting Famine in North China: State, Market and Environmental Decline, 1690s–1990s* (Stanford, CA: Stanford University Press, 2007), 109, 313.

26. Buck, *Land Utilization,* 401.

27. Martin Yang, *A Chinese Village, Taitou, Shantung Province* (New York: Columbia University Press, 1945), 32.

28. Fang Xuejia, *Kejia Minsu,* 9. Other *zaliang* included millet (*sumi*), dried bean curd paste (*doujiao gan*), dried taro (*yu gan*), corn (*yumi*), fava bean (*hudou*), peanuts, and winter wheat (*xiao mai*), which was harvested during the collective era in early March, before the first rice crop was planted.

29. J. Yang, *Tombstone,* 210.

30. Fang, *Kejia Minsu,* 10

31. Dikötter, *Mao's Great Famine,* 136.

32. Ibid.

33. *Meixian Zhi,* 265.

34. Yunpiao Chen, "The Altar and the Table: Field Studies on the Dietary Culture of Chaoshan Inhabitants," in *Changing Chinese Foodways in Asia,* ed. David Y.H. Wu and Tan Chee-beng (Hong Kong: Chinese University Press, 2001), 20.

35. Simmonds, *Food in China,* 362; Buck, *Land Utilization,* 411.

36. J. Yang, *Tombstone,* 342.

37. *Meixian Zhi,* 277.

38. Simmonds, *Food in China,* 87.

39. Fang, *Kejia Minsu,* 11.

40. Charles Stafford, *Separation and Reunion in Modern China* (Cambridge: Cambridge University Press, 2000), 101.

41. See Holtzman, "Food and Memory," 367.

42. Sutton, *Remembrance of Repasts,* 64.

43. Holtzman, "Food and Memory," 363.

CHAPTER FOUR. EXCHANGE

1. Ramon Myers, "The Commercialization of Agriculture in Modern China," in *Economic Organization in Chinese Society,* ed. W. E. Willmott (Stanford, CA: Stanford University Press, 1972), 173.

2. Buck, *Land Utilization,* 16.

3. Ibid., 16, 401.

4. Ibid., 402, 411.

5. Ibid., 233.

6. Ibid., 237.

7. Ibid., 461.

8. Ibid., 467.

9. Ibid., 461.

10. Ibid., 371.

11. Certain industries in Meixian date back to the Qing dynasty and include coal, limestone quarries, iron mines, silica, ceramics, glass, cast-iron cooking pots, plows, pharmaceuticals, and handmade paper (*Meixian Zhi,* 368).

12. Yan Yunxiang, *The Flow of Gifts: Reciprocity and Social Networks in a Chinese Village* (Stanford, CA: Stanford University Press, 1996), 93.

13. Of the Moonshadow Pond population, 11 percent had an overseas connecton during the time of my fieldwork, which was obviously several decades after the Great Leap Forward. It can at least give a rough sense of the proportion of the village with overseas connections.

14. Jonathan Parry and Maurice Bloch, introduction to *Money and the Morality of Exchange,* ed. Jonathan Parry and Maurice Bloch (Cambridge: Cambridge University Press, 1989), 8.

15. Y. Yan, *Flow of Gifts,* 65.

16. Ibid., 65.

17. Stafford, *Separation and Reunion,* 100.

18. Ibid., 109.

19. Ibid., 105.

20. For instance, see Y. Yan, *Flow of Gifts*; Andrew Kipnis, *Producing Guanxi: Sentiment, Self, and Subculture in a North Chinese Village* (Durham, NC: Duke University Press, 1997).

21. Y. Yan, *Flow of Gifts,* 45.

22. Ibid., 46.

23. Ibid.

24. Charles Stafford points out that, while "courtesy demands reciprocity" is the common translation, an actual transliteration is, "ceremonial (*li*) generates back-and-forth (*wang-lai*)" (*Separation and Reunion*, 105).

25. In 2007, a survey I conducted in Moonshadow Pond found that 25 percent of marriages over the last ten years had been with a non-Hakka (Oxfeld, *Drink Water*, 85).

26. Ibid., 106.

27. As Charles Stafford states, both the quality of the meal and the number of guests are "taken as reflections of the status of the groom's family and community" (*Separation and Reunion*, 116).

28. For instance, Songling remembered that, when her eldest daughter married, her family received a gift of 299 yuan from the groom's family (one yuan "is always held back in the belief that a full payment might be inauspicious and prevent the bride from actually leaving her natal family" [Oxfeld, *Drink Water*, 106]). However, by 2006, one family in Moonshadow Pond had received a bride price as high as 9,999 yuan.

29. A "dry daughter" or "dry son" is a ritualized relationship somewhat akin to that of godparent. A dry son or daughter may be ritually adopted by another family. Afterward, this individual may be included in New Year's banquets or other celebratory occasions, and, furthermore, he or she will wear mourning garb during the funeral when the adoptive parent dies. The reasons for creating the relationship are various, but sometimes they are related to difficulties in childhood. For instance, a child might be having health problems or behavioral problems, such as being very picky or demanding. Creating a relationship with a new set of parents is seen as a way to displace their troublesome qualities. However, dry sons or dry daughters do not inherit property from their adoptive parents.

30. While the literature on popular religion in rural China is huge, the classic statement of the relationship between gods, ghosts, and ancestors can be found in Arthur Wolf, "Gods, Ghosts, and Ancestors," in *Studies in Chinese Society*, ed. Arthur Wolf (Stanford, CA: Stanford University Press, 1978).

31. The Chinese name for the bodhisattva is Avalokiteśvara.

32. Michael Puett, "The Offering of Food and the Creation of Order: The Practice of Sacrifice in Early China," in *Of Tripod and Palate: Food, Politics, and Religion in Traditional China*, ed. Roel Sterckx (New York: Palgrave Macmillan, 2005), 75.

33. Stafford, *Separation and Reunion*, 109.

34. S. Thompson, "Death, Food, and Fertility, 73.

35. Examples of this are Caishen, who is a vegetarian, and certain Buddhist deities, such as *Dangjia*, also known as *Jialan Pusa*, and *Chanliang Pusa*, both of whom are also vegetarian. Also, *Dimu*, or *Weituo Pusa*, is concerned with rice planting and therefore gets only vegetarian offerings.

36. Daniel Overmyer, "Comments on the Foundations of Chinese Culture in Late Traditional Times, in *Ethnography in China Today: A Critical Assessment of Methods and Results*, ed. Daniel Overmyer (Taipei: Yuan-Liou, 2002), 318.

37. Among the various Hakka locality gods, those with the appellation *gong-wang* tend to administer larger areas, whereas those with the appellation *baigong* tend to administer smaller areas (Wang Z., *Kejia Wenhua Daolun,* 349). Fang Xuejia points out that many of these locality gods had different origins, but they ultimately became associated with a village or community and became the community gods (*Kejia Meizhou,* 149). He also points out that Gongwang tends to be placed at the village entrance near water because "water brings in wealth" (*shuiji shi cai*). According to Wai Lun Tam, *baigong,* which he translates as "Uncle King," are "spirits of rocks, fields, trees, or bridges," and *gongwang,* which he translates as "Duke King," are often village protectors "with their altar[s] situated at and guarding the place where the river flows out of the village" ("Communal Worship and Festivals in Chinese Villages," in *Chinese Religious Life,* ed. David A. Palmer, Glenn Shive, and Philip L. Wikeri [New York: Oxford University Press, 2011], 42).

38. Oxfeld, *Drink Water,* 17.

39. Caishen and Longshen are both at the back of the temple, and a marker for Tudi Baigong is placed under the ancestral altar.

40. These include the Earth God and the Dragon Spirit or Dragon's Veins, both of which are guardians of the mountains and the graves, since this is where tombs are located.

41. These include Buddhist deities, such as Guanyin, the Sanbao, which are three deities (*Shijiamouni pusa, Xiaozaiyanshouyao fo,* and *Emituo Fo*); the Boddhisatva Dangjia, *Dimu,* also known as *Weituo Pusa;* popular non-Buddhist deities, such as *Weitong, Guandi Laoye, Tiangong,* and *Tianmu,* or the Heavenly Father and Mother; and Caishen.

42. Stafford, *Separation and Reunion,* 102.

43. That day's particular order of sacrifice, with food, and in particular cooked food (the *san sheng,* or three sacrificial meats), offered first to *tian* and later to gods and ancestors, is quite common in Hakka practice. Daniel Overmyer points to the common practice in rural Hakka areas of first offering cooked foods to the "celestial gods" and then offering them to the ancestors ("Comments," 330).

44. Robert L. Chard, "Rituals and Scriptures of the Stove Cult," in *Ritual and Scripture in Chinese Popular Religion,* ed. David Johnson (Berkeley: Institute of East Asian Studies, 1995), 3–54.

45. Families aim to complete this before the Yuan Xiao Festival, which is the fifteenth day and official end of the New Year.

46. These ritual fields are called either *chang tian* or *jitian.* Xiaoping Dong, "The Dual Character of Chinese Folk Ideas about Resources: On Three Western Fujian Volumes in the Traditional Hakka Society Series," in *Ethnography in China Today: A Critical Assessement of Methods and Results,* ed. Daniel Overmyer (Taipei: Yuan-Liou, 2002), 363. In the old society, this ritual land was typically rented to poor or landless peasants, and the proceeds were used to support the banquets that followed yearly worship at the graves of lineage and lineage-branch founders. Because this land supported lineage observances, it could not be partitioned (Oxfeld, *Drink Water,* 180).

47. Fang, *Kejia Meizhou,* 187.

48. This contractual arrangement is also called *zuofu*. It is not to be confused with the Zuofu holiday described earlier. But in both cases, *zuofu* means "to create blessings" or "good fortune."

49. This is called the "small three sacrificial meats" (*xiao san sheng*). Examples of such lesser-order gods include some of the gods in the village temple. For instance, when a child or grandchild is sixteen, he or she is said to enter the "flower garden" (*huayuan*), and offerings are made to the "Flower Father and Mother" (*Huagong* and *Huamu*). Then when the same child turns nineteen, he or she is said to leave the flower garden, and offerings are made to the "Heavenly Father and Mother" (*Tiangong* and *Tianmu*). These offerings include the small three sacrificial meats. The gods are not considered high enough in the celestial hierarchy to warrant a more elaborate offering.

50. Fang, *Kejia Meizhou,* 165. It has also been called the Wandering Souls Festival (*wangren jie*), the Yulanpen Festival, and the Zhong Yuan Festival.

51. *Meixian Zhi,* 1033.

52. Wen Yanyuan, "Customs of Jianqiao Village, Fengshun," in *Village Religion and Culture in Northeastern Guangdong,* ed. Fang Xuejia (Hong Kong: International Hakka Studies Association and the École-Française D'Extrême-Orient, 1997), 212.

53. Overmyer, "Comments," 339.

54. Ibid., 340.

55. Lin Qingshui, "The Folk Customs of Two Townships in Jiaoling County," in *Meizhou heyuan diqu de cunluo wenhua* [Village religion and culture in northeastern Guangdong], ed. Fang Xuejia (Hong Kong: International Hakka Studies Association and École Française D'Extrême Orient, 1997), 5:246.

56. *Yeshen yegui,* "unruly spirits and ghosts."

57. Thus, an old Hakka folk expression states, "Those ghosts without a lineage (or name), those ghosts are very numerous; but when people call their names, they are not actually offering sacrifices." This expression implies that people may call out the equivalent of "what the devil!" But they are not actually sacrificing to, or, in other words, feeding the ghosts (*Wu shi gui, gui wu shu, he shi jiao, jiao wu si*).

58. *Meixian Zhi,* 1033.

59. For instance, see *Meizhou Ribao* [Meizhou Daily]. "Zhongyuan Jie: Kejia Ren de Qi Yue Ban" [the Zhongyuan Festival: the Hakka 7/15]. *Meizhou Ribao.* Accessed August 8, 2012. mzrb.meizhou.cn/data/20120825/html/6/content_11.html.

60. Fang Xuejia, *Kejia Yuanliu Tanao,* (Guangdong: Guangdong Gaodeng Chubanshe, 1994), 232.

61. Fang, *Kejia Yuanliu Tanao,* 233.

62. A. Wolf, "Gods, Ghosts, and Ancestors," 170.

63. Ibid., 171.

64. Ibid., 172.

65. Another example is a specialty soup that includes several ingredients that come from wild grasses—a root called *maidong* (radix ophiopogonis), which origi-

nates in a plant called *shanjmii* (Lophatherum herb); another grass called *dengxin* (soft rush, Juncus effusus.L); and finally a grass called *maogen* (Japanese bloodgrass, imperata cylindrica). All of these grasses can be found in Moonshadow Pond in the wild. Yet the soup made from these ingredients can also be found as a special medicinal soup in higher-quality restaurants.

66. Tang Linzhen, "Medicine Diet: A New Food Trend," *Meizhou Ribao* (April 2, 2007).

67. Some examples are the three grasses used to make Qingming Festival steamed buns: *chou ye* (ramie, China grass), *ai* (Chinese mugwort), and *jishiteng* (Chinese fevervine herb). Another is *fenjidu* (Stephania longa), which is good for sore throat. Additionally, people collect fiddleheads, or edible fern fronds *(jue cai),* which grow by the sides of rivers and are gathered and stir fried. Indeed, in the past, people went to great lengths to gather them, and even went searching for them by mountain streams. People no longer go to such efforts to find them. One more freely gathered food that is still eaten is a bean, somewhat like a fava bean but grown in the wild. It is called *gouzhuadou* (Bengal bean or mucuna pruriens). Again, while people no longer go to great lengths to get it, they enjoy eating it when they find it, or if someone (such as a neighbor or relative) informally gifts it to them.

68. Stephen Gudeman, "Necessity or Contingency: Mutuality and Market," in *Market and Society: The Great Transformation Today,* ed. Chris Hann and Keith Hart (Cambridge: Cambridge University Press, 2009), 24.

69. As David Graeber points out, reciprocal exchange always has the capacity to turn suddenly competitive *(Theory of Value,* 114–15)

70. Paul Eiss and David Pedersen, "Introduction: Values of Value, *Cultural Anthropology* 17, no. 3 (2002): 286.

CHAPTER FIVE. MORALITY

1. Douglas, "Food as a System," 82–104.

2. Douglas, "Deciphering a Meal," 249.

3. Watson, "From the Common Pot."

4. Arjun Appadurai, "Gastro-politics in Hindu South Asia," *American Ethnologist* 8, no. 3 (1981): 494–511.

5. Examples include rules surrounding caste rank and food transactions in India. See Louis Dumont, *Homo Hierarchicus: The Caste System and Its Implications* (Chicago: University of Chicago Press, 1980); McKim Marriott, "Caste-Ranking and Food Transactions: A Matrix Analysis, in *Structure and Change in Indian Society,* ed. Milton Singer and Bernard S. Cohn (Chicago: Aldine, 1968), 133–71.

6. Raj Patel, *Stuffed and Starved: The Hidden Battle for the World Food System* (Brooklyn: Melville House, 2007), 82.

7. Jacob A. Klein, Yuson Jung, and Melissa L. Caldwell, introduction to *Ethical Eating in the Postsocialist and Socialist World,* ed. Yuson Jung, Jacob A. Klein, and Melissa Caldwell (Berkeley: University of California Press, 2014), 9.

8. Kathryn Jean Edgerton-Tarpley, "From 'Nourish the People' to 'Sacrifice for the Nation': Changing Responses to Disaster in Late Imperial and Modern China, *Journal of Asian Studies* 73, no. 2 (2014): 450.

9. Steven Parish, *Moral Knowing in a Hindu Sacred City: An Exploration of Mind, Emotion, and Self* (New York: Columbia University Press, 1994), 285.

10. Ibid. 284.

11. Caroline Humphrey, "Exemplars and Rules: Aspects of the Discourse of Moralities," in *The Ethnography of Moralities,* ed. Signe Howell (London: Routledge, 1997), 26.

12. Oxfeld, *Drink Water,* 29.

13. In his work on Greece, Sutton points out that, while the introduction of processed commodities may destroy some of the local meanings that went into the making and exchanging of local foods, foreign foods may also be locally processed and reinvested with new meanings when they are exchanged (*Remembrance of Repasts,* 64, 66).

14. Fei Xiaotung, *From the Soil: The Foundations of Chinese Society,* trans. Gary Hamilton and Wang Zheng (Berkeley: University of California Press 1992), 30.

15. Ibid.,74.

16. Lien-sheng Yang, "The Concept of *Pao* as a Basis for Social Relations in China," in *Chinese Thought and Institutions,* ed. John K. Fairbank (Chicago: University of Chicago Press, 1957), 291.

17. Jean Levi, "The Rite, the Norm, and the Dao: Philosophy of Sacrifice and Transcendence of Power in Ancient China," in vol. 2 of *Early Chinese religion, Part One: Shang through Han (1250 BC–220 AD),* ed. John Lagerwey and Marc Kalinowski (Leiden, The Netherlands: Brill, 2009), 645–92.

18. Ibid., 659.

19. L. Yang, "Concept of *Pao*," 302.

20. Kathryn Edgerton-Tarpley, *Tears from Iron: Cultural Responses to Famine in Nineteenth-Century China* (Berkeley: University of California Press, 2008), 165.

21. These are either "moral cause and effect" or "moral cause and effect over three lifetimes" (David K. Jordan and Daniel Overmyer, *The Flying Phoenix: Aspects of Chinese Sectarianism in Taiwan* (Princeton, NJ: Princeton University Press, 1986), 112.

22. Lung-ku Sun, "Contemporary Chinese Culture: Structures and Emotionality," *Australian Journal of Chinese Affairs* 26 (July 1991): 25.

23. Richard Madsen, *Morality and Power in a Chinese Village* (Berkeley: University of California Press, 1984), 15.

24. Ibid., 18.

25. The arranged marriage system also meant that a woman's husband and his family were strangers to her. Further, infant betrothal was practiced in many areas of rural China well into the first few decades of the twentieth century. An adopted daughter-in-law was sent to her future husband's home as an infant. She was married with little ceremony, when she came of age, to her "brother" in her adoptive family. Having grown up with her future husband as a virtual sibling, her marital relation-

ship with her spouse was often emotionally cool, and her connection with her natal family was often weak or nonexistent, since they had given her away as an infant. With a weak emotional bond to her husband, and often no natal family to fall back on, an adopted daughter-in-law had even fewer resources to balance against her mother-in-law's authority than a woman who married into the family as an adult. See Arthur Wolf, "Adopt a Daughter-in-Law, Marry a Sister: A Chinese Solution to the Problem of the Incest Taboo," *American Anthropologist* 70, no. 5 (1968): 864–74. However, whether she entered into a "major marriage" as an adult bride, or a "minor marriage," in the case of an infant betrothal, a daughter-in-law gained informal influence within her family of marriage over time.

26. Margery Wolf, *Women and the Family in Rural Taiwan* (Stanford, CA: Stanford University Press, 1972).

27. Neil Diamant, "Re-examining the Impact of the 1950 Marriage Law: State Improvisation, Local Initiative, and Rural Family Change," *China Quarterly* 161 (2000): 187.

28. Ibid., 187.

29. Ibid., 177.

30. Yunxiang Yan, *Private Life under Socialism* (Stanford, CA: Stanford University Press, 2003), 229.

31. Ibid., 89, 103, 109.

32. Everett Yuehang Zhang, "China's Sexual Revolution," in *Deep China: The Moral Life of the Person,* ed. Arthur Kleinman et al. (Berkeley: University of California, 2011).

33. The *New York Times* has also reported on this phenomenon. A reporter who visited one Yunnan village noted almost all the able-bodied adults had migrated to the cities to work, leaving grandparents to raise the grandchildren. The article also mentions a Sichuan Province widow's successful suit against her adult son and daughter, who had refused to give her either a place to live or economic support. See Howard French, "Rush for Wealth in China's Cities Shatters the Ancient Assurance of Care in Old Age," *New York Times,* November 3, 2006.

34. Lihua Pang, Alan deBrauw, and Scott Rozelle, "Working until You Drop: The Elderly of Rural China," *China Journal* 52 (2004): 75.

35. Ibid., 77.

36. Pang, deBrauw, and Rozelle, "Working until You Drop," 90; Ellen Judd, *Gender and Power in Rural China* (Stanford, CA: Stanford University Press, 1994); Tamara Jacka, *Women's Work in Rural China* (Cambridge: Cambridge University Press, 1997), 58.

37. Danyu Wang, "Ritualistic Coresidence and the Weakening of Filial Practice," in *Filial Piety: Practice and Discourse in Contemporary Asia,*" ed. Charlotte Ikels (Berkeley: University of California Press, 2004), 16–33; Eric T. Miller, "Filial Daughters, Filial Sons: Comparisons from Rural North China," in Ikels, *Filial Piety,* 34–52; Jun Jing, "Meal Rotation and Filial Piety," in Ikels, *Filial Piety,* 53–62.

38. Oxfeld, *Drink Water,* 89.

39. See chapter 4 of Oxfeld, *Drink Water.*

40. Mette Halskov Hansen and Cuiming Pang, "Idealizing Individual Choice: Work, Love, Family in the Eyes of Young, Rural Chinese," in *iChina: The Rise of the Individual in Modern Chinese Society,* ed. Mette Halskov Hansen and Rune Svarverud (Copenhagen: NAID Press, 2010), 55.

41. Ibid. 55.

42. Oxfeld, *Drink Water,* 59. This obligation to take care of elderly parents is also written into law in China (see Anni Kajanus, *Journey of the Phoenix: Overseas Study and Women's Changing Position in China,* Research Series in Anthropology [Helsinki: University of Helsinki, 2014], 158). However, Yunxiang Yan points out that affines tend to be part of voluntary networks that address "practical concerns." In this sense, the mutual help that affines may extend to one another varies according to circumstance or even according to how well specific individuals get along. This is different from moral obligations to agnates, which "are inherited from . . . parents or ancestors" (*Flow of Gifts,* 116).

43. Roel Sterckx, "Food and Philosophy in Early China," in *Of Tripod and Palate: Food, Politics, and Religion in Traditional China,* ed. Roel Sterckx (New York: Palgrave Macmillan, 2005), 56.

44. Ibid., 39.

45. Stafford, "Chinese Patriliny and the Cycles of Yang and Laiwang," in *Cultures of Relatedness: New Approaches to the Study of Kinship,* ed. Janet Carsten (Cambridge: Cambridge University Press, 2000), 37–54.

46. Lillian Li, *Fighting Famine,* 272.

47. Edgerton-Tarpley, *Tears from Iron,* 165.

48. Ibid., 175.

49. Ibid., 182.

50. Edgarton-Tarpley states, "During the late imperial period, female infanticide, the discouragement of female remarriage, and the desire of many elite men to possess concubines as well as a legal wife meant that there was a chronic shortage of marriageable women in China" (183). Ironically, it was these very images of trafficked women that led many Chinese elites to write that this was a cause for shame, and to adapt the idea that changing the role and status of women was an indispensable ingredient in Chinese nationalism; in order to save China, women would also have to be saved (*Tears from Iron,* 183, 201, 197).

51. James L. Watson, "Feeding the Revolution: Public Mess Halls and Coercive Commensality in Maoist China," in *Governance of Life in Chinese Moral Experience: The Quest for an Adequate Life,* ed. Everett Zhang, Arthur Kleinman, and Weiming Tu (New York: Routledge, 2011), 36.

52. Ibid.

53. Ibid.

54. Ibid., 37.

55. Ibid.

56. Thaxton, *Catastrophe and Contention,* 309.

57. Ibid., 261.

58. Ibid., 265.

59. J. Yang, *Tombstone.* Yang provides many examples of the decline of intrafamilial morality in the face of famine, including instances of intrafamilial cannibalism (43, 143, 278), keeping one child alive and letting the others starve because there was not enough food for all (143), and killing family members so that the remaining family would have more to eat (290).

60. Ibid., 349.

61. Jing, "Meal Rotation," 56.

62. Fei Wu, "Suicide, a Modern Problem in China," in *Deep China: The Moral Life of the Person. What Anthropology and Psychiatry Tell Us about China Today,* ed. Arthur Kleinman et al. (Berkeley: University of California, 2011), 222–24.

63. Ibid., 224.

64. *Zhong tian de ren zuo gei zuo heng zhuo de ren chi.*

65. The idea of fungi and mushrooms as special substances associated with longevity and good health has a long history in China. Robert Ford Campany points out that mushrooms and fungi were found in "strange realms, vastly different and distant from the agricultural heartland." Thus, they are symbolically opposed to ordinary food (grain, vegetables, and meat), and were seen as "longevity-producing alternatives" to these ordinary staples (see "The Meanings of Cuisines of Transcendence in Late Classical and Early Medieval China," *T'oung Pao,* 2nd ser., 91 [2005]: 45). Seligman and Weller explain that winter worm summer grass, which they translate as "winter insect summer grass," is seen as a power food because of its liminality. It does not fit purely into a plant (vegetable) or animal category, and it is also both dead and alive in that the fungus kills the larva but then shoots up a grass sprout in spring. See Robert Seligman and Robert Weller, *Rethinking Pluralism: Ritual, Experience and Ambiguity* (Oxford: Oxford University Press, 2012), 89.

66. J. Yang, *Tombstone,* 280.

67. Ibid., 281.

68. Ibid., 221.

69. Oxfeld, *Drink Water,* 210.

70. Cui Jia, "Ganbei Culture Killing Officials," *China Daily,* July 20, 2009. www.chinadaily.com.cn/china/2009-07/20/content_8446843.htm. Of course, the cadres often insist that what outsiders view as overindulgence is simply a matter of treating their guests right (an issue we will deal with in the next chapter). Also, for cadres in the contemporary era, another form of food privilege, the access of cadres to special supplies of organic and clean food that many ordinary urbanites cannot get, has less to do with quantity than quality. See Barbara Demick, "In China, What You Eat Tells Who You Are," *Los Angeles Times,* September 16, 2011.

71. Y. Yan, *Flow of Gifts,* 227–28.

72. J. Yang, *Tombstone,* 43, 143, 278.

73. Jia, "Ganbei Culture."

74. John Kieschnick, "Buddhist Vegetarianism in China," in *Of Tripod and Palate: Food, Politics, and Religion in Traditional China,* ed. Roel Sterckx (New York: Palgrave Macmillan, 2005), 201.

75. Ibid., 186.

76. Oxfeld, *Drink Water,* 145–46.

77. Vincent Goossaert and David Palmer, *The Religious Question in Modern China* (Chicago: University of Chicago Press, 2011), 94.

78. Ibid., 137.

79. Myron Cohen, "Souls and Salvation: Conflicting Themes in Chinese Popular Religion," in *Death Ritual in Late Imperial and Modern China,* ed. James L. Watson and Evelyn Rawski (Berkeley: University of California Press, 1988), 199.

80. In Taiwan, many successful Buddhist societies have international reach and are also well known for their charitable and educational activities.

81. Goossaert and Palmer, *Religious Question,* 286.

82. Ibid., 226, 281.

83. Kieschnick, "Buddhist Vegetarianism," in Sterckx, *Of Tripod and Palate,* 193.

84. Xiao Shaobin, "Meishi Yu Xiaodao," *Meizhou Guangbo Dianshi,* March 23, 2007, 6.

85. E. P. Thompson, "The Moral Economy of the English Crowd in the Eighteenth Century," *Past and Present* 50, no. 1 (1971): 136.

86. Ibid., 90.

87. Dan Robotham points out that in *Moral Sentiments,* Adam Smith contended that the free market would liberate people from local parochialisms (afterword to *Market and Society: The Great Transformation Today,* ed. Chris Hann and Keith Hart (Cambridge: Cambridge University Press, 2009), 280).

88. Chris Hann, "Embedded Socialism? Land, Labor and Money in Eastern Xinjiang," in *Market and Society: The Great Transformation Today,* ed. Chris Hann and Keith Hart (Cambridge: Cambridge University Press, 2009), 256–71.

89. Ibid., 258, 265.

90. Thaxton, *Catastrophe and Contention,* 335.

91. Stephen Feuchtwang, "Political History, Past Suffering and Present Sources of Moral Judgement in the People's Republic of China," in *Ordinary Ethnics in China,* ed. Charles Stafford (London: Bloomsbury, 2013), 234.

CHAPTER SIX. CONVIVIALITY

1. Adam Yuet Chau, *Miraculous Response: Doing Popular Religion in Contemporary China* (Stanford, CA: Stanford University Press, 2006), 147.

2. Ibid., 149.

3. Ibid., 150.

4. Oxfeld, *Drink Water,* 136.

5. Hans Steinmüller, "The Moving Boundaries of Social heat: Gambling in Rural China," *Journal of the Royal Anthropological Institute* 17 (2011): 263.

6. Ibid., 269.

7. As Charles Stafford points out, in the case of banquets, this rareness may indeed be the genuine case, and not merely rhetorical, especially if the banquet is to send or see someone off (*Separation and Reunion*, 103).

8. In a very different context—Samburu of northern Kenya—Jon Holtzman observes that a person cannot announce that he or she is going to eat without inviting others to share, and therefore must sometimes actually be secretive about when he or she is going to eat (*Uncertain Tastes*, 133). At the same time, Holtzman observes that willingness to share is related to moral personhood and prestige (139), and refusing to share may subject one to misfortune and curses (137).

9. Raymond Williams, *Keywords,* Routledge Revivals (1976; repr., New York: Routledge, 2011), 243.

10. Overing and Passes, introduction, 14.

11. Emile Durkheim, "What Is a Social Fact? (1895)" in *Anthropological Theory: An Introductory History,* ed. R. Jon McGee and Richard L. Warms (New York: McGraw Hill, 2012), 78–85.

12. Overing and Passes, introduction, 14. They take their cue here from Raymond Williams's *Keywords.*

13. Overing and Passes, introduction, 14.

14. Warren Belasco, *Food: The Key Concepts* (New York: Berg, 2008), 19.

15. Maurice Bloch, "Commensality and Poisoning," Social Research 66, no. 1 (1999): 133.

16. Ibid., 138.

17. Charles Stafford also reports that such polite language is common, even expected, in cases of banqueting or reunion meals. As he states, "People may use, in the presence both of close friends and total strangers, the language of kinship to accompany a meal. They say, 'treat us as your own family' (*gen ziji jia yiyang*), or 'we're all the same family' (*yijiaren*). (*Separation and Reunion,* 103).

18. For a discussion of *da guo fan* in Cantonese village culture, see James Watson, "From the Common Pot," 389–401.

19. Graeber, *Theory of Value,* 225.

20. Ibid.

21. Roel Sterckx, introduction, in *Of Tripod and Palate: Food, Politics, and Religion in Traditional China,* ed. Roel Sterckx (New York: Palgrave Macmillan, 2005), 3.

22. Andrew Kipnis, *Producing Guanxi: Sentiment, Self, and Subculture in a North China Village* (Durham, NC: Duke University Press, 1997), 39–49.

23. Stafford, *Separation and Reunion,* 103.

24. In addition to the spores, the fungus itself can be sliced and put into soup. It is believed to help in longevity, and although some people, such as Lishan and her husband (see ch. 2), now cultivate it, the wild variety is preferred. It is often thought of in ideal terms as coming from a nonpolluted mountain stream where deer drink clear water!

25. Stafford, *Separation and Reunion,* 99.

26. Anni Kajanus, *Journey of the Phoenix: Overseas Study and Women's Changing Position in China*. Research Series in Anthropology (Helsinki: University of Helsinki, 2014). Kajanus adds that even if there was not much conversation when daughters studying overseas returned home, there was always plenty of food, and the food was often "ritually passed from the mother to the child" (150). She recounts the story of one mother who took a week off from work to cook all her daughter's favorite dishes (150).

27. Practical considerations can sometimes alter the timing of this visit.

28. Claude Lévi-Strauss, "The Culinary Triangle," in *Food and Culture: A Reader,* ed. Carole Counihan and Penny Van Esterik, 2nd. ed. (New York: Routledge, 2008), 38.

29. Ibid., 39.

30. Steinmüller, "Moving Boundaries," 268.

31. Ibid.

32. Although I attended many weddings in Meixian and observed the back and forth banter of four-hands tea many times, this particular interchange did not come from a wedding I attended. Instead, as I was anxious to get some verbatim examples, this interchange comes from a recorded wedding video that took place in the spring of 1995. (The groom was the brother of Songling's son-in-law.)

33. Bloch, "Commensality and Poisoning," 135.

34. Ibid.

35. Ibid.

36. Of course, in Cantonese cuisine, the popular *yincha*, or dim sum, departs from this, as tea is the essential accompaniment to the meal. However, while Hakka are familiar with *yincha,* it is definitely a Cantonese import, and not a part of Hakka cuisine.

37. Wang Z., *Kejia Yinshi Wenhua,* 154.

38. Kipnis, *Producing Guanxi,* 53.

39. Ibid., 54.

40. Katherine Mason," To Your Health! Toasting, Intoxication and Gendered Critique among Banqueting Women," 118.

41. Katherine Mason," To Your Health! Toasting, Intoxication and Gendered Critique among Banqueting Women," *China Journal* 69 (2013): 108–33.

42. Ibid.

43. Quoted in Astrid Møller-Olsen, "Dissolved in Liquor and Life: Drinkers and Drinking Cultures in Mo Yan's Novel *Liquorland,*" in *Commensality: From Everyday Food to Feast,* ed. Suzanne Kerner, Cynthia Chou, and Morten Warmind (London: Bloomsbury, 2015), 180.

44. Wang Z., *Kejia Yinshi Wenhua,* 153.

45. Charles Stafford, "Some Good and Bad People in the Countryside," in *Ordinary Ethics in China,* ed. Charles Stafford, (London: Bloomsbury, 2013), 107.

46. Wang Z., *Kejia Yinshi Wenhua,* 153.

47. Melissa Caldwell, "The Compassion of Strangers: Intimate Encounters with Assistance in Moscow," in *Ethnographies of Social Support,* ed. Markus Schlecker and Friederike Fleischer (New York: Palgrave Macmillan, 2013), 106.

48. Stanley J. Tambiah, *Magic, Science, Religion, and the Scope of Rationality* (Cambridge: Cambridge University Press, 1990), 108.

49. Ibid.

50. Ibid.

51. Banqueting in Meixian is replete with specific culinary requirements for specific occasions, such as long-life noodles at birthday celebrations, and a first dish consisting of a soup with red dates, peanuts and lotus seeds for weddings. These are chosen because the homonyms for these foods can be found in the four-character phrase, "May you give birth to illustrious sons. The phrase is *zaosheng guizi,* and the ingredients in the soup are *hongzao* (red dates), *huasheng,* (peanuts), and *lianzi* (lotus seeds).

52. Stanley Tambiah, *Culture, Thought, and Social Action* (Cambridge: Harvard University Press, 1985), 134.

53. Roy Rappaport, *Ritual and Religion in the Making of Humanity* (Cambridge: Cambridge University Press, 1999), 108.

54. Ibid., 117.

55. Tambiah, *Magic, Science, and Religion*

56. Ibid, 203.

57. Ibid., 72.

58. Marcel Mauss, *The Gift: The Form and Reason for Exchange in Archaic Societies,* trans. W D. Halls (New York, W. W. Norton, 1990).

59. Kipnis, *Producing Guanxi,* 10.

60. Ibid., 108.

61. In using the words "magnetic fields of human feeling," Kipnis is quoting from Lung-ku Sun's 1991 article "Contemporary Chinese Culture."

62. Sara Ahmed, "Affective Economies," *Social Text* 22, no. 2 (2004), 117–39.

63. Ibid., 117.

CONCLUSION

1. Jon Holtzman, *Uncertain Tastes,* 44.

2. Eric Holt-Giménez and Raj Patel, *Food Rebellions: Crisis and the Hunger for Justice* (Oakland, CA: Food First Books, 2009), 111.

3. The study was conducted by the International Assessment of Agricultural Knowledge, Science, and Technology for Development. Among its conclusions was that "The way the world grows its food will have to change radically." For that to occur, of course, the study concluded that there would need to be a "supportive trade, policy, and institutional environment. That is why IAASTD recommends improving the conditions for sustainable agriculture." Quoted in Ibid., 127, 128.

4. Mayfair Yang, "Postcoloniality and Religiosity in Modern China: The Disenchantments of Sovereignty," *Theory, Culture, and Society* 28, no. 2 (2011): 20.

5. Ibid., 3.

6. Kleinman et al., 4.

7. Ibid., 10.

8. Y. Yan, "Changing Moral Landscape," in Kleinman et al., *Deep China,* 45.

9. Lisa Rofel, *Desiring China: Experiments in Neoliberalism, Sexuality, and Public Culture* (Durham, NC: Duke University Press, 2007), 5.

10. Y. Yan, "Changing Moral Landscape," in Kleinman et al., *Deep China,* 70.

11. Michael Puett, "Economies of Ghosts, Gods, and Goods: The History and Anthropology of Chinese Temple Networks," in *Radical Egalitarianism: Local Realities, Global Relations,* ed. Felicity Aulino, Miriam Goheen, and Stanley Tambiah (New York: Fordham University Press, 2013), 98.

12. Ibid.

GLOSSARY

PINYIN	CHINESE	ENGLISH
ai	艾	Chinese mugwort
Baigong	佰公	Uncle King, spirit of rocks, trees, bridges
banliren	板栗仁	Chinese chestnut
bao	报	reciprocity
bao gutou	煲骨头	(soup) protects bones
baoying bushu	包赢不输	to ensure victory rather than loss
baozi	包子	buns
binggan	饼干	factory-made cookies and biscuits
bo	薄	thin, meager
bojie cao	驳节草	scouring rush herb, or horsetail grass
bu hao yisi	不好意思	to feel embarrassed
bu wenming	不文明	lack of civility
cai	朵	vegetable trimmings
Caishen	财神	God of Wealth
changtian	尝田	ritual fields
chashu gu	茶树菇	*Agrocybe aegerita*
chayang	插秧	to insert seedlings
chi	吃	to eat
chi daguo fan	吃大锅饭	to eat from one big pot
chidiao	吃掉	to eat up
chi fan	吃饭	to eat rice, or to have a meal
chouye	抽叶	ramie, or China grass
cunmin xiaozu	村民小组	villagers' small units
da laoban	大老板	big manager
Dangjia Pusa	当家菩萨	Dangjia Bodhisattva, same as Sangharama Bodhisattva
danwei	单位	office work unit
dengxin cao	灯芯草	soft rush, *Juncus effusus*
Dimu	嫡母	Skanda Bodhisattva

dongcongxiaca	冬虫夏草	"winter worm summer grass," a form of fungus that parasitizes caterpillar larvae and makes a precious herbal medicine
doufu	豆腐	bean curd
doufu tou	豆腐头	paste that comes out at the conclusion of the fermenting process that produces bean curd
doujiao gan	豆角干	dried bean curd paste
du	赌	to gamble
dugu	渡孤	orphan souls
dui	碓	large stone pestle
Emituo Fo	阿弥陀佛	Amitabha Buddha
ernai	二奶	literally means "second milk," a mistress
faban/fajiao ban	发粄／发酵粄	fermented rice cake
facai	发财	to prosper
fan	饭	cooked rice
fangxin rou	放心肉	trustworthy meat
fanshu	番薯	sweet potato
fanshu gan	番薯干	dried sweet potato
fanshu mo	番薯末	bits of sweet potato
fengche	风车	windmill
fengfu	丰富	abundant
fenjidu	粪箕笃	*Stephania longa*
fu	福	blessing and good fortune
gaige kaifang	改革开放	reform and opening (of China's political economy)
ganbu	干部	cadre
ganqing	感情	feelings, emotions
gaobing	糕饼	cakes or pastries (either factory made, or made commercially)
geng	羹	porridge made from rice flour
gengtian	耕田	to plow the fields
gen ziji jia yiyang	跟自己家一样	(*told by hosts to guests*) Make yourself at home.
Gongwang	公王	locality god, Duke King
gouzhuadou	狗爪豆	Bengal bean, or *Mucuna pruriens*
Guandi Laoye	关帝老爷	Lord Guan, a mythical figure originating from historical character Guan Yu, a general during the Three Kingdoms period
guazhi	挂纸	"hang paper," the ritual of hanging "spirit money" on graves when offerings are made

gui	鬼	ghosts
handi	旱地	dry fields
hao hua	好话	good words
haoxiang hen ben	好象很笨	seems very silly
heixin	黑心	evil, untrustworthy
he shi jiao gui wu shu, jiao wu si wu shi gui	何事叫 鬼无数, 叫无祀 无氏鬼	Even if someone calls out the name of one of the numerous ghostly spirits without a lineage, they are not actually offering sacrifices to them.
hongbao	红包	a red envelope
hongmen rou	红焖肉	braised pork
hong qu mi	红曲米	red yeast rice
hongzao	红枣	red dates
Huagong and *Huamu*	花公花母	Flower Father and Mother
huangshan	黄鳝	swamp eel that used to be found in flooded rice paddies
huasheng	花生	peanuts
huayuan	花园	flower garden
hu dou	胡豆	fava beans
hukou	户口	the household registration system
jia	家	family
Jialan Pusa	伽蓝菩萨	Sangharama Bodhisattva
jian ban	煎粄	deep-fried sesame seed balls
jiangjiu	讲究	to be particular about
jiang you ji	姜油鸡	steamed chicken with ginger and red chilies
jian sanzi	煎馓子	deep-fried wheat treats
jian yupian	煎芋片	fried shredded taro cakes
jian yuyuan	煎芋圆	fried taro ball
jiaoban	薯粄	sticky rice cake with the vegetable jiaocai, a kind of leek
jijiu	鸡酒	"chicken wine," dish made of braised chicken in ginger and fermented rice wine
jin	斤	unit of weight, one jin is equivalent to 0.5 kilograms or 1.34 pounds
jingjiu jiao qing	敬酒交情	to exchange feeling by toasting
jishiteng	鸡屎藤	Chinese fevervine herb
jitian	祭田	sacrificial land
jiu shehui	旧社会	old society
juecai	蕨菜	fiddleheads, or edible fern fronds
kaoshan chishan	靠山吃山	While relying on the mountains, eat the mountain's produce.

keqi	客气	polite, courteous
kumai	苦荬, 苦脉	the "bitter-veined," sow thistle leaf Ixeris, a ubiquitous leafy green vegetable
kumai kao zhou	苦脉靠粥	kumai accompanies congee
laorenhui	老人会	Council of Elders
lengxing	冷性	cold
liangxin	良心	good or virtuous heart/mind, conscience
liangxing	凉性	cool
liangxing xunhuan	良性循环	the circle of good things
liangxue	凉血	cool blood
lianzi	莲子	lotus seeds
liao	聊	to chat, talk aimlessly
lingzhi baozi fen	灵芝孢子粉	dried powder from a fungus that can be used as a medicine
li shang wanglai	礼尚往来	Courtesy demands reciprocity.
long	砻	large grinding stone
longmai	龙脉	dragon's veins
Longshen	龙神	the Dragon God
longyan	龙眼	*Dimocarpus longan*
longzhong	隆重	(holidays or events) grand
lunliu	轮流	to rotate
luobo	萝卜	daikon radish
luobo yuan	萝卜圆	steamed dumplings made from daikon radish and pork
luohou	落后	backward
maidong	麦冬	*Radix ophiopogonis*
maogen	茅根	Japanese bloodgrass, *Imperata cylindrica*
meicai kourou	梅菜扣肉	braised pork and dried salted greens
meiyou cai	没有菜	There are no dishes.
mianzi	面子	literally "face," connotes status
min yi shi wei tian	民以食为天	"People consider food as heaven," meaning that people rely on food to survive.
mu	亩	unit of area, one acre is equivalent to 6.07 mu
muzeicao	木贼草	scouring rush herb, or horsetail grass
nanba zhuanqian, mama gengtian	男爸赚钱, 妈妈耕田	Dad makes money and mom ploughs the field.
nande	难得	difficult to attain, rare
nianban	年粄	New Year's treats made with glutinous rice flour or wheat flour
niang doufu	酿豆腐	special dumpling in which chopped meat is pressed into bean curd
nianliang pusa	碾粮菩萨	Nianliang Bodhisattva
ni bu shi nanren ma?	你不是男人吗	Aren't you a man?

ni chi an men jiu le	你吃俺们就乐	We feel so happy when you eat.
niu er gong	牛耳公	deep-fried wheat dough filled with sesame seeds, peanuts, and sweet bean paste
niunai shugen	牛奶树根	*Ficus hispida,* a tropical fig root
nongren	农人	peasant
nongyao	农药	farm chemicals
nuanfu	暖福	"Warm up the good fortune," a step in the cycle of praying to a god
paoyang	抛秧	to toss the seedlings
qi	气	a vital energy, vapor, or breath that circulates through one's body
Qiao Baigong	桥佰公	God of the Bridge, "Earl of the Bridge"
qifu	起福	to pray to a god to raise good fortune
qin	芹	celery
qing	清	bright
qing	青	green
qing kun fan	清困饭	rice cleared of tiredness and fatigue
qingming ban	清明粄	Qingming buns
qingre, runfei	清热，润肺	(soup) counteracts heat and moistens lungs
qinlao	勤劳	industrious
qinqi	亲戚	affines, relatives through marriage
renao	热闹	bustling and busy
renqing de cilichang	人情的磁力场	magnetic fields of human feeling
ren yi zou, cha jiu liang	人一走，茶就凉	Once the people leave, the tea turns cold.
rexing	热性	hot
roushizhe	肉食者	meat eaters
Sanbao	三宝	the three deities (Shakyamuni Buddha, Bhaiṣajyaguru, and Amitabha Buddha)
san ji di tang	三及第汤	three-levels soup, a popular morning soup
sansheng	三牲	three sacrificial meats (pork, chicken, and fish)
sanshi yinguo	三世因果	moral cause and effect over three lifetimes
sanzi	馓子	a snack made of thin ropes of wheat flour
shancha shugen	山茶树根	*Camellia sinensis* roots
shangban	上班	to work in an office
shanjimi	山鸡米	Lophatherum herb
shaohuo	烧火	to start up a fire, usually referring to tending the kitchen fires to prepare for a meal

Sheguan Laoye	社官老爷	a local guardian god, also a god of earth and grain
shen	神	spirits
shengcai	生菜	lettuce
shengchi jianyong	省吃俭用	to live frugally
shengdi	生地	Chinese foxglove
shifan	食饭	to eat rice
shiganlan	石橄榄	*Pholidota chinensis* Lindl
Shijiamouni Pusa	释伽牟尼	Shakyamuni Buddha
shijiu	食酒	to "eat" liquor, to consume liquor
shufanshu	树番薯	the starch of the cassava
shui ji shi cai	水即是财	Water brings in wealth.
shuitian	水田	wet fields
sigua	丝瓜	towel gourd
sishou cha	四手茶	four-hands tea, the wedding tradition in which the bride and groom serve the guests tea while receiving gifts and money
song jiangjiu	送姜酒	to send ginger wine, the Hakka tradition of sharing ginger wine with other families when a woman gives birth
suan	蒜	garlic
sumi	粟米	millet
suomu cao	锁幕草	scouring rush herb, or horsetail grass
sushi	素食	vegetarian diet
tian	天	heaven
tianban	甜粄	glutinous rice flour with brown sugar steamed overnight
Tiangong and *Tianmu*	天公天母	the Heavenly Father and Mother
tiaojian	条件	conditions, living conditions
tiejia cao	铁甲草	*Dictyocline griffithii*
tongyangxi	童养媳	adopted daughter-in-law
tuanyuan fan	团圆饭	(family) reunion dinner
Tudi Baigong	土地佰公	Earth God, "Earl of the Earth"
tufuling	土茯岭	Chinaroot greenbier rhizome
wan	玩	to play
wan fu	完福	to complete the praying cycle by redeeming one's vow to the god
Wangren Jie	亡人节	Wandering Souls Festival
wan xinniang	玩新娘	"to play jokes on the bride," a Hakka wedding tradition in which the bride and groom go from table to table to toast the guests

wei	味	sapor
weijiao ban	味酵粄	fermented rice flour pasta
Weituo Pusa	韦驮菩萨	Skanda Bodhisattva, also known as Dimu
wenxing	温性	warm
wushi gui	无氏鬼	ghosts without a lineage or name
wuwei	五味	the five flavors
wuzhi maotao	五指毛桃	wild peach root
xiancai	苋菜	Chinese spinach
xiang yi qian	香仪钱	incense-rites money
xiao	孝	filiality
xiaomai	小麦	winter wheat
xiaozai yanshou yaofo	消灾延寿药佛	Bhaisajyaguru, the Buddha of healing and medicine in Mahāyāna Buddhism
xing	性	quality
xiuxin	修心	to cultivate one's heart or mind
xuyuan	许愿	to make a vow
yang	养	to support or nourish (one's family)
yaocai	药材	medicinal grasses
yeshen yegui	野神野鬼	unruly spirits and ghosts
yidian xinyi	一点心意	a small token of regard
yiku fan	忆苦饭	"recalling bitterness meal," unappetizing dish eaten for Lunar New Year's unity meal during Cultural Revolution, supposed to prompt memories of "bitterness" of pre-Liberation era and "sweetness" of the present
yiku sitian	忆苦思甜	to recall the bitter before thinking of the sweet
yincha	饮茶	to drink tea
ying fantou	硬饭头	Chinaroot Greenbier Rhizome
yinguo	因果	cause and effect
yin shui si yuan	饮水思源	When you drink water, remember the source.
you wenhua shuiping	有文化水平	(people) with education, or a certain cultural level
you xin	有心	"to have heart/mind," to demonstrate care and concern
yu	鱼	fish
yu	裕	fortune
yuanlanpen jie	盂兰盆节	the Yulanpen Festival, sometimes known as the Ghost Festival, or Zhongyuan
yuanxiao jie	元宵节	the Yuan Xiao Festival
yu gan	芋干	dried taro
yumei	愚昧	ignorance

yu mi	玉米	corn
yuyan yulie zhi shi	愈演愈烈之势	to become increasingly more intense
zaliang	杂粮	miscellaneous staples
zaosheng guizi	早生贵字	"May you have a distinguished son early," a common wish to newly married couples
zaoxing	燥性	dry
zhaima	斋妈	"vegetarian mothers," referring to the Buddhist lay female practitioners in Meixian
zhaipan	斋盘	vegetarian offerings
Zhongyuan Jie	中元节	the Zhong Yuan Festival
zhongxing	中性	neutral
zhou	粥	congee, or rice porridge
ziliudi	自留地	private plots
zuigui	醉鬼	drunken ghosts
zui xiao de yi tian	最小的一天	one's youngest day
zuofu	作福	to create blessings, or good fortune
zuogong	做工	to do physical work or factory work

REFERENCES

Ahmed, Sara. "Affective Economies." *Social Text* 22, no. 2 (2004): 117–39.

Anderson, Eugene. *The Food of China*. New Haven, CT: Yale University Press, 1988.

Appadurai, Arjun. "Gastro-politics in Hindu South Asia." *American Ethnologist* 8, no. 3 (1981): 494–511.

Baudrillard, Jean. "The Ideological Genesis of Needs." In *The Consumer Society Reader*, edited by Douglas B. Holt and Juliet B. Schor, 57–80. New York: New Press, 2000.

Becker, Jasper. *Hungry Ghosts: Mao's Secret Famine*. New York: Free Press, 1996.

Belasco, Warren. *Food: The Key Concepts*. New York: Berg, 2008.

Benewick, Robert, and Stephanie Hemelryk Donald. *The State of China Atlas*. Berkeley: University of California Press, 2005.

Bloch, Maurice. "Commensality and Poisoning." *Social Research* 66, no. 1 (1999): 133–49.

Bourdieu, Pierre. *Distinction: A Social Critique of the Judgement of Taste*. Translated by Richard Nice. London: Routledge and Kegan Paul, 1984.

Buck, John Lossing. *Land Utilization in China*. Chicago: University of Chicago Press, 1937.

Caldwell, Melissa. "The Compassion of Strangers: Intimate Encounters with Assistance in Moscow." In *Ethnographies of Social Support*, edited by Marcus Schlecker and Friederike Fleischer, 103–20. New York: Palgrave Macmillan, 2013.

Campany, Robert Ford. "The Meanings of Cuisines of Transcendence in Late Classical and Early Medieval China." *T'oung Pao*, 2nd ser., 91 (2005): 1–57.

Carstens, Janet. "Cooking Money: Gender and the Symbolic Transformation of Means of Exchange in a Malay Fishing Community." In *Money and the Morality of Exchange*, edited by Jonathan Parry and Maurice Bloch, 117–41. Cambridge: Cambridge University Press, 1989.

Chang, K. C. Introduction to *Food in Chinese Culture: Anthropological and Historical Perspectives*, edited by K. C. Chang, 1–22. New Haven, CT: Yale University Press, 1977.

Chard, Robert L. "Rituals and Scriptures of the Stove Cult." *Ritual and Scripture in Chinese Popular Religion,* edited by David Johnson, 3–54. Institute of East Asian Studies. Berkeley: University of California, 1995.

Chau, Adam Yuet. *Miraculous Response: Doing Popular Religion in Contemporary China.* Stanford, CA: Stanford University Press, 2006.

Chengbei Xiang [Chengbei township]. *Ge Guanliqu Zhuyao Jiben Qingkuang* 成北 乡各管理区主要基本情况 [Basic information on each administrative district]. Unpublished Information Sheet. Chengbei Township, 1997, 2007, 2012.

Chen, Yunpiao. "The Altar and the Table: Field Studies on the Dietary Culture of Chaoshan Inhabitants." In *Changing Chinese Foodways in Asia,* edited by David Y. H. Wu and Tan Chee-beng, 19–34. Hong Kong: Chinese University Press, 2001.

China Statistical Yearbook 2015. Beijing: China Statistics Press, 2015.

Cohen, Myron. "Souls and Salvation: Conflicting Themes in Chinese Popular Religion." In *Death Ritual in Late Imperial and Moden China,* edited by James L. Watson and Evelyn Rawski, 180–222. Berkeley: University of California Press, 1988.

Counihan, Carole M. *Around the Tuscan Table: Food, Family, and Gender in Twentieth Century Florence.* New York: Routledge, 2004.

Cui, Jia. "Ganbei Culture Killing Officials." *China Daily,* July 20, 2009. www .chinadaily.com.cn/china/2009-07/20/content_8446843.htm.

Demick, Barbara. "In China, What You Eat Tells Who You Are." *Los Angeles Times,* September 16, 2011.

Diamant, Neil. "Re-examining the Impact of the 1950 Marriage Law: State Improvisation, Local Initiative, and Rural Family Change." *China Quarterly* 161 (2000): 171–98.

Dikötter, Frank. *Mao's Great Famine: The History of China's Most Devastating Catastrophe.* New York: Bloomsbury, 2010.

Dong, Xiaoping. "The Dual Character of Chinese Folk Ideas about Resources: On Three Western Fujian Volumes in the Traditional Hakka Society Series." In *Ethnography in China Today: A Critical Assessement of Methods and Results,* edited by Daniel Overmyer, 343–67. Taipei: Yuan-Liou, 2002.

Douglas, Mary. "Deciphering a Meal." In *Implicit Meanings: Essays in Anthropology,* 249–75. London: Routledge and Kegan Paul, 1975.

———. "Food as a System of Communication." In *In the Active Voice,* 82–104. London: Routledge and Kegan Paul, 1982.

Dumont, Louis. *Homo Hierarchicus: The Caste System and Its Implications.* Chicago: University of Chicago Press, 1980.

Durkheim, Emile. "What Is a Social Fact? (1895)." In *Anthropological Theory: An Introductory History,* edited by R. Jon McGee and Richard L. Warms, 78–85. New York: McGraw-Hill, 2012.

Edgerton-Tarpley, Kathryn Jean. "From 'Nourish the People' to 'Sacrifice for the Nation': Changing Responses to Disaster in Late Imperial and Modern China." *Journal of Asian Studies* 73, no. 2 (2014): 447–69.

———. *Tears from Iron: Cultural Responses to Famine in Nineteenth-Century China.* Berkeley: University of California Press, 2008.

Eiss, Paul, and David Pedersen. "Introduction: Values of Value." *Cultural Anthropology* 17, no. 3 (2002): 283–90.

Fang, Xuejia 房学嘉. *Kejia Minsu* 客家民俗 [Hakka folk customs]. Guangzhou: Huanan Ligongdaxue Chuban She 华南理工大学出版社 [South China University of Technology Press], 2005.

———. *Kejia Yuanliu Tanao* 客家源流探奥 [An investigation into the origins and development of the Hakka]. Guangdong: Guangdong Gaodeng Chuban She 广东高等教育出版社 [Guangdong Higher Educational Press], 1994.

———, ed. *Meizhou heyuan diqu de cunluo wenhua* 梅州河源地区的村落文化 [Village religion and culture in northeastern Guangdong]. Traditional Hakka Society Series, Overseas Chinese Archives. Vol. 5. Hong Kong: Internatonal Hakka Studies Association and École Française D"Extrême Orient, 1997.

Fang, Xuejia, Song Dejian, Xiao Wenping, and Zhou Jianxin 房学家,宋德剑,肖文评,周建新. *Kejia Wenhua Daolun* 客家文化导论 [An introduction to Hakka culture]. Guangzhou: Huacheng Chuban She [Huacheng Press], 2002.

Fang, Xuejia, Xiao Wenping, and Zhong Pulan 房学嘉 肖文评 钟普兰. *Kejia Meizhou* 客家梅州 [Hakka Meizhou]. Guangzhou: Huanan Ligong Daxue Chuan She 华南理工大学出版社 [Huagong University of Science and Engineering Press], 2009.

Fantasia, Rick. "Fast Food in France." *Theory and Society* 24, no. 2 (1995): 201–43.

Fei, Hsiao-tung, and Chih-I Chang. *Earthbound China: A Study of Rural Economy in Yunnan.* Chicago: University of Chicago Press, 1945.

Fei, Xiaotung. *From the Soil: The Foundations of Chinese Society.* Translated by Gary Hamilton and Wang Zheng. Berkeley: University of California Press, 1992.

Feuchtwang, Stephen. "Political History, Past Suffering and Present Sources of Moral Judgement in the People's Republic of China." In *Ordinary Ethics in China,* edited by Charles Stafford, 222–41. London: Bloomsbury, 2013.

Fitting, Elizabeth. *The Struggle for Maize: Campesinos, Workers, and Transgenic Corn in the Mexican Countryside.* Durham, NC: Duke University Press, 2011.

French, Howard. "Rush for Wealth in China's Cities Shatters the Ancient Assurance of Care in Old Age." *New York Times,* November 3, 2006.

Giddens, Anthony. *The Consequences of Modernity.* Stanford, CA: Stanford University Press, 1990.

Goossaert, Vincent, and David Palmer. *The Religious Question in Modern China.* Chicago: University of Chicago Press, 2011.

Graeber, David. *Toward an Anthropological Theory of Value: The False Coin of Our Own Dreams.* New York: Palgrave, 2001.

Gudeman, Stephen. "Necessity or Contingency: Mutuality and Market." In Hann and Hart, *Market and Society,* 17–37.

Hann, Chris. "Embedded Socialism? Land, Labor and Money in Eastern Xinjiang." In Hann and Hart, *Market and Society* 256–71.

Hann, Chris, and Keith Hart, eds. *Market and Society: The Great Transformation Today.* Cambridge: Cambridge University Press, 2009.

Hansen, Mette Halskov, and Cuiming Pang. "Idealizing Individual Choice: Work, Love, Family in the Eyes of Young, Rural Chinese." In *iChina: The Rise of the Individual in Modern Chinese Society,* edited by Mette Halskov Hansen and Rune Svarverud, 39–64. Copenhagen: NIAD Press, 2010.

Hemelryk, Stephanie, and Donald Robvert Benewick. *The State of China Atlas.* Berkeley: University of California Press, 2005.

Holt-Giménez, Eric, and Raj Patel. *Food Rebellions: Crisis and the Hunger for Justice.* Oakland, CA: Food First Books, 2009.

Holtzman, Jon D. "Food and Memory." *Annual Review of Anthropology* 35 (2006): 361–78.

———. *Uncertain Tastes: Memory, Ambivalence, and the Politics of Eating in Samburu, Northern Kenya.* Berkeley: University of California, 2009.

Humphrey, Caroline. "Exemplars and Rules: Aspects of the Discourse of Moralities." In *The Ethnography of Moralities,* edited by Signe Howell, 25, 47. London: Routledge, 1997.

Ikels, Charlotte, ed. *Filial Piety: Practice and Discourse in Contemporary Asia.* Berkeley: University of California Press, 2004.

Jacka, Tamara. *Women's Work in Rural China.* Cambridge: Cambridge University Press, 1997.

Jing, Jun, ed. *Feeding China's Little Emperors: Food, Children and Social Change.* Stanford, CA: Stanford University Press, 2000.

———. "Meal Rotation and Filial Piety." In *Filial Piety: Practice and Discourse in Contemporary Asia,* edited by Charlotte Ikels, 53–62. Berkeley: University of California Press, 2004.

Jordan, David K. *Gods, Ghosts and Ancestors: The Folk Religion of a Taiwanese Village.* Berkeley: University of California Press, 1977.

Jordan, David K., and Daniel Overmyer. *The Flying Phoenix: Aspects of Chinese Sectarianism in Taiwan.* Princeton, NJ: Princeton University Press, 1986.

Judd, Ellen. *Gender and Power in Rural China.* Stanford, CA: Stanford University Press, 1994.

Kajanus, Anni. *Journey of the Phoenix: Overseas Study and Women's Changing Position in China.* Research Series in Anthropology. Helsinki: University of Helsinki, 2014.

Kieschnick, John. "Buddhist Vegetarianism in China." In Sterckx, *Of Tripod and Palate,* 186–212.

Kipnis, Andrew. *Producing Guanxi: Sentiment, Self, and Subculture in a North China Village.* Durham, NC: Duke University Press, 1997.

Klein, Jakob. "Creating Ethical Food Consumers? Promoting Organic Foods in Urban Southwest China." *Social Anthropology* 17, no. 1 (2009): 74–89.

Klein, Jacob A., Yuson Jong, and Melissa L. Caldwell. Introduction to *Ethical Eating in the Postsocialist and Socialist World,* edited by Yuson Jung, Jacob A. Klein, and Melissa L. Caldwell, 1–24. Berkeley: University of California Press, 2014.

Kleinman, Arthur, Yunxiang Yan, Jing Jun, Sing Lee, Everett Zhang, Pan Tianshu, Wu Fei, and Jinhua Guo. *Deep China: The Moral Life of the Person. What Anthropology and Psychiatry Tell Us about China Today.* Berkeley: University of California, 2011.

———. Introduction. In Kleinman et al., *Deep China*, 1–35.

Ku, Hok Bun. *Moral Politics in a Chinese Village.* Lanham, MD: Rowman and Littlefield, 2003.

Lambek, Michael. Introduction to *Ordinary Ethics: Anthropology, Language, and Action,* edited by Michael Lambek, 1–36. New York: Fordham University Press, 2010.

Levi, Jean. "The Rite, the Norm, and the Dao: Philosophy of Sacrifice and Transcendence of Power in Ancient China." In Vol. 2 of *Early Chinese Religion, Part One: Shang through Han (1250 BC—220 AD),* edited by John Lagerwey and Marc Kalinowski, 645–92. Leiden, The Netherlands: Brill, 2009.

Lévi-Strauss, Claude. "The Culinary Triangle." In *Food and Culture: A Reader,* edited by Carole Counihan and Penny Van Esterik, 36–43. 2nd ed. New York: Routledge, 2008.

Li, Lillian M. *Fighting Famine in North China: State, Market and Environmental Decline, 1690s–1990s.* Stanford, CA: Stanford University Press, 2007.

Lin, Qingshui 林清水. "The Folk Customs of Two Townships in Jiaoling County" 蕉嶺縣新铺镇徐稀镇民俗. In *Meizhou heyuan diqu de cunluo wenhua* 梅州河源地区的村落文化. [Village religion and culture in northeastern Guangdong], edited by Fang Xuejia 房学家, 219–66. Vol. 5. Hong Kong: Internatonal Hakka Studies Association and École Française D'Extrême Orient, 1997.

Liu, Xin. *In One's Own Shadow: An Ethnographic Account of the Condition of Postreform China.* Berkeley: University of California Press, 2000.

Lo, Vivienne. "Pleasure, Prohibition, and Pain: Food and Medicine in Traditional China." In Sterckx, *Of Tripod and Palate*, 163–85.

Lora-Wainwright, Anna. "Of Farming Chemicals and Cancer Deaths: The Politics of Health in Contemporary Rural China." *Social Anthropology* 17.1 (2009): 56–73.

Luo, Shunhui 罗双辉, Chen Yuanxia 陈苑霞, and Zhang Zhenping（张振平. 梅州市观光农业与休闲旅游农业发展现状及优势 [Current Situation and Advantages of the Development of Sightseeing Agriculture and Leisure Agriculture in Meizhou]. *Modern Agricultural Technology* 现代农业科技2013年11期 (November 2013). mall.cnki.net/magazine/magadetail/ANHE201311.htm.

Lu, Yonglung, Yonglong Lu, Shuai Song, Ruoshi Wang, Zhaoyang Liu, Jing Meng, Andrew J. Sweetman, Alan Jenkins, Robert C. Ferrier, Hon Li, Wei Luo, and Tieyu Wang. "Impacts of Soil and Water Pollution on Food Safety and Health Risks in China." *Environment International* 77 (2015): 5–15.

Madsen, Richard. *Morality and Power in a Chinese Village.* Berkeley: University of California Press, 1984.

Marriott, McKim. "Caste-Ranking and Food Transactions: A Matrix Analysis." In *Structure and Change in Indian Society,* edited by Milton Singer and Bernard S. Cohn, 133–71. Chicago: Aldine, 1968.

Mason, Katherine A. "To Your Health! Toasting, Intoxication and Gendered Critique among Banqueting Women." *China Journal* 69 (2013): 108–33.

Mauss, Marcel. *The Gift: The Form and Reason for Exchange in Archaic Societies.* Translated by W. D. Halls. With a foreword by Mary Douglas. New York, W. W. Norton, 1990.

Mayers, Ramon. "The Commercialization of Agriculture in Modern China." In *Economic Organization in Chinese Society,* edited by W. E. Willmott, 173–92. Stanford, CA: Stanford University Press, 1972.

Meizhou City People's Government. "Meixian Qu, 2008." Accessed July 14, 2015. www.meizhou.gov.cn/mzgk/xyjjjs/2008–04–14/1208159025d17809.html.

Meizhou Ribao [Meizhou Daily]. "Zhongyuan Jie: Kejia Ren de Qi Yue Ban" 中元 节 : 客家人的七月半 [the Zhongyuan Festival: the Hakka 7/15]. *Meizhou Ribao.* Accessed August 8, 2012. mzrb.meizhou.cn/data/20120825/html/6 /content_11.html.

Miller, Eric T. "Filial Daughters, Filial Sons: Comparisons from Rural North China." In Ikels, *Filial Piety,* 34–52.

Millstone, Erik, and Tim Lang. *The Atlas of Food: Who Eats What, Where, and Why.* Berkeley: University of California Press, 2008.

Mintz, Sidney. *Sweetness and Power.* New York: Viking, 1985.

———. *Tasting Food, Tasting Freedom.* Boston: Beacon Press, 1997.

Møller-Olsen, Astrid. "Dissolved in Liquor and Life: Drinkers and Drinking Cultures in Mo Yan's Novel *Liquorland.*" In *Commensality: From Everyday Food to Feast,* edited by Suzanne Kerner, Cynthia Chou, and Morten Warmind, 177–94. London: Bloomsbury, 2015.

Meixian Zhi 梅县志 [Mei County Gazetteer]. Edited by Meixian Difangzhi Bianzuan Weiyuanhui 梅县地方志编纂委员会 [Meixian Gazetteer Compiling Committee]. Guangzhou: Guangdong Renmin Chubanshe, 1994.

Myers, Ramon. "The Commercialization of Agriculture in Moden China." In *Economic Organization in Chinese Society,* edited by W. E. Willmott, 173–92. Stanford, CA: Stanford University Press, 1972.

Ngai, Pun. *Made in China: Women Factory Workers in a Global Workplace.* Durham, NC: Duke University Press, 2005.

Overing, Joanna, and Alan Passes. Introduction to *The Anthropology of Love and Anger: The Aesthetics of Conviviality in Native Amazonia,* edited by Joanna Overing and Alan Passes, 1–30. New York: Routledge, 2000.

Overmyer, Daniel. "Comments on the Foundations of Chinese Culture in Late Traditional Times." In *Ethnography in China Today: A Critical Assessment of Methods and Results,* edited by Daniel L. Overymyer, 313–42. Taipei: Yuan-Liou, 2002.

Oxfeld, Ellen. *Drink Water, but Remember the Source: Moral Discourse in a Chinese Village.* Berkeley: University of California Press, 2010.

Pang, Lihua, Alan deBrauw, and Scott Rozelle. "Working until You Drop: The Elderly of Rural China." *China Journal* 52 (2004): 73–96.

Parish, Steven. *Moral Knowing in a Hindu Sacred City: An Exploration of Mind, Emotion, and Self.* New York: Columbia University Press, 1994.

Parry, Jonathan, and Maurice Bloch. Introduction to *Money and the Morality of Exchange,* edited by Jonathan Parry and Maurice Bloch, 1–32. Cambridge: Cambridge University Press, 1989.

Patel, Raj. *Stuffed and Starved: The Hidden Battle for the World Food System.* Brooklyn: Melville House, 2007.

Puett, Michael. "Economies of Ghosts, Gods, and Goods: The History and Anthropology of Chinese Temple Networks." In *Radical Egalitarianism: Local Realities, Global Realities,* edited by Felicity Aulino, Miriam Goheen, and Stanley Tambiah, 91–100. New York: Fordham University Press, 2013.

———. "The Offering of Food and the Creation of Order: The Practice of Sacrifice in Early China." In Sterckx, *Of Tripod and Palate,* 75–95.

Rappaport, Roy. *Ritual and Religion in the Making of Humanity.* Cambridge: Cambridge University Press, 1999.

Redfield, Robert. *The Little Community, and Peasant Society and Culture.* Chicago: University of Chicago Press, 1960.

Reed-Danahay, Deborah. "Champagne and Chocolate: 'Taste' and Inversion in a French Wedding Ritual." *American Anthropologist* 98, no. 4 (1996): 750–61.

Robotham, Dan. Afterword. In Hann and Hart, *Market and Society: The Great Transformation Today,* 272–83.

Rofel, Lisa. *Desiring China: Experiments in Neoliberalism, Sexuality, and Public Culture.* Durham, NC: Duke University Press, 2007.

Rohsenow, John S, ed. *ABC Dictionary of Chinese Proverbs.* Honolulu: University of Hawaii Press, 2002.

Roy, Krishnendu. *The Migrants Table. Meals and Memoires in Bengali-American Households.* Philadelphia: Temple University Press, 2005.

Seligman, Robert, and Robert Weller. *Rethinking Pluralism: Ritual, Experience and Ambiguity.* Oxford: Oxford University Press, 2012.

Shanin, Teodor. *Defining Peasants: Essays Concerning Rural Societies, Expolary Economies, and Learning from Them in the Contemporary World.* Oxford: Blackwell, 1990.

———. *Peasants and Peasant Societies.* Oxford: Blackwell, 1987.

Simmonds, Frederick J. *Food in China: A Cultural and Historical Inquiry.* Boca Raton, FL: CRC Press, 1991.

Smil, Vaclav. *China's Past, China's Future: Energy, Food, Environment.* New York: Routledge Curzon, 2005.

Spence, Jonathan. "Ch'ing." In *Food in Chinese Culture: Anthropological and Historical Perspectives,* edited by K. C. Chang, 259–94. New Haven, CT: Yale University Press, 1977.

Stafford, Charles. "Chinese Patriliny and the Cycles of Yang and Laiwang." In *Cultures of Relatedness: New Approaches to the Study of Kinship,* edited by Janet Carsten, 37–54. Cambridge: Cambridge University Press, 2000.

———. *Separation and Reunion in Modern China.* Cambridge: Cambridge University Press, 2000.

———. "Some Good and Bad People in the Countryside." In *Ordinary Ethics in China,* edited by Charles Stafford, 101–114. London: Bloomsbury, 2013.

Statistical Bureau of Meixian District. "Meizhou Statistical Report on National Economy and Social Development, 2013" 梅州市梅县区统计局关于2013年国民经济和社会发展的统计公报. Meizhou City: Statistical Bureau of Meixian District. Accessed August 22, 2015. www.mxtjj.gov.cn/tjfx/2014-01-27/271.html.

Steinmüller, Hans. "The Moving Boundaries of Social Heat: Gambling in Rural China." *Journal of the Royal Anthropological Institute* 17 (2011): 263–80.

Sterckx, Roel. "Food and Philosophy in Early China." In Sterckx, *Of Tripod and Palate,* 34–61.

————. Introduction. In Sterckx, *Of Tripod and Palate,* 1–18.

Sun, Lung-ku. "Contemporary Chinese Culture: Structures and Emotionality." *Australian Journal of Chinese Affairs* 26 (1991): 1–41.

Sutton, David. "Comment on 'Consumption' by David Graeber." *Current Anthropology* 52, no. 4 (2011): 507.

————. *Remembrance of Repasts: An Anthropology of Food and Memory.* New York: Berg, 2001.

Tambiah, Stanley. *Culture, Thought, and Social Action.* Cambridge: Harvard University Press, 1985.

————. *Magic, Science, Religion and the Scope of Rationality.* Cambridge: Cambridge Univesity Press, 1990.

Tam, Wai Lun. "Communal Worship and Festivals in Chinese Villages." In *Chinese Religious Life,* edited by David A. Palmer, Glenn Shive, and Philip L. Wikeri, 30–49. New York: Oxford University Press, 2011.

Tan, Chee Beng, and Ding Yuling. "The Promotion of Tea in South China: Reinventing Tradition in an Old Industry." *Food and Foodways* 18 (2010): 121–44.

Tang, Linzhen 唐林珍. "Medicine Diet: A New Food Trend" 药膳引领新潮流. *Meizhou Ribao* 梅州日报 (April 2, 2007).

Thaxton, Ralph A. *Catastrophe and Contention in Rural China: Mao's Great Leap Forward Famine and the Origins of Righteous Resistance in Da Fo Village.* Cambridge: Cambridege University Press, 2008.

Thompson, E. P. "The Moral Economy of the English Crowd in the Eighteenth Century." *Past and Present* 50, no. 1 (1971): 76–136.

Thompson, Stuart. "Death, Food, and Fertility." In *Death Ritual in Late Imperial and Modern China,* edited by James L. Watson and Evelyn S. Rawski, 71–108. Berkeley: University of California Press, 1988.

Unger, Jonathan. *The Transformation of Rural China.* Armonk, NY: M. E. Sharpe, 2002.

University of Michigan China Data Center. "China Data Online, County Data." n.d. Accessed August 11, 2015. http://chinadataonline.org/member/county/countytshow.asp.

Wang, Danyu. "Ritualistic Coresidence and the Weakening of Filial Practice." In Ikels, *Filial Piety,* 16–33.

Wang, Zengneng 王增能干. *Kejia Yinshi Wenhua* 客家饮食文化 [Hakka food culture]. Fuzhou: Fujian Jiaoyu Chuban She 福建教育出版社 [Fujian Educational Press], 1995.

Watson, James L. "Feeding the Revolution: Public Mess Halls and Coercive Commensality in Maoist China." In *Governance of Life in Chinese Moral Experience: The Quest for an Adequate Life,* edited by Everett Zhang, Arthur Kleinman, and Weiming Tu, 33–46. New York: Routledge, 2011.

———. "From the Common Pot: Feasting with Equals in Chinese Society." *Anthropos* 82 (1987): 389–401.

Wen, Yanyuan. "Customs of Jianqiao Village, Fengshun" 丰顺县建桥围的宗祖與民俗. In *Village Religion and Culture in Northeastern Guangdong* 梅州河源地区的村落文化, edited by Xuejia Fang, 198–219. Hong Kong: International Hakka Studies Association and the École-Française D'Extrême-Orient, 1997.

Wilk, Richard. "Morals and Metaphors: The Meaning of Consumption." In *Elusive Consumption,* edited by Karin Ekström and Helen Brembeck, 11–26. New York: Berg, 2004.

Williams, Raymond. *Keywords.* Routledge Revivals. 1976. Reprint, New York: Routledge, 2011.

Wolf, Arthur. "Adopt a Daughter-in-Law, Marry a Sister: A Chinese Solution to the Problem of the Incest Taboo." *American Anthropologist* 70, no. 5 (1968): 864–74.

———. "Gods, Ghosts, and Ancestors." In *Studies in Chinese Society,* edited by Arthur Wolf, 131–82. Stanford, CA: Stanford University Press, 1978.

Wolf, Eric. *Peasants.* Englewood Cliffs, NJ: Prentice-Hall, 1966.

Wolf, Margery. *Women and the Family in Rural Taiwan.* Stanford, CA: Stanford University Press, 1972.

Wu, Fei. "Suicide, a Modern Problem in China." In Kleinman et al., *Deep China,* 213–36.

Xiao, Shaobin 肖绍彬. "Meishi Yu Xiaodao" 美食与孝道. *Meizhou Guangbo Dianshi* 梅州广播电视 (March 23, 2007): 6.

Yan, Hairong. "Spectralization of the Rural: Reinterpretng the Labor Mobility of Rural Young Women in Post-Mao China." *American Ethnologist* 30, no. 4 (2003): 578–96.

Yan, Yunxiang. "The Changing Moral Landscape." In Kleinman et al., *Deep China,* 36–77.

———. *The Flow of Gifts: Reciprocity and Social Networks in a Chinese Village.* Stanford, CA: Stanford University Press, 1996.

———. "Food Safety and Social Risk in Contemporary China." *Journal of Asian Studies* 71, no. 3 (2012): 705–29.

———. *Private Life under Socialism.* Stanford, CA: Stanford University Press, 2003.

Yang, Jisheng. *Tombstone: The Great Chinese Famine, 1958–1962.* Edited by Edward Freidman, Guo Jian, and Stacy Mosher. Translated by Stacy Mosher and Guo Jian. New York: Farrar, Straus and Giroux, 2008.

Yang, Lien-Sheng. "The Concept of Pao as a Basis for Social Relations in China." In *Chinese Thought and Institutions,* edited by John K. Fairbank, 291–309. Chicago: University of Chicago Press, 1957.

Yang, Martin. *A Chinese Village, Taitou, Shantung Province.* New York: Columbia University Press, 1945.

Yang, Mayfair. *Gifts, Favors, and Banquets: The Art of Social Relationships in China.* Ithaca, NY: Cornell University Press, 1994.

———. "Postcoloniality and Religiosity in Modern China: The Disenchantments of Sovereignty." *Theory, Culture, and Society* 28, no. 2 (2011): 3–45.

Zhang, Everett Yuehang. "China's Sexual Revolution." In Kleinman et al., *Deep China,* 106–51.

Zhang, Qian Forrest, and John A. Donaldson. "The Rise of Agrarian Capitalism with Chinese Characteristics: Agricultural Modernization, Agribusiness and Collective Land Rights." *China Journal* 60 (2008): 25–47.

Zhou, Xun, ed. *The Great Famine in China, 1958–1962: A Documentary History.* New Haven, CT: Yale University Press, 2012.

Zigon, Jarrett. *Morality: An Anthropological Perspective.* Oxford: Berg, 2008.

INDEX

adoption, 81–82, 85, 149, 214n29; adopted daughters-in-law, 107–8, 218–19n25
adulteration of food, 4, 44, 87
affective economies (Ahmed), 183
agriculture: collectivization, 8–9, 28, 45–47, 140; de-collectivization, 3, 37, 39; domestic production and production for the market, 34; future of, 34, 186; gender roles in, 43–47, 59–60, 70; *gengtian*, 12–13, 16, 34, 35–43; government direction of, 11–14; market-based, 14, 34, 44, 47, 70–71, 204–5n41, 205n42; mechanized, 6, 36, 202n9; percent of population engaged in, 6, 12; petrochemicals in, 4, 202n9; as a safety net, 51, 53; subsistence, 34–35, 40, 48, 50, 53, 97, 126, 187; sustainable, 186–87, 190–91, 225n3; tilling, 34, 36–37, 50, 52, 145. *See also* garden plots
Ahmed, Sara, 183
A Hui, 190
Aihua, 41, 49, 52, 108
Ailing, 43–44, 55, 75
alcohol consumption: at banquets, 16–17, 151, 173–74, 175–76, 177; excessive, 151, 175–76; gendered nature of, 174–75; and morality, 137, 151–52, 174, 176; and sociality, 171, 172, 173–74. *See also* toasting
Analects, 176
ancestors: food offerings, 28, 92*fig.,* 113, 115, 118, 127, 215n43; graves, 2, 80, 114, 116–17, 118, 158, 215n46; memorial halls,

164; patrilineal, 118; spirits, 112–13, 123; temples, 114. *See also guazhi* (hang paper); filiality; lineage branches; Lunar New Year; three sacrificial meats
apples, 93, 105, 106
aquaculture, 42, 196, 209n11. *See also* fishponds
aquifers, 21, 22*fig.,* 58
arranged marriage, 218–19n25
A Xie, 143

"backyard furnaces," 9
baigong locality gods, 215n37
Baining of Papua, New Guinea, 208n80
ban (buns), 1, 2, 20, 90–91. See also *nianban*
bananas, 13, 14*fig.*
bandits, 122
banquet halls, 23, 111, 125, 145
banquets: associated with calendrical celebrations and rituals, 76, 107; catering for, 66–69; compared with family holiday meals, 64–65; consumption of meat, 177; and corruption, 145; culinary requirements for specific occasions, 225n51; definition of, 65; example of multiple categories, 30, 33; food preparation for, 65, 66, 68, 69; and gift exchange, 28, 107, 110–11, 126; and hierarchy, 129, 164–66; host-guest distinction, 129, 164–66, 181; lineage branch, 158–61, 159*fig.,* 164; liquor and, 16–17, 151, 173–74, 175–76, 177; mahjong and, 169; as medium of exchange,

banquets *(continued)*
30, 32, 126; menus, 68–69, 160, 162;
organization of, 67; for parental visit,
175; participatory and causative features
of, 179; as rare opportunity, 161–62,
223n7; rice and, 16; as ritual, 179–80; in
rural North China, 165; seating at, 165;
and sociality, 158, 160, 162, 180; specialty
foods, 82, 86; of spring 2010, 161; toasting, 161, 169, 171, 173–75, 175–76, 180; in
urban contexts, 174; wedding, 107,
108–9, 160, 169, 171, 214n27; for Zuofu,
66, 109, 121, 126
bao (reciprocity), 132. *See also* reciprocity
Baoli, 41, 52. *See also* Songling and Baoli
Baudrillard, Jean, logics of "value," 30,
208n76
bean curd: association with Hakka identity, 89–90; consumed in restaurants,
23; as food homonym, 94; history of, 89;
and memory, 93; *niang doufu,* 89; paste
from fermentation process, 90; prepared
for market, 45, 46*fig.;* prepared for
Zuofu, 66; as source of protein, 87
beef, 19; beef balls, 154
beggars, 119, 122; at Zuofu banquets, 111–12,
112*fig.,* 123, 126
Belasco, Warren, 163
Big Gao, 147
binggan (biscuits), 72, 77, 90–92, 95
birthdays, 225n51
bitterness and sweetness, 15, 81–82, 144
Bloch, Maurice, 31–32, 163, 171–72
boiling, 168
Bourdieu, Pierre: "habitus," 74, 185–86;
study of taste in France, 207n72
breast feeding, 1, 138, 142
bride price, 109, 110, 214n28
Bright Ling, 153–54, 155
Buck, John Lossing, 4–5, 83, 97, 205n43
Buddhism: deities, 114, 117, 215n41; Ghost
Festival and, 119; and moral obligation,
133, 218n21; in Taiwan, 222n80; vegetarianism and, 152–54. *See also* Guanyin
butchers, 18

cadres: banqueting by, 145–46, 147, 151,
221n70; and corruption, 89, 145–47;

food consumption of, 29, 221n70; gifts
for, 146
Caishen (God of Wealth), 78, 114, 215n39,
215n41
Caldwell, Melissa, 178
calendrical rituals, 29, 73–74, 76–77, 117.
See also Lunar New Year; Mid-Autumn
Festival; Qingming Festival; Zuofu
Campany, Robert Ford, 221n65
candy, 92, 94, 105
cannibalism, 140, 148, 221n59
canteens, 9, 10, 86, 139
Cantonese food culture, 2, 206n54, 224n36
capitalism, 33, 208n76. *See also* market
economy
car ownership, 12, 44, 204n37
Carstens, Janet, 32
caste system (India), 129, 150, 207n68,
217n5
catering, 66–69
caterpillar fungus, 145, 221n65
causality, 179
celery, 79, 94
Chang Chih-I, 48
Chang, K. C., 2–3
chang tian (ritual fields), 117, 215n46
Chaoshan, 8, 86
Chaozhou (Guangdong Province), 84
Chau, Adam, 160
chayang (inserting the seedlings), 37
chemical fertilizers, 16, 205n42, 205n43.
See also *nongyao* (farm chemicals);
petrochemicals
chickens, 15, 44, 88, 209n11. *See also*
poultry
chi da guo fan (eating from one big pot),
164, 165*fig.,* 223n18
childbirth, dishes prepared for, 1, 2, 142
childcare, 12, 52, 87, 101, 136, 139, 219n33
children: agricultural activities of, 46, 50;
cooking by, 61, 63*fig.;* milk consumption
of, 20, 87; rice consumption of, 55–56;
schooling of, 46, 137
Chunyu, 47
"circle of good things" (*liangxing xunhuan*),
15
"circulatory perspective" (Eiss and Pedersen),
126

food as medium of connection, 2, 190

food as metaphor, xii, 132, 144, 146, 149–50

food and novelty, 72, 73

food exchanges: from a "circulatory perspective," 126–27; familial, 28, 100–103; marriage and, 109; moral dimension of, 129, 131; and mutual obligation, 143, 189; to smooth an interaction, 104–5; with spirits, 112–15, 215n43. *See also* gift exchange

food homonyms, 2, 78–79, 89, 91, 93, 94, 111, 225n51

food orientation, 2–3

food offerings, 28, 117–18, 123–24. *See also* three sacrificial meats

food preparation, 34, 54, 58–59, 59*fig.*, 59–64

food prices, 29, 139, 148

food riots, 155

food safety, 3, 87, 148, 187

food scarcity, 5, 76, 148, 149. *See also* famines

foraging, 20, 82, 124, 212n21, 217n67

Four Cleanups Campaign (1965), 147

four-hands tea (*si shou cha*), 170–71, 172, 224n32

France, 203n31, 207n72

fruit: in British working-class system of food, 26; citrus, 14, 44, 93; consumption of, 5, 20, 206n50; cultivation of, 13, 42, 43, 44, 195, 209nn9,11; used to delay end of gathering, 168. *See also* pomelos

Fujian Province, 83

funerals, 91, 97, 106, 115, 120, 123, 160, 214n29

fungus, 44–45, 145, 166, 221n65, 223n24

gaige kaifang (reform and opening), 3, 10–11, 28

gambling, 160, 169, 175, 176

ganqing. See emotion

gaobing, 91, 93

garden plots, 10, 11, 13, 13*fig.*, 29, 43, 208n80, 209n11

garlic, 79, 94

gender roles: in agriculture, 43–47, 59–60, 70; fetching water, 58; and food preparation, 54, 59–60, 70

generational roles, 43, 47–48, 50–53, 59–64

geng (porridge made from rice flour), 87

gengtian (farming), 12–13, 16, 34, 35–43. *See also* agriculture

Ghost Festival, 118–19, 120–21, 122–23, 216n50

ghosts, 113, 118, 120, 122–23, 189, 216n57

Giddens, Anthony, 72

gift exchange: balanced, 164; banqueting and, 28, 107, 110–11, 126; with cadres, 146; familial, 101–3; food and, 29, 33, 96–97, 105, 182, 183–84, 189; inalienability of, 99–100; instrumental and expressive, 105; money and, 106–7, 109, 111–12, 122, 214n28; reciprocity and, 104–6, 182; ritualized and nonritualized, 104. *See also* food exchanges; reciprocity

ginger, 1, 2, 201n3. See also *jijiiu*

glutinous rice wine, 17, 19, 20, 78, 102, 151, 167, 174, 183, 198

goat curry, 177

goats, 19, 20, 44, 45*fig.*

God of Wealth (*Caishen*), 78, 114, 215n39, 215n41

gods: locality, 114, 116, 117, 121, 215nn37, 40; offerings to, 113, 214n35 215n43, vegetarian, 214n35; village guardian, 78. *See also* God of Wealth; Stove God

Gongwang, 78, 114, 121, 215n37

good fortune, 117, 118, 216n48

Graeber, David, 30–31, 164, 208n80, 217n69

grain: area sown, 194, 209n11; consumption, 193, 204n35; government distribution of, 129; output of, 193–94; payment in, 98, 99, 124; tax, 11, 40–41. *See also* rice

Great Leap Forward: cadre indulgence during, 146–47; collectivization, 5, 8–9; exaggeration of production, 10; famine following, 5, 10, 84, 85, 138, 139–40, 148, 157, 211n17, 221n59; foods associated with, 10, 82, 86; mentioned, 144; and the "recall bitterness meal," 80; requisitioning of eggs, 88; social relationships and access to food, 98–99; taxation during, 40; wheat production in, 209n3

Greece, 203n27, 218n13

greenhouse gas emissions, 4

greens, cooling and neutral, 22
Guangzhou, labor migration to, 12
Guanyin, 113, 114, 119, 152, 215n41
Guanzi, 137
guazhi (hang paper), 116–17, 120, 158
Gudeman, Stephen, 126
Guizhen, mother-in-law of, 88

"habitus" (Bourdieu), 74, 185–86
Hakka: identity and food customs, 16,
   89–90, 185, 201n3; industriousness of
   women, 43, 47, 210n13; of Meizhou area,
   2, 8; migration of, 8, 89–90
Hann, Chris, 156–57
Hansen, Mette Halskov, 137
hao shi (happy occasion), 65
heart, 22
heating qualities, 1, 21–22, 27, 206n55
holidays, 29, 65–66, 73–74, 76–77, 117,
   211n32. *See also* Lunar New Year; Mid-
   Autumn Festival; Qingming Festival;
   Zuofu
Holtzman, Jon, 74, 223n8
home repair, 203–4n31
hongbao (red envelope), 105, 106, 109, 110
Hong Kong: gifts from, 64, 175; gifts taken
   to, 183; emigration to, 49, 84, 128; work
   in, 56
hong qu mi (dried red yeast rice), 19
hongzao (red dates), 206n52
host-guest relationship, 129, 164–66, 178,
   181
hotpot, 167–68
household registration system (*hukou*), 49
household surveys, 204nn38–39,
   205nn43,44
house moving, 91
huangshan (swamp eel), 82, 124
hungry ghosts, 118, 120. *See also* ghosts

incense-rites money, 106
India, 47, 84. *See also* caste system
individualism, 3–4, 188, 202n8
Indonesia, 47
industrialized food, 4, 72–73, 150, 186. *See
   also* fast food; factory-made treats
infant betrothal, 218–19n25
infant mortality, 5

inflammation, 22, 206n55
International Assessment of Agricultural
   Knowledge, Science, and Technology
   for Development, 225n3
international food aid, 3
"iron rice bowl," 144
irrigation, 36, 42

Jiabing (son of Yanhong), 198
jianban (deep-fried sesame seed balls), 64,
   211n31
Jiang Yizhou, 146
Jieguo, 149
jijiu (chicken and ginger braised in rice
   wine), 1, 1–2, 20, 88–89, 142, 201n3
Jinchenggong, 158–59, 161, 164
Jing, Jun, 141
jitian (ritual fields), 117, 215n46
Jordan, David, 55

Kajunus, Anna, 166, 224n26
kaoshan chishan (rely on the mountains, eat
   the mountain's produce), 124–25
Kentucky Fried Chicken, 23
kidneys, 22, 206n55
kindling, 58
Kipnis, Andrew, 165, 174, 182, 225n61
kitchens: collective, 9, 10, 86, 139; equipment in, 58; families and, 54–55; "sharing a stove," 54–55, 56; traditional,
   57–58; with view to courtyard, 60*fig.*
Kleinman, Arthur, *Deep China*, 188, 202n8
kumai cai (bitter veined vegetable), 81–82,
   85, 95, 124, 211–12n18; *kumai kao zhou*
   (*kumai* accompanies congee), 82
kumquats, 94
Kundera, Milan, 178

labor, 32, 71, 92, 95, 179. *See also* agriculture;
   cooking; meals, preparation of; wage
   labor
laiwang (comings and goings), 103–4, 107,
   110
lamb, consumption of, 19
land, loss of, 97
landlord class, 48–49, 177
land tenure, 5, 39, 40, 42, 43, 51, 53
Lantern Festival, 94

Levi, Jean, 132
Lévi-Strauss, Claude, 168, 207n68
Leviticus, 25
Li, Teacher, 102, 104, 106, 168
Lianfeng, 116
liangxin (good heart/mind), 128, 133
Liji, 137
Lin Xingfu, 146
lineage branches, 158–60, 159*fig.*
lingzi baozi fen (a Chinese medicine), 44–45
Liqiao, 45, 90
Lishan and Wende, 44, 223n24
Liu, Teacher, 76–77
Liu, Xin, 6
liver, 22, 206n55
Lo, Vivienne, 22
locality gods, 78, 114, 116, 117, 121, 215nn37,40
logics of "value" (Baudrillard), 30–32, 208n76
Longshen (Dragon God), 114, 215n39
Lora-Wainwright, Anna, 204–5n41, 205n42
Lunar New Year: consumption of meat and
    poultry, 19, 177; during the Cultural
    Revolution, 79–80; customary foods
    for, 1, 61–62, 77, 79, 90; family visits, 79,
    105; food homonyms and, 78–79, 94;
    gift exchange, 124; help with cooking,
    61–64; offerings to gods and ancestors,
    77–78, 78*fig.*, 91, 92*fig.*, 115–16, 215n43;
    as "out of ordinary time," 73–74; prepa-
    ration of treats for, 62–64, 63*fig.*; remi-
    niscences of, 72; return home for, 80,
    140–41; reunion meals, 56, 65, 78–79,
    80, 116, 144, 166–67; and rice cultiva-
    tion, 35–36; tea drinking and, 21. See
    also *nianban*
lungs, 22
lunliu (meal rotation), 57, 136, 141

Macy, R. H., 175
Madsen, Richard, 133–34
"magical" acts, 181
mahjong, 168, 169, 175
Malay households, 32
market economy, 155–57, 222n87
market exchange, 33, 97–100, 130
marriage, 107–8, 135, 167, 176, 214nn25,28.
    See also weddings
Marriage Law of 1950, 134–35

Marx, Karl, 31
Mason, Katherine, 174
Mazu, 189
meal rotation (*lunliu*), 57, 136, 141
meals: during the collective era, 75; eating
    alone, 128; "eating from one big pot,"
    164, 165*fig.*; eating space for, 58; families
    and, 54–55, 137; family reunion, 56, 65,
    78–80, 107, 116, 140–41, 144, 166–68,
    224n26; holiday, 64–65; invitations to
    share, 162–63, 223n8; "recall bitterness
    meal" (*yi ku fan*), 79–80; requirements
    of, 26, 27, 61. *See also* cooking; food
    preparation
meat: and banqueting, 177; and caste in
    India, 207n68; consumption of, 5, 6, 17,
    18, 88, 177, 206n48; for the elderly, 137,
    154; as food offering, 28, 114–15, 117, 118,
    216n14; meat balls, 23, 154; and moral-
    ity, 150, 154–55; price of, 148; produc-
    tion and procurement of, 18, 204n35,
    206n49; and reciprocity, 132; regula-
    tions concerning, 148; and sociality,
    176; varieties of, 18–19. *See also* pork;
    poultry; three sacrificial meats
medicinal herbs (*yaocai*), 20, 124–25, 127,
    206nn51,52,55, 212n21. *See also* wild
    grasses; medicinal soups
medicinal soups, 22, 145, 124–25, 125*fig.*,
    206n55, 212n21, 216–17n65
meicai kourou (braised pork and dried
    salted greens), 17
Meirong, 128, 141–42
Meixian County (Guangdong), 7–8; grain
    consumption, 204n35; population of,
    204n35; rice cultivation in, 35–36
Meiying (daughter of Songling and Baoli),
    11, 167, 168, 198
Meizhou, 2, 8, 9*map*, 204n32
memory: bean curd and, 89–90; congee
    and, 86–87; eggs and, 87–89; embodied,
    32, 74, 81; industrialized food and,
    72–73, 91–92, 93, 95; historicized foods,
    32, 93–95; and labor, 91–92, 96; and
    local culinary traditions, 73–74, 75–76;
    nianban and, 90–91; sweet potatoes
    and, 10, 75, 82–86, 93–95, 189; vegeta-
    bles and, 81–82

yang, cycle of, 103, 113, 129, 154. *See also* mutual nourishment

Yang Jisheng, 84, 140, 146, 221n59

Yang, Lien-sheng, 132

Yang, Martin, 83

Yang, Mayfair, 187–88

Yanhong (son of Songling and Baoli), 11–12, 64, 161, 183, 197–99, 204n37

yaocai. See medicinal herbs

yi ku fan (recall bitterness meal), 79–80

yincha (drinking tea/dim sum), 183–84, 206n54, 224n36

Yinglei, 1, 2

Yinzhao: continuing responsibilities of, 142; cultivation of sweet potatoes, 85; and familial exchange of vegetables, 101; family New Year's celebration of, 80; family rice of, 56; home of, 57; preparation of *nianban,* 62–64, 142; rice cultivation and harvesting by, 39

Yuan Xiao Festival, 215n45

Yulanpen Festival, 121, 216n50. *See also* Ghost Festival

zaliang (miscellaneous staples), 83, 209n3, 212n28

Zhong Yuan Festival. *See* Ghost Festival

zhou. See congee

Zuofu: appearance of the beggars, 111–12, 112*fig.,* 121–22, 123, 126; banquets for, 109, 110–11, 121, 123, 126, 145; celebration of, 66, 70*fig.;* consumption of meat, 177; contrasted with family reunions, 167; feeding of beggars, 119; festival for orphan souls, 119; food preparation for, 66–69; and the Ghost Festival, 120–21, 122, 123; gift exchange 110–11, 121; mentioned, 74; packaged biscuits for, 91

zuofu (create blessings), 216n48

CALIFORNIA STUDIES IN FOOD AND CULTURE

Darra Goldstein, Editor